Techniques in the Clinical Supervision of Teachers

Techniques in the Clinical Supervision of Teachers

Preservice and Inservice Applications

Fourth Edition

Keith A. Acheson

Meredith Damien Gall

University of Oregon

 LONGMAN

An imprint of Addison Wesley Longman, Inc.

New York • Reading, Massachusetts • Menlo Park, California • Harlow, England
Don Mills, Ontario • Sydney • Mexico City • Madrid • Amsterdam

**Techniques in the Clinical Supervision
of Teachers: Preservice and Inservice
Applications, Fourth Edition**

Copyright © 1997, 1992, 1987, 1980 by Longman Publishers USA.,
A Division of Addison Wesley Longman, Inc.

Longman, 10 Bank Street, White Plains, N.Y. 10606

Acquisitions editor: Virginia L. Blanford
Associate editor: Arianne J. Weber
Editorial assistant: Mike Lee
Production editor: Linda Moser
Production supervisor: Edith Pullman
Cover design: Dorothy Wachtenheim
Compositor: University Graphics

Library of Congress Cataloging-in-Publication Data

Acheson, Keith A.
    Techniques in the clinical supervision of teachers : preservice
and inservice applications / Keith A. Acheson, Meredith Damien Gall.
    —4th ed.
        p.   cm.
    Includes bibliographical references and index.
    ISBN 0-8013-1509-3
    1. Student teaching.   2. Teachers—Inservice training.   3. School
supervision.   4. Observation (Educational method)   5. Teachers'
workshops.   I. Gall, Meredith D.   II. Title.
LB2157.A3A29   1997   96-20130
371.1'46—dc20   CIP

2 3 4 5 6 7 8 9 10-MA-00999897

Contents

v

Preface

This book is about the clinical supervision of teachers. Several texts on clinical supervision have been published in the last 15 years, but in general they have emphasized theory and research on clinical supervision. Our book is practical. We emphasize the techniques of clinical supervision, the "nuts and bolts" of how to work with teachers to help them improve their classroom teaching.

In preparing the text, we were guided by a set of objectives to help you, the supervisor, develop

- an understanding of the three phases of clinical supervision: planning conference, classroom observation, and feedback conference
- knowledge and skill in using specific techniques in conferences with teachers and in observing their classroom teaching
- understanding of issues and problems in clinical supervision
- understanding of role differences of the supervisor as facilitator, evaluator, counselor, and curriculum adviser
- a positive attitude toward clinical supervision as a method of promoting teacher growth
- insights into the roles that teachers and principals can play in using the techniques of clinical supervision

The textbook format is better suited for helping you to attain knowledge and for understanding objectives than it is for helping you to achieve skill-related objectives. If you are typical of most educators, you did not learn how to teach by reading textbooks. You learned how to teach by practicing the act of teaching in actual classroom situations. (We hope you had a skillful supervisor to assist you!) Textbooks may have facilitated this process by suggesting specific techniques for you to try.

The same principle applies to acquiring skill as a clinical supervisor. We would like to think that this textbook is sufficient to train you to be a highly skilled supervisor. Our experience suggests otherwise. You will need to practice and receive feedback on each conference and observation technique if you are to incorporate them into your supervisory repertoire. It will help, too, if you have the opportunity to observe supervisors who can demonstrate these techniques.

Building principals, school district personnel, and teacher educators in colleges and universities may be required to do teacher supervision as part of their duties. These professional educators need to be skilled in the processes of clinical teacher supervision. If you currently supervise teachers or if you plan to do so in the future, this book was written with you in mind.

In this edition, we have updated examples and reordered chapters to reflect what we see as trends in the field. The shift toward shared leadership in schools has an impact on supervision arrangements, and interest in collaborative activities for teachers has grown. This phenomenon is addressed in a new chapter, Peer Consultation (chapter 13). A prime source for our understanding of this process comes from the work of the British Columbia Teachers Association over a twelve-year period. Their Program for Quality Teaching has been developed, implemented, researched, expanded, and disseminated, and the techniques employed in that program are the ones described in this book.

The book is organized into five units. Unit I provides background necessary for understanding techniques of clinical supervision. Unit II deals with setting goals for a series of observations and planning for individual observations. Units III and IV describe specific techniques for collecting observation data and conducting feedback conferences. Unit V includes some speculation about the future roles of principals, teachers as instructional leaders, and more, including questions you may not have asked yet, and answers you may not be ready for. (Like the child who asked, "Ma, what's a penguin?," was told, "Ask your father," and replied, "I don't want to know *that* much about penguins!")

A NOTE TO THE INSTRUCTOR

The content of this book can be taught in several formats. We recommend taking up observation techniques as early as possible, giving the participants opportunities to practice in a live setting whenever possible and to share experiences and data with other class members. Planning conferences can be introduced as a topic related to trying out different observation systems. An analysis of a planning conference is a reasonable assignment. Teachers should be selected for their willingness to let observers practice their skills. Observers who have student teachers assigned to them and principals who have a faculty to work with should have no difficulty finding opportunities to apply their new skills. After feedback conferences have been discussed, students should have a chance to work through several complete cycles with a teacher.

Simulated situations can be set up to allow participants to practice observing short lessons taught by classmates to their peers. Participants can also practice conference skills in role-playing sessions with classmates, using data supplied by the instructor; an observer for each pair of role players allows for subsequent debriefing and discussion. Tape recordings of conferences are useful in the analysis process, but we find that many teachers are reluctant to permit tape recording unless they understand clearly what use will be made of the tapes and that they will not be evaluated or embarrassed in the process.

A number of activities, exercises, and assignments can be used in conjunction with the printed materials and instructor presentations. Listing what class members feel to be the crucial competencies of teaching will stimulate interest in the aspects of teaching effectiveness discussed in chapter 2.

Tape recordings of classroom interaction can be used to practice writing selected verbatim comments, questions, or responses. Films or videotapes showing nonverbal behaviors also can be useful. A prepared tape (or psychodrama) of a conference gives class members something tangible to react to when studying conference techniques. Overhead projector transparencies of data from seating charts or other observation instruments can serve as a focus for analysis and discussion.

Teaching the skills for coding interaction requires some structured practice. We suggest using a tape recording that has been carefully coded by an expert so that class members can be given feedback when they practice.

Instructor presentations on such topics as research on teaching or supervision or teacher evaluation can augment the material on these topics in this book. Small-group discussions in which participants share their experiences, data, and opinions have been valuable activities in our courses.

ACKNOWLEDGMENTS

Some of the ideas for this book originally were developed at Stanford University in the early 1960s, along with techniques for using videotapes and other forms of feedback in the training of preservice teachers. Influential in that project were Robert Bush, Dwight Allen, Fred McDonald, Norman Boyan, Horace Aubertine, Bill Johnson, Jim Olivero, Frank MacGraw, Al Robertson, and Jimmy Fortune. Both authors, along with John Hansen, worked on earlier versions of the techniques presented here as part of a project sponsored by the Far West Laboratory for Educational Research and Development, where the support and suggestions of Walter Borg and Ned Flanders were especially helpful. Others who have provided valuable research or support for the first and later editions include colleagues and students at the University of Oregon, in particular Peter Titze, Wes Tolliver, Michael Carl, Colin Yarham, Gary Martin, Jim Shinn, Judy Aubrecht, John Suttle, and Kathy Lovell; the Confederation of Oregon School Administrators and Ozzie Rose, the Oregon State Department of Education and Ron Burge, the Nevada Association of School Administrators; various principals' and administrators' associations in Washington State, British Columbia, and Nebraska; Dale Bolton at the University of Washington and Rob Spaulding at San Jose State

University; Paul Tucker and Cal Zigler; and members of the Teachers Corps Research Adaptation Cluster.

We also thank countless students, teachers, and administrators who have given feedback about the techniques (and the writing), and for this edition in particular we would like to thank the following reviewers:

Donald Hackmann, Eastern Michigan University

Martha Livingston, Valdosta State College

Wendy London, Bank Street College of Education

George Kozitza, Western Oregon State College

Marilyn Tallerico, Syracuse University

unit 1

Introduction to Clinical Supervision

OVERVIEW

Clinical supervision has as its goal the professional development of teachers, with an emphasis on improving teachers' classroom performance. Chapter 1 introduces the basic characteristics of clinical supervision and compares it with other forms of teacher supervision. As the goal of clinical supervision is effective teaching, chapter 2 presents criteria of effective teaching that have been verified through research. Supervisors and teachers can use these criteria to define for themselves what is meant by "effective teaching" and to set goals for professional growth.

OBJECTIVES

The purpose of this unit is to help you develop understanding of:

The basic processes and goals of clinical supervision

Why teachers traditionally have had negative attitudes toward supervision

How clinical supervision differs from other forms of teacher supervision

The relationship between clinical supervision and teacher evaluation

The current state of research on the effectiveness of clinical supervision

Different perspectives from which to define effective teaching and the research that supports them

Criteria of effective teaching that have been verified through research

What is meant by effective teaching

chapter 1

The Nature of Clinical Supervision

What gripes me about this so-called supervision is that the principal only comes into my classroom once a year for about an hour. It's a scary, unpleasant experience. I wouldn't mind if I was being supervised by someone who's been a success in the classroom; but usually it's someone who was a poor teacher who's been pushed into an administrative position; and, to top it off, that person usually has had no training whatsoever in how to supervise.
From a conversation with a sixth-grade teacher

The spirit of clinical supervision is difficult to capture in words. Clinical supervision is a process, a distinctive style of relating to teachers. For this process to be effective, the clinical supervisor's mind, emotions, and actions must work together to achieve the primary goal of clinical supervision: the professional development of the preservice or in-service teacher.

Although we acknowledge the unitary nature of clinical supervision, our book is primarily analytical. It attempts to tease out and describe the components and techniques of clinical supervision. This analytical approach is useful as an instructional device, but it does not allow you to view clinical supervision as a whole. As a way of dealing with this problem, we present an episode from an actual case of clinical supervision.

AN EXAMPLE

Arthur Harris, a university supervisor, was assigned to supervise Jim, a student teacher at a local junior high school. Arthur had an initial meeting with Jim to get acquainted, discuss the supervisory role, and answer questions. He then met with the two teachers in whose classrooms Jim would work and with the school's principal. The two teachers gave Jim several weeks to observe their classes, become acquainted with the students, and prepare several social studies units.

Arthur viewed his initial role as providing support and encouragement to Jim. Once Jim had found his bearings, Arthur explained the procedures of clinical supervision and initiated a supervisory cycle by asking Jim to state his lesson plan for the class on Africa that Arthur would observe later in the week. Jim's plan was to organize the students into three groups and have each group read a different article about Rhodesia [Zimbabwe]. Then Jim wanted students in each group to state what they learned from the articles and answer questions about them.

Arthur and Jim agreed that it would be helpful to collect data on verbal interaction patterns in the lesson. Two specific areas of focus were selected: (1) Jim's responses to students' answers and ideas, which Arthur would record using selective verbatim (technique 9), and (2) the distribution of student talk during the lesson, which would be recorded on a seating chart (technique 12).

Figure 1.1 shows a sample of the data collected by Arthur Harris using each technique. When he and Jim met the following day for a feedback conference, Jim was able to use the data to reach his own conclusions about how the lesson went. Arthur initiated this process by asking, "What do these data tell you about your teaching?" (technique 23). Jim realized that he had not praised or elaborated on student ideas; he had simply acknowledged them. Also, Jim saw that he was successful in getting students to talk, but the distribution of talk was unbalanced: Students nearest the teacher, and one student in particular, did most of the speaking.

Arthur's next move in the feedback conference was to ask Jim how he would explain why these verbal patterns occurred (technique 24). Jim commented that he had heard in his methods courses about the importance of responding constructively to student ideas, but he had not made the connection to his own teaching behavior until now. As for the distribution of student talk, Jim stated he was simply unaware that the imbalance had occurred. He realized, though, that he probably called a number of times on the student who talked the most because he could depend on her to give good answers.

Arthur asked Jim what he might do based on these observations (technique 24). Jim said he would practice using praise in his next lessons and would make an effort to call on more students. Harris suggested several ways that Jim might acknowledge student ideas and incorporate them in the lesson. He also suggested that a different arrangement of desks—perhaps a semicircle or circle—might encourage students to express more ideas and engage in discussion among themselves.

This brief example illustrates the three phases of the clinical supervision cycle: planning conference, classroom observation, and feedback conference. The example also makes clear that clinical supervision focuses on the teacher's actual classroom performance and includes the teacher as an active participant in the supervisory process. To see what teachers want supervisors to do, study Figures 1.2 and 1.3 (pp. 6 and 7).

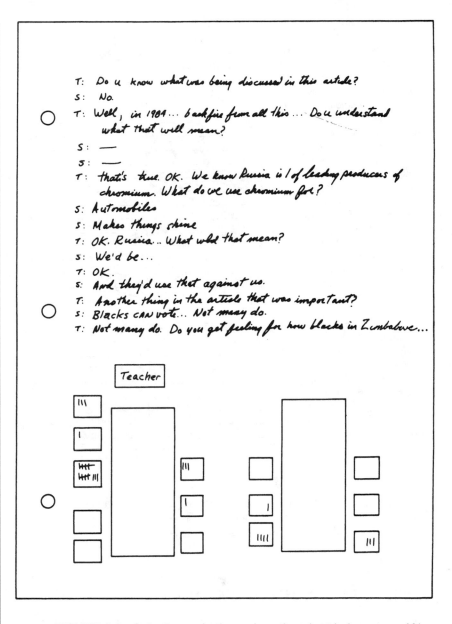

FIGURE 1.1 Selective verbatim and seating chart in lesson on Africa.

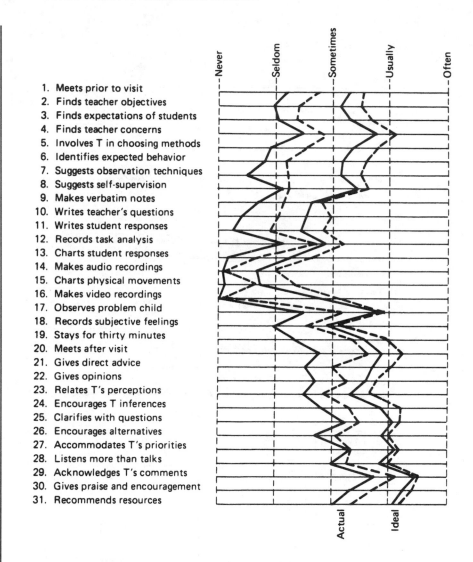

FIGURE 1.2 Actual and ideal behaviors as judged by teachers of trained (dotted lines) and untrained (solid lines) principals.

SOURCE: From James L. Shinn, "Teacher Perceptions of Ideal and Actual Supervisory Procedures Used by California Elementary Principals" (Ph.D. diss., University of Oregon, 1976), p. 52.

THE "PROBLEM" OF TEACHER SUPERVISION

Most teachers do not like to be supervised, even though it is a required part of their training and professional work. They react defensively to supervision and do not find it helpful.

This generalization undoubtedly has exceptions. Some teachers profit from su-

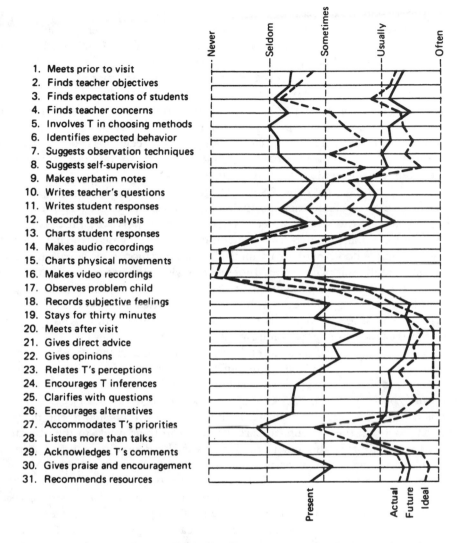

	Never	Seldom	Sometimes	Usually	Often

1. Meets prior to visit
2. Finds teacher objectives
3. Finds expectations of students
4. Finds teacher concerns
5. Involves T in choosing methods
6. Identifies expected behavior
7. Suggests observation techniques
8. Suggests self-supervision
9. Makes verbatim notes
10. Writes teacher's questions
11. Writes student responses
12. Records task analysis
13. Charts student responses
14. Makes audio recordings
15. Charts physical movements
16. Makes video recordings
17. Observes problem child
18. Records subjective feelings
19. Stays for thirty minutes
20. Meets after visit
21. Gives direct advice
22. Gives opinions
23. Relates T's perceptions
24. Encourages T inferences
25. Clarifies with questions
26. Encourages alternatives
27. Accommodates T's priorities
28. Listens more than talks
29. Acknowledges T's comments
30. Gives praise and encouragement
31. Recommends resources

Present   Actual Future Ideal

FIGURE 1.3 Supervisor behavior at the present and in the future as perceived by teachers (solid lines); actual and ideal supervisor behavior as perceived by supervisors (dotted lines).

SOURCE: From Saad Adwani, "The Relationship between Teacher and Supervisor as Perceived by Teachers, Supervisors and Principals in Secondary Schools in Saudi Arabia" (Ph.D. diss., University of Oregon, 1981), p. 184, and Saleh al-Tuwaijri, "The Relationship between Ideal and Actual Supervisory Practice as Perceived by Supervisors in Saudi Arabia" (Ph.D. diss., University of Oregon, 1985), p. 159.

pervision, and some gifted supervisors are popular and effective with teachers. Yet the weight of evidence supports the generalization. In a study of 2500 teachers, Kimball Wiles found that only a small fraction of them (1.5 percent) perceived their supervisor as a source of new ideas.[1] Morris Cogan conducted several studies of teacher supervision, on the basis of which he concluded that "psychologically [supervision] is almost inevitably viewed as an active threat to the teacher, possibly endangering his professional standing and undermining his confidence."[2] Arthur Blumberg reviewed studies of teacher supervision and found that teachers view supervision "as a part of the system that exists but that does not play an important role in their professional lives, almost like an organizational ritual that is no longer relevant."[3]

The prevalence of teacher hostility to supervision would suggest that schools abandon it entirely. A more hopeful conclusion is that teachers are hostile, not to supervision, but to the style of supervision they typically receive. Teachers might react positively to a supervisory style that is more responsive to their concerns and aspirations. Clinical supervision is based on this premise.

Before describing what clinical supervision is, let us examine some supervisory practices to which teachers react negatively. In traditional inservice supervision, the supervisor—usually the school principal—initiates the supervisory process to evaluate the teacher's performance. The evaluation function may be mandated by state law, by the local school board, or by ministries of education. This situation creates two problems at the start. First, supervision becomes equated with evaluation. People tend to be anxious when they know they are being evaluated, especially if negative evaluations threaten their jobs. No wonder, then, that teachers react negatively to supervision. The second problem is that supervision arises from a need of the supervisor, rather than from a need felt by the teacher.

Because traditional supervision tends to be unpleasant, interaction between supervisor and teacher is avoided or minimized. Unfortunately, this practice compounds the problem. The supervisor may show up unannounced at the teacher's classroom to observe what is happening. The teacher has no knowledge of what the supervisor might observe and evaluate. Is the supervisor interested in the neatness of the classroom, in the students' apparent interest in their work, in the objectives and teaching strategy of the lesson, or perhaps in the degree to which classroom control is maintained? The supervisor, on the other hand, may not have planned what to observe and evaluate. The result is that classroom observation data are likely to be unsystematic, highly subjective, and vague. The follow-up to classroom visitation is not likely to improve matters. Typically the supervisor completes a rating checklist and writes an evaluative report on the teacher's performance. The teacher may not have an opportunity to confer with the supervisor about the observational data and evaluative criteria used in the report, even though the report may be used in important decisions relating to the teacher's promotion and tenure.

This highly directive form of supervision reflects the historical role of supervisors as school "inspectors." As far back as the early eighteenth century, lay committees in Boston were charged with inspecting schools periodically. The purpose of inspection was to determine whether instructional standards were being maintained. School inspection by lay committees continued until schools grew large enough to require more than one teacher in each school. The inspection function then became the responsibility of one of the teachers, who was known as the "principal teacher." Eventually the title was shortened to "principal." Although other models of supervision have been advocated in recent years, many principals probably still perceive their supervisory role as that of inspector.

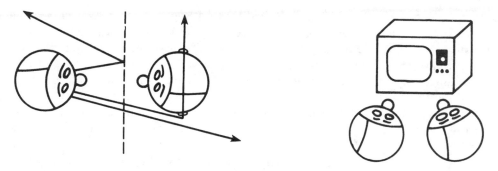

FIGURE 1.4   Nose to nose versus side by side.

Another misconception of the supervisor's role can be represented graphically as "talking heads," where the supervisor emits sage advice that appears to go in one ear and out the other, goes right on by, or bounces off an invisible shield that protects (i.e., is defensive for) the teacher. A better model than the "nose to nose" scheme is the "side by side" version, where both participants look at factual information, analyze, interpret, and make decisions as colleagues rather than as adversaries. (See Figure 1.4.)

CLINICAL SUPERVISION—A DEFINITION

The preceding descriptions of teacher supervision are overdrawn, yet they characterize what some supervisors do some of the time. To the extent that the portrayals are accurate, they account for teachers' pervasive negative feelings about supervision. We wish to promote an alternative model of supervision that is interactive rather than directive, democratic rather than authoritarian, teacher-centered rather than supervisor-centered. This supervisory style is called clinical supervision.

We use the label *clinical supervision* because the model presented here is based directly on the methods developed by Morris Cogan, Robert Goldhammer, and others at the Harvard School of Education in the 1960s.[4] Clinical is meant to suggest a face-to-face relationship between teacher and supervisor and a focus on the teacher's actual behavior in the classroom. As Goldhammer puts it, "Given close observation, detailed observational data, face-to-face interaction between the supervisor and teacher, and an intensity of focus that binds the two together in an intimate professional relationship, the meaning of 'clinical' is pretty well filled out."[5] We might substitute "side-by-side" for "face-to-face" given the context of Figure 1.4.

The word *clinical* can also connote pathology, a connotation that should not be applied to the model of teacher supervision presented here. We certainly do not wish you to think that clinical supervision is always a "remedy" applied by the supervisor to deficient or unhealthy behavior exhibited by the teacher. To avoid this implied meaning of clinical supervision, we considered using the term *teacher-centered supervision.* One nice feature of this label is that it parallels the method of "person-centered counseling" popularized by Carl Rogers, with which clinical supervision has much in common.[6] Nevertheless, we settled on clinical supervision as the more descriptive term because it continues the tradition of the group at Harvard who originated this model of supervision.

Clinical supervision acknowledges the need for teacher evaluation, under the condition that the teacher participate with the supervisor in this process. However, the primary emphasis of clinical supervision is on professional development, and the primary goal of this supervision is to help the teacher improve his or her instructional performance.

How is this goal to be accomplished? The supervisor begins the process of supervision by holding a conference with the teacher. In the conference, the teacher has an opportunity to state personal concerns, needs, and aspirations. The supervisor's role is to help the teacher clarify these perceptions so that both have a clear picture of the teacher's current instruction, the teacher's view of ideal instruction, and whether there is a discrepancy between the two. Next, supervisor and teacher explore new techniques that the teacher might try in order to move the instruction toward the ideal.

This first phase of supervision, done properly, can be helpful to the teacher. Teaching is a lonely profession. Most teachers (i.e., those who do not work in a team teaching context) are deprived of access to colleagues with whom they can share perceptions. Supervision can satisfy this important need of teachers.

The planning conference also provides teachers with an opportunity to reflect on their teaching. Many teachers have a vague anxiety about the effectiveness of their teaching. They do not know whether they are doing a good job, whether a "problem" student can be helped, whether their instruction can be improved. Teachers rarely have the opportunity to observe other teachers' classroom performance, which might provide a basis for reflecting on their own performance. Supervisors can meet this need by using a different approach—helping the teacher clarify goals, collecting observational data on classroom events, and analyzing the data for discrepancies. For teachers who are not aware of their goals or how they "come across" in the classroom, this process can be a useful guide.

The planning conference often results in a cooperative decision by teacher and supervisor to collect observational data. For example, a teacher we know had a vaguely defined concern that he was turning off the brighter students in the class. In the planning conference, the teacher developed the hypothesis that perhaps he was spending the majority of his time with the slower students and ignoring the needs of the brighter students. Together, teacher and supervisor decided to do a verbal flow analysis (technique 12) of the teacher's discussion behavior. This analysis involves observation of the students with whom the teacher initiates interaction and how he responds to each student's ideas. The teacher and the supervisor also decided it would be worthwhile for the teacher to collect class assignments over a two-week period to determine their level of difficulty and challenge.

It is curious how rarely we collect data on different aspects of the teacher's classroom performance. In the field of sports, for example, the athlete watches closely the statistical data that summarize observations of his performance—number of home runs in baseball, percentage of completed passes in football, final and intermediate times in track events, and so forth. Also, athletes are exposed constantly to videotape replays of their performance so that they can perfect their techniques. In such professions as medicine, business, and law, the practitioner has access to many indicators that directly reflect quality of performance—number of lives saved, salary based on fees, sales figures. Additionally, practitioners often hear expressions of satisfaction or dissatisfaction from their clients. We need to provide teachers with similar indicators of performance, based on direct or indirect observation.

The final phase of clinical supervision is for teacher and supervisor to participate in a feedback conference. Together they review the observational data, with the supervisor encouraging the teacher to make his or her own inferences about teaching effectiveness. For example, in viewing a videotape of their performance, teachers usually notice a number of areas in which they need to improve. They comment that they hadn't known how much they talk in class, that they tend to ignore or fail to acknowledge student comments, that they do not speak forcefully enough, and the like. As the teacher reviews the observational data, the feedback conference often turns into a planning conference—with teacher and supervisor deciding cooperatively to collect further observational data or plan a self-improvement program.

In brief, clinical supervision is a model of supervision that contains three phases: planning conference, classroom observation, and feedback conference. The model is shown graphically in Figure 1.5. The most distinctive features of clinical supervision are its emphases on direct teacher-supervisor interaction and on the teacher's professional development.

Richard Weller has offered a formal definition of clinical supervision: "Clinical supervision may be defined as supervision focused upon the improvement of instruction by means of systematic cycles of planning, observation, and intensive intellectual analysis of actual teaching performances in the interest of rational modification."[7] In addition to providing this succinct but accurate definition, Weller isolated the essential characteristics and assumptions of clinical supervision as described in

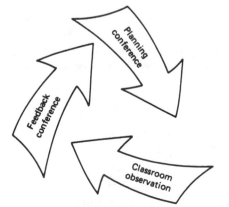

FIGURE 1.5 The three phases of the clinical supervision cycle.

the literature. An adaptation of this list of characteristics and assumptions is presented below.[8] The characteristics are made operational in the set of conference and observation techniques presented in chapters 3 through 10.

Essential Characteristics and Assumptions of Clinical Supervision

1. To improve instruction, teachers must learn specific intellectual and behavioral skills.
2. Supervisors should take responsibility for helping teachers develop (a) skills for analyzing the instructional process based on systematic data; (b) skills for experimentation, adaptation, and modification of the curriculum; and (c) a broader repertoire of teaching skills and techniques.
3. Supervision emphasizes what and how teachers teach. The aim is to improve instruction, not change the teacher's personality.
4. The planning and analysis focus on making and testing instructional hypotheses based on observational evidence.
5. The conferences deal with a few instructional issues that are important, relevant to the teacher, and amenable to change.
6. The feedback conference concentrates on constructive analysis and the reinforcement of successful patterns rather than on the condemnation of unsuccessful patterns.
7. It is based on observational evidence, not on unsubstantiated value judgments.
8. The cycle of planning, observation, and analysis is continuous and cumulative.
9. Supervision is a dynamic process of give-and-take in which supervisors and teachers are colleagues in search of mutual educational understanding.
10. The supervisory process is primarily centered on the analysis of instruction.
11. Individual teachers have both the freedom and the responsibility to initiate issues, analyze and improve their own teaching, and develop personal teaching styles.
12. Supervision can be perceived, analyzed, and improved in much the same manner as teaching can.
13. Supervisors have both the freedom and the responsibility to analyze and evaluate their own supervision in a manner similar to teachers' analysis and evaluation of their instruction.

The Goals of Clinical Supervision

Planning conferences, classroom observation, and feedback conferences are the major activities of clinical supervision. The major aim of these activities is the improvement of teachers' classroom instruction. In this respect, clinical supervision is a key technique for promoting the professional development of teachers.

The aim of clinical supervision can be analyzed into more specific goals as follows:

- *To Provide Teachers with Objective Feedback on the Current State of Their Instruction.* Clinical supervision, in its most basic form, holds up a mirror so that teachers can see what they are actually doing while teaching. What teachers are doing may be quite different from what teachers think they are doing. For example, many teachers believe they are good at encouraging students to express their ideas until they listen to audiotapes of their lessons. Then they discover the extent to which they dominate the lesson. Typically, two-thirds of classroom talk is by the teacher. Receiving objective feedback is often sufficient stimulus for teachers to initiate a self-improvement process.

- *To Diagnose and Solve Instructional Problems.* Clinical supervisors use conference techniques and observational records to help teachers pinpoint specific discrepancies between what they are doing and what they ought to do. At times teachers are able to diagnose these discrepancies on their own. On other occasions the skilled intervention of a supervisor is necessary. A parallel situation exists in classroom instruction. Sometimes students can self-diagnose learning problems and take remedial steps on the basis of this information. At other times, students are stymied by their inability to learn a particular subject, and the teacher is needed to diagnose and remediate.

- *To Help Teachers Develop Skill in Using Instructional Strategies.* If the only purpose of clinical supervision were to help the teacher solve immediate problems and crises, its value would be severely limited. The supervisor would be needed each time the teacher had a "brush fire" to be put out. This is not true. The skillful supervisor uses the clinical conference and observation data to help the teacher develop enduring patterns of behavior—what we call instructional strategies. These strategies are effective in promoting learning, motivating students, and managing the classroom. The observational techniques presented in chapters 5–8 and the criteria for effective teaching in chapter 2 deal with instructional strategies most educators believe effective. Teachers can practice these strategies and can receive objective data on improvement resulting from practice.

- *To Evaluate Teachers for Promotion, Tenure, or Other Decisions.* This is the most controversial function of clinical supervision. Some supervisors avoid evaluation, but most supervisors are required by the school district or college of education to evaluate the teacher's competence, usually at the end of the supervisory cycle. Although clinical supervision emphasizes the teacher's professional development, the objective data collected through systematic classroom observation provide one basis for evaluating the teacher's competence. As we discuss later in the chapter, the "sting" of evaluation can be lessened if, as part of the clinical supervision process, the supervisor shares with the teacher the criteria and standards to be used in the evaluation report.

- *To Help Teachers Develop a Positive Attitude about Continuous Professional Development.* A major goal of clinical supervision is to help the teacher realize that training does not end with the completion of certification requirements. Teachers need to view themselves as professionals, which means, in part, that they engage in self-development and skill training as a career-long effort. The clinical supervisor can model this aspect of professionalism through a willingness to develop new supervisory skills.

OTHER TYPES OF TEACHER SUPERVISION

The purpose of clinical supervision can be further clarified by comparing it with other kinds of teacher supervision.

Counseling.   Many teachers—especially student teachers and first-year teachers—have overt anxiety and insecurity about their ability to perform in the classroom. Also teachers may experience temporary crises in their personal lives that interfere with classroom performance. Some teachers may suffer from chronic emotional problems (e.g., depression or unprovoked outbursts of anger) that disrupt their teaching effectiveness. Sensitive supervisors respond to teachers' anxiety and insecurity by providing emotional support and reassurance. They also may make an effort to deal with more serious problems or may refer a teacher to appropriate specialists. In carrying out these functions, the supervisor is performing the role of counselor. Clinical supervision may also incorporate these functions, but its focus is on the teacher's instructional performance rather than the teacher's personal problems.

Another problem that arises in teacher supervision centers on career decisions. Student teachers often wonder whether they are cut out to be teachers. They may ask for assistance in seeking a teaching position or for advice about additional education. Experienced teachers may feel undecided about whether to remain in the teaching profession, to seek a transfer to another school, or to teach a different content area and grade level. The supervisor who advises a teacher about such problems is performing a counseling function rather than a clinical supervision function.

Curriculum Support.   Teachers sometimes ask their supervisors for advice about curriculum materials they are using. Are the materials suitable? How should they be used? Are alternative materials available? A teacher may have other curriculum concerns as well: the amount of time to spend on each curriculum topic, procedures for organizing a course of study, or new curriculum policy and guidelines in the school district.

Supervision in the form of curriculum support can be very helpful to the teacher, but it should not be equated with clinical supervision. Clinical supervision focuses directly on actual observable events of teaching. In contrast, curriculum support focuses on materials, objectives, and philosophy of instruction. These are major influences on teaching, but they are not the teaching act itself.

A Note of Caution. Counseling and curriculum support are important, legitimate functions of teacher supervision. Teachers do experience emotional problems and curriculum concerns that may impede their instructional effectiveness. Nevertheless, a teacher may use these problems and concerns as an excuse to avoid dealing with difficulties in the act of teaching. For example, a teacher may feel uncomfortable about the fact that students in class are generally unruly. Yet, the teacher does not wish to confront this problem and does not want the supervisor to notice what is happening. Thus the teacher steers the supervisory conference in the direction of problems and events that exist outside the classroom. (We know of instances where teacher and supervisor used their time together to talk about the problems of other teachers in the school.) When these situations occur, the clinical supervisor should listen sensitively to the teacher's comments but then tactfully steer the conference back to the teacher's own classroom behavior.

TEACHER EVALUATION AND CLINICAL SUPERVISION

Supervisors face a conflict caused by being caught between two roles—evaluator and facilitator. Supervisors often ask, "How can I help teachers grow as persons and as classroom instructors when they know that, eventually, I must make a written evaluation of their effectiveness?" So great is the conflict that some educators have argued for a separation in roles, as we shall see in unit 5. Thus, some supervisors would evaluate teachers' performance in a manner similar to the traditional "inspector" role. Other supervisors would devote themselves to promoting teachers' development. Teachers feel the conflict, too. They do not know whether to rely on the supervisor for support or avoid the supervisor for fear of being criticized.[9]

This book is strongly oriented toward the role of clinical supervisor as facilitator, but we acknowledge that most supervisors must also evaluate teachers. Preservice teachers are usually evaluated at the end of their student-teaching experience by the university supervisor and cooperating teachers. These evaluations are put in placement files or reflected in written recommendations and influence their chances of obtaining teaching positions. Evaluation reports of in-service teachers may influence salary increases, promotions, and tenure decisions.

We have no easy solution for the problem created by the supervisor's dual role of facilitator and evaluator. But the following observation may help you and the teachers you supervise work toward your own resolution of the problem.

The conflict between facilitation and evaluation is not unique to teacher supervision; supervisors in all occupations and professions face the same problem. Even teachers must play the dual role of evaluator and facilitator. Teachers are charged with the responsibility of helping their students learn, but they also are required to evaluate how well students have learned relative one to another.

Remember that the "sting" of evaluation can be lessened by a skillful supervisor. Teachers are most threatened when they are unaware of the criteria by which they will be judged and when they do not trust the evaluator's ability to be fair. These concerns can be alleviated by involving the teacher in the evaluative process—

for example, by sharing the evaluative criteria beforehand and by basing the evaluation on objective observational data shared with the teacher. This process of sharing ideally results in teacher and supervisor working together rather than at cross-purposes.

The experience of our colleagues in the teaching profession and our own experience indicates that the vast majority of teachers are effective and can improve with supervision and training. Less effective teachers usually self-select out of the profession either during the preservice phase or during the first few years in the field. The realization that probability is working for them (i.e., they are more likely to be evaluated positively than negatively) helps many teachers accept the evaluative function of supervision.

Finally, we remind you of the old truism that people often learn more from their failures than from their successes. Even a negative evaluation may provide a growth experience. Supervisor and teacher may find that a negative evaluation of the teacher's performance is painful for both of them, especially if it results in the teacher's leaving the profession. One can only hope that the teacher views this leave-taking as a positive process that frees him or her to explore and be successful in another profession.

We have more to say about the roles of clinical supervision in teacher evaluation in chapter 11. The techniques presented there can be used to promote teacher growth in addition to their application to evaluation. Planning and feedback conferences can be used to identify and share evaluative criteria. Classroom observation data can be used not only as feedback to the teacher but also as the basis for objective evaluation of the teacher's performance. The way that planning conferences, observation, and feedback fit into a state-mandated teacher evaluation process is illustrated in Figure 11.1. Chapters 12, 13, and 14 consider some additional functions and roles that can make use of the techniques of clinical supervision.

THE NEED FOR CLINICAL SUPERVISION

Is it necessary to make clinical supervision available to teachers? This question is worth asking, especially because research findings raise doubts about the value of this kind of supervision.

The need for clinical supervision can be defended by considering another question, "Do students need teachers?" Most educators would answer in the affirmative. All students need a teacher's assistance at one time or another; some students need more assistance than others. Very few students are so independent that they can learn solely by studying curriculum materials.

Teachers are in a similar situation. They, too, are learners. The content they need to learn is the profession of teaching. At various points in their professional development they need the skillful assistance of a clinical supervisor if they are to make progress.

In many instances, the interventions of a clinical supervisor have made a significant impact on a teacher's growth. We recall a preservice teacher no one thought would survive student teaching. Continuous supervision of her classroom performance and consultation with school personnel helped her overcome feelings of insecurity and learn appropriate role behaviors.

Clinical supervision can also make a difference for an in-service teacher. We recall a teacher who was on probationary status because of low ratings on teaching effectiveness. A sympathetic supervisor helped the teacher through this difficult period, with the result that he eventually was taken off probationary status. It would have been almost impossible for that teacher to pull himself up by his own bootstraps. The supervisor's intervention was critical.

A less serious case involved an experienced primary grade teacher who had difficulty after accepting an invitation to teach a class of sixth graders. The supervisor assigned to help her quickly discovered that the teacher was trying to teach the sixth-grade class in the same manner that she had taught her second-grade classes. The supervisor collected observational data that helped the teacher see that her lesson plans and verbal behaviors were too simple for her new instructional situation. With the supervisor's assistance, the teacher was able to adjust her teaching style so that both she and the class felt more satisfied.

THE CLINICAL SUPERVISOR

Any educator responsible for the professional development of teachers can use the techniques of clinical supervision: Methods instructors, practicum supervisors, student teaching supervisors, cooperating teachers,[10] and school administrators to varying degrees guide the development of preservice teachers. All these educators can make use of clinical supervision techniques.

It has been estimated that as many as a quarter of a million persons in the United States provide in-service education to teachers on a full-time or part-time basis.[11] These educators include 80,000 education professors, supervisors, and consultants; 100,000 principals and vice principals; and perhaps 50,000 support personnel, such as reading instructors, media experts, and mental health specialists. Each of these professionals, at one time or another, may hold conferences with individual teachers or visit their classrooms for the purpose of making observations. Anyone who interacts with teachers in these contexts may find it necessary or useful to employ the techniques of clinical supervision.

Are clinical techniques useful to those whose primary or only responsibility is the evaluation of teachers? The answer is, "Yes, under certain conditions." If the evaluator intends to use classroom observation data as a basis for the evaluation, the observation techniques in chapters 5–8 will be useful. If the evaluator wishes to involve the teacher in determining the criteria for evaluation, the conference techniques in chapters 9 and 10 will facilitate this process.

We may seem to be promoting clinical supervision as a panacea to be used by all supervisors with all teachers. To a certain extent this is true. As you become familiar with the techniques of clinical supervision, you will find that they deal with basic processes—speaking, listening, influencing, observing—that occur in any supervisory contact. Because clinical supervision is built around these processes, it has a certain universality. Not all supervisors will use the "full" model of clinical supervision, however, and some will do so only under certain conditions. Other supervisors, perhaps those who see their primary role as counselor or curriculum specialist, will use only a few techniques from the clinical supervision model.

HOW EFFECTIVE IS CLINICAL SUPERVISION?

Educators ask three important questions about the effectiveness of clinical supervision.

1. Do teachers and supervisors have a positive attitude toward the clinical supervision model? Do they like it? Is it what they want?
2. Does clinical supervision result in improved teaching in the classroom?
3. Does clinical supervision result in improved learning by the teacher's students?

This section briefly considers the research relating to each question. The discussion is necessarily brief because relatively little research has been done on teacher supervision. The available research has been characterized by Richard Weller as "unsystematic, unrelated to other research, globally evaluative, and of very limited scope."[12]

Attitudes toward Clinical Supervision

Arthur Blumberg and Edmund Amidon studied the reactions of a large group of in-service teachers to supervisory conferences with their principals.[13] Specifically, they were interested in how teachers perceived supervisors' use of "direct" behaviors (e.g., giving information, directions or commands, and criticism) and "indirect" behaviors (e.g., accepting feelings and ideas, giving praise and encouragement, and asking questions). The researchers attempted to relate these perceptions of direct and indirect supervisory behavior to the same teachers' ratings of conference effectiveness.

Blumberg and Amidon found that supervisors who emphasized indirect behaviors tended to receive high ratings from teachers on the productivity of their conferences. Teachers valued indirect supervisory conferences. As indirect communication is a major element in clinical supervision, we infer that teachers would be favorable to this model of supervision (see techniques of indirect communication in chapter 10).

James Shinn's research study[14] asked a large sample of in-service teachers to rate the ideal frequency with which they would like school principals to use various techniques of clinical supervision and the actual frequency of such use (see Figure 1.2). The most significant finding is that teachers believe all the techniques of clinical supervision are worthwhile; each technique was rated as meriting occasional or frequent use. The data also confirm Blumberg and Amidon's findings: several of the highest-rated techniques (e.g., 31, 32, 33) are indirect supervisory behaviors. A number of subsequent studies have used the questionnaire used by Shinn, and the results indicate that the kinds of supervisory behavior teachers want are surprisingly stable, even across cultures.

A study by Gary Martin[15] provides further evidence of teachers' acceptance of the clinical supervision model. Martin surveyed a group of in-service teachers and supervisors trained in the systematic observation techniques (see chapters 5–8). A comparison group of teachers and supervisors had not received this training. Martin found that the trained teachers believed that their annual evaluation was more helpful to them than did the untrained teachers. Also, the trained teachers were more likely to accept evaluation as a basis for promotion and tenure decisions than were the untrained teachers. Although Martin's study focused on teacher evaluation, the findings suggest that teachers also would have a positive attitude toward the observation component of clinical supervision.

How well do supervisors like clinical supervision? Two studies in Saudi Arabia (which, until recent years, used an inspector model of supervision) asked supervisors what supervisory techniques were being used and which should be used in the future or ideally. (See Figure 1.3.)[16] An Oregon study asked evaluators (administrators) to report what techniques they used before and after a new state law had mandated goal setting, observation, and other aspects of clinical supervision and before and after brief training had been provided by the school district. A more recent study in the same district showed that the only factor that had changed significantly over the years was the confidence the teachers had (less) in programs of assistance versus that of administrators (more). In our experience and in the experience of colleagues conducting workshops on clinical supervision, the workshops have been well received by thousands of school principals, teacher educators, and others who have participated in them. Several studies shed some light on what supervisors say they do, and how teachers perceive it. How well teachers and supervisors like the program varies from district to district, as might be expected since the programs vary. The most promising programs we have studied are those that use nonjudgmental peer observers.

Effects of Clinical Supervision on Teaching

Does clinical supervision help teachers improve their performance in the classroom? Norman Boyan and Willis Copeland developed an extensive training program for supervisors based on the clinical supervision model.[17] They found that supervisors trained in the model were able to help teachers make significant improvements in a variety of teaching behaviors.

In a study cited earlier, Blumberg and Amidon related teacher perceptions of supervisors' direct and indirect behaviors in conferences to teacher perceptions of learning outcomes.[18] The researchers made an interesting discovery: teachers felt they learned most about themselves, as teachers and as individuals, from conferences high in both indirect and direct supervision.

Indirect support for the effectiveness of clinical supervision can be found in the research literature on microteaching, which is a widely used set of techniques for training teachers. Microteaching techniques parallel key techniques in clinical supervision. For example, in microteaching the teacher seeks to improve specific, operationally defined teaching skills; in clinical supervision the supervisor helps the teacher translate general teaching concerns into specific, observable behaviors (technique 2). Another key ingredient of microteaching is that the teacher presents a lesson in which he or she practices several teaching skills. This lesson is recorded on audiotape or videotape, then played back so that the teacher can receive feedback on the teaching performance. The practice and feedback techniques of microteaching are paralleled by the classroom observation (techniques 8–23) and feedback phases (techniques 24–35) of clinical supervision. Many research studies have demonstrated that microteaching is effective in helping teachers improve specific teaching skills. It seems reasonable to infer that if the clinical supervisor uses techniques parallel to microteaching, similar improvements in teaching performance will be obtained.

Effects of Clinical Supervision on Students

Ultimately, clinical supervision should improve student learning. The clinical supervisor believes that if he or she can improve teacher performance, the teacher in turn will be able to improve student performance. If clinical supervision is effective, we should be able to observe its effects in the supervised teacher's students. Improvements in student attitude, classroom behavior, and scholastic achievement represent the range of possible student effects.

Unfortunately, we have not been able to locate any convincing research on student effects associated with clinical supervision, although our studies and those of our students clearly point in the direction of a positive relationship. A possible reason for the lack of research is the time span required to observe effects. Such research would require a group of supervisors who would use the clinical supervision model with a group of teachers. After supervision had occurred for a period of time, the researcher would look for possible improvements in teacher performance. After more time had elapsed, the researcher would look for possible improvements in student performance. The research would be costly, but it is methodologically feasible.

Indirect evidence suggests that good clinical supervision results ultimately in improved student performance. Chapter 2 presents teaching techniques researchers have found to be associated with student learning. For example, students of teachers who emphasize such teaching behaviors as praise and encouragement tend to learn more than students of teachers who emphasize criticism and punishment. If clinical supervision focuses on these techniques, and if teachers show improvement in their use, then we have reason to expect that students, too, will benefit.

In summary, the links between clinical supervision and teacher performance, and between clinical supervision and student performance, have not been convincingly demonstrated. Although indirect evidence suggests that these linkages exist, research directly focused on the clinical supervision process should be encouraged.

One of the most promising lines of investigation related to the techniques of clinical supervision is their application to new settings and situations. For example, we have followed rather closely over a 12-year period the development and implementation of peer consultation programs in western Canada and in northwest states. Interviews and surveys with teachers who have volunteered and actively participated in these programs (which require training and practice to develop the skills necessary to be effective) indicate unusual satisfaction and positive attitudes toward the programs. The British Columbia Teachers' Federation "Program for Quality Teaching" has achieved striking results with teachers who practice "peer consultation" after learning the techniques of observation and feedback. Peer consultation is less prescriptive than most "peer coaching" programs. Teachers set their own goals, and the consultant does not play a directive role.

Other examples of new or different applications of techniques in units II, III, and IV can be found in community colleges, medical schools, and other forms of teaching. Modifications of the clinical supervision cycle can have positive effects when used collegially in elementary and secondary schools. Studies of mid-career teachers, collaborative or restructured schools, and programs of intensive assistance for teachers with problems all point to successful applications of these techniques. They also disclose instances where the techniques have not been applied appropriately.

Summaries and syntheses of the literature[19] along with points of view expressed by a number of writers[20] point to the need for substantial changes in how supervision is conducted in the schools and in teacher preparation programs.

NOTES

1. Kimball Wiles, *Supervision for Better Schools*, 3d ed. (Englewood Cliffs, NJ: Prentice-Hall, 1967).
2. Morris L. Cogan, *Supervision at the Harvard-Newton Summer School* (Cambridge, MA: Harvard Graduate School of Education, 1961).
3. Arthur Blumberg, *Supervisors and Teachers: A Private Cold War* (Berkeley, CA: McCutchan, 1974).
4. Their work is described in several books: Robert Goldhammer, *Clinical Supervision* (New York: Holt, Rinehart and Winston, 1969); Ralph L. Mosher and David E. Purpel, *Supervision: The Reluctant Profession* (Boston: Houghton Mifflin, 1972); Morris L. Cogan, *Clinical Supervision* (Boston: Houghton Mifflin, 1973).
5. Goldhammer, *Clinical Supervision*, p. 54.
6. Carl R. Rogers, *Client-Centered Therapy* (Boston: Houghton Mifflin, 1951).
7. Richard H. Weller, *Verbal Communication in Instructional Supervision* (New York: Teachers College Press, 1971).
8. Adapted from *ibid.*, pp. 19–20. The list has been rephrased and items pertaining to group clinical supervision have been omitted.
9. A poignant description of the conflicts caused by the teacher's dual role is presented in Susan Edgerton, "Teacher in Role Conflict: The Hidden Dilemma," *Phi Delta Kappan* (1977): 120–22.

10. By cooperating teacher we mean a classroom teacher who supervises a preservice intern or practice teacher.

11. Bruce R. Joyce, Kenneth R. Howey, Sam J. Yarger, and Teacher Corps Recruitment and Technical Resource Center Directors, *Inservice Teacher Education Report 1: Issues to Face* (Palo Alto, CA: Stanford Center for Research and Development in Teaching, 1976).

12. Weller, *Verbal Communication*, p. 20.

13. Arthur Blumberg and Edmund Amidon, "Teacher Perceptions of Supervisor-Teacher Interaction," *Administrators Notebook* 14 (1965): 1–8.

14. James L. Shinn, "Teacher Perceptions of Ideal and Actual Supervisory Procedures Used by California Elementary Principals: The Effects of Supervisory Training Programs Sponsored by the Association of California School Administrators" (Ph.D. diss., University of Oregon, 1976).

15. Gary S. Martin, "Teacher and Administrator Attitudes toward Evaluation and Systematic Classroom Observation" (Ph.D. diss., University of Oregon, 1975).

16. Saad Adwani, "The Relationship between Teacher and Supervisor as Perceived by Teachers, Supervisors and Principals in Secondary Schools in Saudi Arabia" (Ph.D. diss., University of Oregon, 1981); Saleh al-Tuwaijri, "The Relationship between Ideal and Actual Supervisory Practice as Perceived by Supervisors in Saudi Arabia" (Ph.D. diss., University of Oregon, 1985).

17. Norman J. Boyan and Willis D. Copeland, "A Training Program for Supervisors: Anatomy of an Educational Development," *Journal of Educational Research* 68 (1974): 100–116.

18. Blumberg and Amidon, "Teacher Perceptions."

19. For further references we recommend the annotated bibliographies and syntheses produced by the ERIC Clearinghouse on Educational Management at the University of Oregon in collaboration with the North Central Regional Educational Laboratory, 1987. The annotated bibliographies are titled: *Models of Instructional Leadership; Teacher Evaluation; The Social and Organizational Context of Teaching.* The synthesis papers are *Instructional Leadership: A Composite Working Model; Teacher Evaluation as a Strategy for Improving Instruction; From Isolation to Collaboration; Improving the Work Environment of Teaching.*

20. Several prominent writers have begun to address the need for variations in the kinds of supervision needed by different individuals: Carl Glickman, Alan Glatthorn, Thomas Sergiovanni, John Smyth, Noreen Garman. Others have addressed the need for accountability through teacher evaluation: Richard Mannatt, Ronald Hyman, Daniel Duke and Richard Stiggens, Thomas McGreal. A host of articles and books on reflection, restructuring, collaboration, cooperation, collegiality, and related topics has also added to the knowledge base that can illuminate one's conception of the nature of clinical supervision.

chapter 2

Clinical Supervision and Effective Teaching

> *They who educate children well are more to be honored than they who produce them.*
>
> *Aristotle*

We reviewed various models of clinical supervision in chapter 1. One of their common elements is the goal of helping teachers become more effective. But what does "effective" mean?

Research has not yielded a simple answer to this question. Instead, researchers have discovered that it is a complex question because effective teaching has many dimensions. We will describe each of these dimensions with the intention of helping you clarify your notions about what it means to be an effective teacher. In turn, you can help your supervisees develop their notions. The ultimate goal is to develop a personal philosophy of teaching and use it to set supervision goals.

Some educators argue that teaching cannot be researched and analyzed because the criteria of effective teaching differ for every instructional situation and every teacher. We are sympathetic to this argument, but our experience suggests that most teachers and supervisors can develop serviceable definitions of effective teaching to guide the supervision process.

As a demonstration of this point, we suggest that you list five characteristics of a good elementary, secondary, or college teacher. (You can elaborate on this task by listing characteristics of an *ineffective* teacher.) Most educators find this task relatively easy to perform. Moreover, they usually agree with one another's lists. Rarely do we find a controversial characteristic—one that some educators think represents good teaching and other educators think represents bad teaching. Disagreement, if it occurs, usually concerns the relative importance of characteristics.

Here is a list of characteristics of good teaching generated in a workshop on teacher supervision. To what extent do these characteristics agree with your list? Would you change the order of this list?

Characteristics of a Good Teacher
- has positive relationships with students
- deals with students' emotions
- maintains discipline and control
- creates a favorable environment for learning
- recognizes and provides for individual differences
- enjoys working with students
- obtains students' involvement in learning
- is creative and innovative
- emphasizes teaching of reading skills
- gives students a good self-image
- engages in professional growth activities
- knows subject matter in depth
- is flexible
- is consistent
- displays fairness

Before you finalize your list of characteristics of good teaching, we recommend that you read the research findings in this chapter. To understand the research, however, you need to know something about how researchers conduct their studies. The most common approach is to compare the teaching practices of more effective teachers and less effective teachers. This type of inquiry is commonly called causal-comparative or correlational research. Another approach is to have a group of teachers (the experimental group) try a particular teaching practice. Another group of teachers (the control group) is asked to follow their usual practices or try a different teaching practice. If the experimental teaching method produces superior results, it is considered effective. This type of inquiry is commonly called experimental research.

It is necessary in correlational research to identify a criterion by which to define the more effective and less effective teachers whose teaching practices are to be compared. Similarly, in experimental research, it is necessary to identify a criterion to determine the relative effectiveness of the experimental and control groups.

Researchers have used various criteria in their studies. These criteria reflect different perspectives about what is important in schooling. If you do not agree with the criteria used by the researchers, you probably will disagree with their conclusions about what constitutes effective teaching. Because the criteria are so important to understanding this research, we have organized the following review into sections that correspond to different criteria of teaching effectiveness.

EFFECTIVE TEACHING OF ACADEMIC KNOWLEDGE AND SKILLS

Many educators and members of the general public believe that the major purpose of school is to help students acquire the knowledge and skills associated with reading, mathematics, history, geography, music, art, foreign languages, and other academic disciplines studied in the K–12 curriculum. From this perspective, a teacher is more or less effective depending on how much of the academic curriculum is mastered by his or her students.

The usual research procedure to determine how much is learned by the students of a particular teacher is to give the entire class a standardized achievement test before and after a period of instruction (usually, at the start and end of a school year). Teachers whose students make substantial gains in their test scores are considered more effective, whereas teachers whose students make small gains are considered less effective.

The meaning of teacher effectiveness in this type of research obviously depends on the achievement test or tests that are used. If a teacher's students make large gains on a reading test, the teacher can be judged to be effective in teaching reading, but that does not mean he is necessarily effective in teaching mathematics. It would be necessary to give the students a mathematics achievement test to make this determination.

The achievement test that is used in research places limits on the generalizability of the testing methods that are discovered to be effective. Teachers who are effective in teaching reading may rely on Method A more extensively than teachers who are less effective in teaching this subject. However, this does not necessarily mean that Method A is effective for teaching another academic subject, such as mathematics. The general effectiveness of a teaching method must be determined by correlating it with student gains on a variety of achievement tests. In the following research review, we emphasize teaching methods that were found to be effective across at least several school subjects.

Nine Teacher Characteristics Associated with Gains in Student Academic Achievement

Barak Rosenshine and Norma Furst synthesized the research that was done on teacher effectiveness up until approximately 1970.[1] They identified nine characteristics of teachers whose students make greater gains in academic achievement than students of other teachers. Those characteristics are:

1. clarity
2. variety in use of materials and methods
3. enthusiasm
4. task-oriented, businesslike approach to instruction
5. avoidance of harsh criticism
6. indirect teaching style

7. emphasis on teaching content covered on the criterion achievement test
8. use of structuring statements that provide an overview for what is about to happen or has happened
9. use of questions at multiple cognitive levels

Research studies reported after 1970 have continued to demonstrate the effectiveness of these teacher characteristics in promoting student learning. Procedures for observing each characteristic are described in unit III.

Direct and Indirect Teaching

Ned Flanders initiated an important line of research on effective teaching in the 1960s.[2] He identified two contrasting styles of teaching—direct and indirect. Direct teaching is characterized by teacher reliance on:

1. lecture
2. criticism
3. justification of authority
4. giving directions

Indirect teaching is characterized by teacher reliance on:

1. asking questions
2. accepting students' feelings
3. acknowledging students' ideas
4. giving praise and encouragement

Many research studies have found that students of "indirect" teachers learn more and have better attitudes toward learning than students of "direct" teachers.[3]

Flanders believed, though, that both direct and indirect behaviors are necessary in good teaching. For example, teachers can effectively use a direct teaching strategy, such as lecture and demonstration, to clarify a difficult curriculum topic. Even in this situation, however, the teacher can make the lecture and demonstration more indirect by asking questions occasionally to determine whether students are following the presentation. Effective teaching behavior, then, seems to involve appropriate use of indirect teaching techniques, not total reliance on them.

The Explicit Teaching Model

In recent years researchers have made a concerted effort to identify teacher behaviors that facilitate student learning in specific curriculum areas. Much of this research has focused on reading and mathematics instruction at the primary and elementary school levels.

Barak Rosenshine synthesized the findings of this body of research into an organized model of teaching, which he calls "explicit teaching."[4] The teaching is "explicit" because the teaching goals and steps are predictable and can be clearly analyzed and described. The six parts of the explicit teaching model are described in the list below. You will note that the first five parts of the model correspond approximately to a daily lesson plan. The sixth part—review—is incorporated into the lesson plan at periodic intervals.

The Six Elements of the Explicit Teaching Model

1. *Review.* Each day, start the lesson by correcting the previous night's homework and reviewing what students have recently been taught.
2. *Presentation.* Tell students the goals of today's lesson. Then present new information a little at a time, modeling procedures, giving clear examples, and checking often to make sure students understand.
3. *Guided practice.* Allow students to practice using the new information under the teacher's direction; ask many questions that give students abundant opportunities to correctly repeat or explain the procedure or concept that has just been taught. Student participation should be active until all students are able to respond correctly.
4. *Correction and feedback.* During guided practice, give students a great deal of feedback. When students answer incorrectly, reteach the lesson if necessary. When students answer correctly, explain why the answer was right. It is important that feedback be immediate and thorough.
5. *Independent practice.* Next, allow students to practice using the new information on their own. The teacher should be available to give short answers to students' questions, and students should be permitted to help each other.
6. *Weekly and monthly reviews.* At the beginning of each week, the teacher should review the previous week's lesson. At the end of the month, the teacher should review what students have learned during the last four weeks. It is important that students not be allowed to forget past lessons once they have moved on to new material.[5]

There is an interesting correspondence between the explicit teaching model and Madeline Hunter's model of effective teaching.[6] Her model, sometimes called Instructional Theory into Practice (ITIP), has had a major influence on American education for several decades. The seven components of the model and their counterpart in the explicit teaching model (in parentheses) are as follows:

1. anticipatory set (review)
2. stating of objectives (presentation)
3. information input (presentation)
4. modeling (presentation)
5. checking for understanding (presentation; correction and feedback)
6. guided and independent practice (guided practice; independent practice)
7. closure (weekly and monthly review)

Hunter based her model on a different, older base of research knowledge than did Rosenshine, yet they drew similar conclusions about the elements of effective teaching.

Rosenshine claims that the explicit teaching model is applicable to any "well-structured" school subject, such as "mathematical procedures and computations, reading decoding, explicit reading procedures such as distinguishing fact from opinion, science facts and concepts, social studies facts and concepts, map skills, grammatical concepts and rules, and foreign language vocabulary and grammar."[7] These examples represent what is generally known as lower-cognitive objectives. Effective teaching of higher cognitive objectives requires different methods, which are discussed in the next section. Rosenshine further delimited the situations for which the explicit teaching model is effective:

> It would be a mistake to say that this small-step approach applies to all students or all situations. It is most important for young learners, slow learners, and for all learners when the material is new, difficult, or hierarchical. In these situations, relatively short presentations are followed by student practice. However, when teaching older, brighter students, or when teaching in the middle of a unit, the steps are larger, that is, the presentations are longer, less time is spent in checking for understanding or in guided practice, and more independent practice can be done as homework because the students do not need as much help and supervision.[8]

These qualifications about the use of the explicit teaching model have an important implication for the supervision of teachers. Specifically, they imply that a supervisor should not use the explicit teaching model, or any other teaching model, as an absolute set of criteria for evaluating a teacher or for setting improvement goals. Instead, the supervisor needs first to determine the teacher's instructional context through a planning conference (see unit II). Then the supervisor and teacher can discuss appropriate teaching methods to use in that context. This discussion, in turn, provides a basis for determining which aspects of the teacher's behavior to record during the observation phase of the supervision cycle.

Effective Teaching of Thinking Skills

The distinction between lower-cognitive and higher-cognitive learning outcomes is often made. In Bloom's taxonomy, for example, six cognitive levels of learning are distinguished.[9] The knowledge, comprehension, and application levels are generally considered to be lower-cognitive learning outcomes, whereas the analysis, synthesis, and evaluation levels are higher-cognitive learning outcomes. (These outcomes sometimes are called "thinking skills.") Many educators are concerned about the development of students' thinking skills in addition to their mastery of the basic school curriculum. Nancy Cole, a vice-president of Educational Testing Service, recently observed that lower-cognitive and higher-cognitive objectives in the curriculum reflect different theories about learning and different measurement approaches.[10] With respect to lower-cognitive learning, Cole observed:

By the 1960s, behavioral psychology dominated conceptions of learning in psychology and in education. The learning theory with which a generation of educators grew up came directly from this field. It was heavily based on studies of animal learning and was closely connected with the learning of specific, discrete skills described as precise, well-delimited behaviors. . . .

The theories that supported behavioral psychology were well suited to the political times of increasing public concern that children were not learning to read, write, nor perform basic arithmetic operations. There was also public concern that students were not learning basic factual information. The result of this merging of theoretical and political orientation was a decade (the seventies) in which the strongly dominant conception of educational achievement in public discussion was in terms of specific, separate, basic skills and facts.[11]

Much of the research that led to the development of the explicit teaching model described above involved this conception of learning.

Cole observed that another conception of learning recently has come into prominence:

Alongside the conception of achievement as mastery of basic skills and facts, and often competing with it, stands a dramatically different conception of educational achievement. This conception focuses on a more complex level of achievement—the achievement of higher order skills (using such terms as critical thinking or problem solving) and of advanced knowledge of subjects (using words such as understanding or expertise).[12]

The importance of thinking skills is supported by recent advances in cognitive psychology. Also, measurement experts are currently working to develop tests that assess students' learning of these skills. These tests are strikingly different from the multiple-choice response tests traditionally used to assess student achievement.[13]

If you and your supervisee value the teaching of thinking skills, you will need to decide which teaching practices and assessment techniques are effective for this purpose. Research on this problem is still fragmentary, but it does provide general guidance.

The discussion method is, at this time, the best validated approach for promoting higher cognitive learning.[14] Most of this research, however, has involved college students and other adult learners. There is no reason why younger students would not benefit from discussion teaching, but it may be more difficult to create the necessary classroom conditions. For example, Meredith Gall and Joyce Gall stated that the essential elements of a discussion are small group size (six to eight students) and students talking to each other rather than to the teacher.[15] The teacher may set the problem for discussion, but then serves primarily as moderator and facilitator of student-to-student interaction. We, and others, have found it possible to train even young students in discussion skills and to organize them into small groups.

Another teaching practice that can be used to promote the development of thinking skills is asking higher-cognitive questions. These questions can be asked in a variety of instructional contexts: in discussions, in inquiry teaching, in reviewing what students have read (i.e., the traditional recitation), and even interspersed in a lecture or demonstration.

Researchers have not yet determined for certain the effectiveness of higher-cognitive questions. Philip Winne reviewed the research and concluded that it made no difference to student learning whether the teacher emphasized higher-cognitive or lower-cognitive questions. Doris Redfield and Elaine Rosseau reviewed essentially the same research, but concluded that teacher emphasis on higher-cognitive questions led to more learning. Complicating the picture is Barak Rosenshine's review of three major classroom studies, from which he concluded that lower-cognitive questions were more effective.[16] Also complicating the picture is that most of the studies included in the reviews did not differentiate the effects of higher-cognitive questions on thinking skills and on lower-cognitive learning outcomes.

Our view of the situation is that higher-cognitive questions are probably necessary, but not sufficient, for the development of students' ability to think. Higher-cognitive questions cue students that thinking is expected and important. However, these questions may be ineffective if the student is unable to respond appropriately. For example, the three studies reviewed by Rosenshine were done in primary-grade classrooms in low-achieving urban schools. Higher-cognitive questions, in the absence of any other intervention, might very well have no effect on—or even frustrate—these students. By contrast, Christiaan Hamaker found in his review of research that higher-cognitive questions inserted in reading passages had a consistently positive effect on students' thinking skills.[17] The research he reviewed was mostly done with college students, which is a population that would be able to handle the response demands of questions at the higher-cognitive levels.

For younger students, we think teachers should ask higher-cognitive questions routinely, but also they should provide appropriate instruction and conditions for answering them. This means, for example, modeling the appropriate thinking processes, which can be done by "thinking aloud" for students. Also in contrast to explicit teaching, the teacher needs to give students opportunities for self-expression (rather than carefully defined tasks), substantial projects and tasks (rather than drill-type worksheets), and elaborated, open-ended feedback (rather than correct-incorrect feedback).

The implication of the preceding discussion for clinical supervision is that the supervisor and teacher concerned about the development of students' thinking skills need to analyze carefully the teaching task. They need to examine not only the cognitive level of the teachers' questions, but also the teacher's use of teaching practices that model and encourage use of thinking skills.

Effective Use of Time in Teaching

Only a certain amount of time is available for instruction. Research has found that teachers' use of this time has a major impact on how well students master the curriculum.

One aspect of time use is allocated time, which is the amount of time that the teacher provides for instruction on each subject or topic. David Berliner and his colleagues found that some elementary teachers spend as little as 16 minutes per average day on mathematics instruction, whereas other teachers spend as much as 50 minutes per average day. The range of allocated time was even greater in reading instruction: from a low of 45 minutes per average day to a high of more than two hours per average day. Walter Borg concluded from his review of research on allocated time that the more time a teacher allocates to instruction in a particular content area, the more students learn about that content area.[18]

If allocated time is the focus of supervision, the supervisor and teacher can review how the teacher plans the time to be spent on each subject during a typical school day. In secondary school instruction, this type of planning is not relevant because the length of class periods and course subjects are fixed. However, most secondary teachers have discretion about allocation of time for particular topics—for example, in a U.S. history class, how much time to spend on the Civil War versus the Reconstruction Period following the war. Similarly, the teacher may have discretion about how much time to allocate to historical facts versus historical concepts. The supervisor and teacher can discuss alternative time allocation patterns and their respective merits.

Students are seldom attentive during the total time allocated for each subject. The percentage of allocated time that students are attentive is sometimes called engaged time or at-task time. Walter Borg concluded from the review of research mentioned above that classes with a high percentage of at-task time have better academic achievement than classes with a low percentage of at-task time. For this reason, at-task time is a frequent focus of clinical supervision. Chapters 6 and 8 present procedures for collecting observational data on this important instructional variable.

If students' at-task time is found to be low, the supervisor and teacher should consider methods for improving it. One possibility is for teachers to increase substantive interaction with students. (Substantive interaction involves explaining content to students, asking them questions, giving feedback, and providing assistance during seatwork.) We make this suggestion because Charles Fisher and his colleagues found that teachers who had more substantive interaction with their students had a higher percentage of student at-task time.[19] Their research involved elementary teaching, but it seems reasonable that a similar relationship would be found in secondary school teaching.

A high rate of substantive interaction may not be necessary if students are motivated and have good independent learning skills. Students who are lacking in these areas, however, can easily get off task if left to work on their own for substantial periods of time. Therefore, like so many aspects of teaching, substantive interaction is not necessarily effective. It depends on the characteristics of the teacher's students.

Homework extends the amount of possible time that students can be engaged in mastering the curriculum. Harris Cooper found in his extensive review of the research on homework that it has relatively little effect on elementary school students' achievement, but a substantial effect on the achievement of older students.[20] The supervisor and teacher can review the teacher's homework policy to determine whether homework is desirable for his or her students; and if so, the amount and type of homework that should be assigned, and how it should be reviewed in class and graded.

EFFECTIVE DEVELOPMENT OF STUDENT ATTITUDES AND MOTIVATION TO LEARN

Attitudes and motivation to learn involve the affective domain of education. They are not easy terms to define, but their manifestations are easy to recognize. We usually can tell through observation whether students are eagerly involved in a learning task, bored by it, or repelled by it. Also, most students, if asked, will tell you which subjects they like and dislike.

Researchers generally distinguish three components of attitudes: beliefs, feelings, and actions. For example, a student who has a positive attitude toward mathematics might believe that math plays an important role in the world of work, might experience positive feelings when working on a challenging math problem, and might act by choosing to learn something new about mathematics rather than engaging in some other activity. Of the three components of attitudes, the most observable—and probably the most important—is action.

By observing how students act in situations that allow choice, we can tell fairly well whether they have a positive or negative attitude toward an "object" (a person, event, book, place, etc.). A positive attitude is manifested by choosing to approach the object, whereas a negative attitude is manifested by choosing to avoid the object. School attitudes can be internalized at different levels of personality. At a superficial level of internalization, the student is motivated to learn, but only with proper stimulation by the teacher. At the deepest level of internalization, the attitude has become an integral part of the student's personality. We can say that the attitude has become a value because it motivates much of the student's life without external prompting. David Krathwohl and his colleagues developed a taxonomy that differentiated the various levels at which attitudes can be internalized.[21]

Each of us has many different attitudes. In other words, we have opinions and feelings about virtually everything with which we come into contact. With respect to education, students usually have an attitude toward each subject they study, toward their teachers, toward their school, and even toward themselves (sometimes called academic self-concept or academic self-esteem).

The development of positive academic attitudes is an important outcome of instruction. One of the most famous of educators, John Dewey, made this point compellingly:

> Perhaps the greatest of all pedagogical fallacies is the notion that a person learns only the particular thing he is studying at the time. Collateral learning in the way of formation of enduring attitudes of likes and dislikes, may be and often is much more important than the spelling lesson or lesson in geography or history that is learned. For these attitudes are fundamentally what counts in the future.[22]

In the public school curriculum, academic knowledge and skills are given more emphasis than attitudes, yet some instructional outcomes involving attitudes can be found. Teachers of social studies usually want students to develop informed beliefs about important social issues and to act as responsible citizens. Teachers of foreign languages usually want students to appreciate the cultures that use the language they are teaching. And teachers of scientific disciplines want students to value scientific inquiry and to develop an appreciation of the natural world.

Which teaching methods are effective for helping students develop these and other attitudes? Some research has been done to answer this question, but the results tend not to be firm or focused on well-defined attitudes. Therefore, the findings that we review below should be considered tentative and used cautiously in clinical supervision.

Several researchers have investigated the effects of teacher enthusiasm on student attitudes. A. Guy Larkins and his colleagues reviewed this research and concluded that teaching with enthusiasm generally promotes positive student attitudes.[23] Procedures for observing a teacher's level of enthusiasm are described in chapter 7.

Another teaching technique whose effect on student attitudes has been investigated is use of praise. N. L. Gage reviewed this research and concluded that teacher praise has a positive effect on student attitudes. More recent research suggests that the effectiveness of teacher praise depends on its content and context.[24] Guidelines for effective use of praise are presented in chapter 5.

Wilbert McKeachie and James Kulik reviewed research at the college level comparing the effectiveness of the lecture method and the discussion method in changing attitudes. They concluded that discussion is the more effective method. In a review of research involving younger students, Joyce and Meredith Gall concluded that the discussion method has positive effects on the attitudes of elementary and high school students. The Galls claim that the distinguishing characteristic of discussion is its emphasis on student-to-student interaction, which is lacking in lecture and other common methods such as recitation and seatwork.[25]

Although discussion is effective in developing student attitudes, it has the potential to be misused. For example, discussion can change students' attitudes by exposing them to new information that changes their belief system (a component of attitudes). Therefore, the teacher must be careful that students do not learn inaccurate information. Another pitfall is that a discussion can reinforce existing negative attitudes, such as racial prejudice, if all the students in the group feel the same way about the topic being discussed.[26] This problem usually can be avoided by forming heterogeneous discussion groups.

Cooperative learning has become a popular teaching method in recent years. It is similar to the discussion method in that students contribute to each other's learning by working together in small groups. It differs from the discussion method, however, because it usually requires the completion of a specific academic task—such as a list of ideas, a visual display, or the solution to a problem—that can be evaluated and graded. By contrast, discussion does not usually have a tangible goal that can be evaluated, and students are not required to cooperate with each other more than to avoid personal attacks and to listen carefully to each other.

Research on cooperative learning has found that it is effective both for improving students' academic achievement and for developing important social attitudes. Robert Slavin, who reviewed this body of research, stated that these attitudinal outcomes include: increased liking and respect among students of different racial or ethnic backgrounds, improved social acceptance of mainstreamed students by their classmates, more friendships among students, gains in self-esteem, and liking of school and of the subject being discussed.[27]

Student motivation to learn is not quite the same thing as an attitude, but it is similar. We can think of motivation to learn as how the student feels about becoming engaged in instruction, whereas an attitude is how the student feels following instruction.

Jere Brophy identified various teaching methods that can increase student motivation to learn. The methods stem from two basic principles:

> In order to motivate their students to learn, teachers need both to help their students appreciate the value of academic activities and to make sure that the students can succeed in these activities if they apply reasonable effort.[28]

For example, if students feel that they are likely to fail their general science course even if they apply effort, they will lack motivation and develop a negative attitude toward the course and toward science generally. Also, if students do not see the relevance of science to their lives or do not value the consequences of doing well in the course (e.g., a good grade, teacher and parent approval), they will not be motivated to learn. Teaching methods that allow students to be successful or that show them the importance of the topic being studied are likely to be effective in improving students' motivation to learn.

To summarize, various teaching methods can improve students' attitudes and motivation to learn. The implications for clinical supervision are clear. If the teacher is concerned about his or her students' attitude to instruction, the supervisor and teacher can plan to collect observation data on the teacher's use of the practices described above—enthusiastic teaching style, praise, discussion and cooperative learning, the opportunity for students to experience academic success, and helping students see the relevance and value of learning. What all these teaching practices have in common is the development of a positive classroom climate involving all participants: teacher with students and students with each other.

TEACHER EFFECTIVENESS IN RESPONDING TO INTELLECTUAL, CULTURAL, AND GENDER DIFFERENCES AMONG STUDENTS

In typical research on teacher effectiveness, the usual criterion is how much the teacher's class as a whole learns over a period of time. This means that the mean score of the class on an achievement test can show a gain, but the gain may result from a small number of students benefitting substantially from instruction, while other students learn relatively little or nothing at all.

Some researchers deal with this problem by investigating whether teachers behave differently toward different groups of students. Other research concerns whether different teaching practices are effective for these groups. For example, teaching method A may be effective for male students, whereas teaching method B is effective for female students.

In this section, we briefly review major findings on effective teaching of different groups of students present in a typical classroom.

Effective Teaching of Students Who Differ in Achievement Level

Thomas Good recently reviewed the research on differential teacher treatment of high-achieving and low-achieving students. He identified 17 teaching practices that are used with different frequencies with these two groups of students. The teaching practices are listed below.[29] They define a pattern of diminished expectations for low-achieving students' ability to learn, and perhaps a lower regard for their personal worth as learners.

> ### Differences in Teacher Behavior Toward High-Achieving and Low-Achieving Students
>
> 1. Wait less time for "lows" to answer questions.
> 2. Give "lows" the answer or call on someone else rather than try to improve their responses by giving clues or using other teaching techniques.
> 3. Reward inappropriate behavior or incorrect answers by "lows."
> 4. Criticize "lows" more often for failure.
> 5. Praise "lows" less frequently than "highs" for success.
> 6. Fail to give feedback to the public responses of "lows."
> 7. Pay less attention to "lows" or interact with them less frequently.
> 8. Call on "lows" less often to respond to questions, or ask them only easier, nonanalytical questions.
> 9. Seat "lows" farther away from the teacher.
> 10. Demand less from "lows."
> 11. Interact with "lows" more privately than publicly and monitor and structure their activities more closely.
> 12. Grade tests or assignments in a differential manner, so that "highs" but not "lows" are given the benefit of the doubt in borderline cases.
> 13. Have less friendly interaction with "lows," including less smiling and less warm or more anxious voice tones.
> 14. Provide briefer and less informative feedback to the questions of "lows."
> 15. Provide less eye contact and other nonverbal communication of attention and responsiveness in interacting with "lows."
> 16. Make less use of effective but time-consuming instructional methods with "lows" when time is limited.
> 17. Evidence less acceptance and use of ideas given by "lows."

Academic achievement is highly correlated with social class, meaning that low-achieving students are more likely to come from disadvantaged home backgrounds, whereas high-achieving students are likely to come from advantaged home backgrounds. Therefore, the differential teaching practices listed by Good suggest a pattern of discrimination based on students' social class as well as their achievement level.

If observational data reveal that a teacher treats high-achieving and low-achieving students differently, the clinical supervisor can help the teacher recognize this pattern of behavior and adopt more equitable, effective patterns. For example, suppose a teacher discovers that he waits less time for low-achieving students to respond than he waits for high-achieving students. This teacher might set the goal of giving low-achieving students at least as much time to respond, and perhaps more time if they need it. Similar goals for equitable treatment of low-achieving or socially disadvantaged students could be set for the other 16 teacher behaviors listed.

Effective Teaching of Ethnically and Racially Different Students

There is evidence that some teachers act differently toward students depending upon their ethnic background or race. An important study of this phenomenon was done by Gregg Jackson and Cecilia Cosca. Their study was sponsored by the U.S. Commission on Civil Rights to determine whether teachers in the Southwest distribute their verbal behavior differentially among Anglo and Chicano students.[30] Observers recorded verbal behaviors in fourth-, eighth-, tenth-, and twelfth-grade classes in 52 schools. A modified form of the Flanders Interaction Analysis System (see chapter 8) was used to classify each verbal interaction and whether it was directed to, or initiated by, an Anglo student or a Chicano student.

Jackson and Cosca found that teachers directed significantly more of their verbal behaviors toward Anglo students than toward Chicano students. The most striking results were that teachers "praised or encouraged Anglos 35% more than they did Chicanos, accepted or used Anglos' ideas 40% more than they did those of Chicanos, and directed 21% more questions to Anglos than to Chicanos." The researchers also found that Anglo students initiated more verbal behaviors than did Chicano students. In a review of similar research, Meredith and Joyce Gall found that black students tend to participate less in discussions than white students.[31]

The research discussed above consists of older studies, so they may not accurately represent current practices. However, because of the importance of student ethnicity and race, clinical supervisors should be sensitive to whether teachers provide equal opportunities for students of all ethnic backgrounds and races to learn, and also to whether teachers include multicultural dimensions of the curriculum in their instruction. Educators differ in what they consider effective teaching practices for these purposes. These differences reflect different philosophies of multicultural education. James Banks distinguished between three such philosophies.[32] They are as follows:

1. *Cultural pluralism:* the goal of the curriculum is to help students function more effectively in their own ethnic culture and to help liberate them from ethnic oppression.

2. *Assimilationism:* the goal is to help students develop a commitment to the common culture and its values.
3. *Multiethnicism:* the goal is to help students learn how to function effectively within the common culture, their own ethnic culture, and other ethnic cultures.

It is important for teachers to be clear about which of these philosophies, or some other philosophy, guides their instruction. Otherwise, they run the risk of ignoring multicultural aspects of teaching, or, worse, succumbing to their prejudices and thereby depriving some students of equal opportunity for learning.

Margaret Pusch and her colleagues reviewed the literature on effective multicultural teaching practices and teacher characteristics.[33] They concluded that effective teachers

1. have an open mind to new ideas and experiences.
2. have empathy for people from other cultures.
3. perceive similarities and differences between a student's culture and their own accurately.
4. describe a student's behavior without judging it.
5. are free from ethnocentrism.
6. express respect and positive regard for all students through eye contact, body posture, and voice tone and pitch.
7. are knowledgeable about the contributions of minority groups to America and to the world.
8. use multicultural materials in the classroom.
9. recognize and accept both the language spoken in the home and the standard language.
10. help students develop pride in and identification with their native culture.

These probably are effective teaching practices and qualities, irrespective of the teacher's philosophy of multicultural education. The picture that emerges from the list is of a teacher who respects all students and who takes responsibility for knowing about their cultural backgrounds and using this knowledge in his or her teaching.

Effective Teaching of Male and Female Students

There is strong evidence that some teachers treat boys and girls differently during classroom instruction. For example, Jere Brophy found that teachers interact more frequently with boys, give them more feedback and help, and criticize and praise them more frequently.[34] These differences may be more pronounced in traditionally male-stereotyped subjects, such as mathematics. In research on fourth-grade mathematics classes, for example, Elizabeth Fennema and Penelope Peterson found that teachers

1. initiated more interactions with boys for the purpose of socializing and classroom management.

2. received and accepted more "call out" responses from boys.
3. more frequently called on boys for both the answers and the explanations of how the answers were obtained when working on word problems.[35]

These findings indicate that teachers tend to treat boys more favorably than girls. If a teacher is observed to do this, the clinical supervisor can help the teacher reallocate interaction patterns so that girls are treated more equitably. In the case of traditionally male-stereotyped subjects, more radical changes may be necessary. Fennema and Peterson found that competitive games tended to help boys learn basic math skills but tended to harm girls' learning of these skills. A different pattern was found for cooperative learning activities: they tended to help girls, but not boys, learn math problem-solving skills. These findings suggest that teachers need to learn how to maintain a delicate balance of competitive and cooperative activities so that both boys and girls have equal opportunity to use learning styles that are effective for them.

Fennema and Peterson also make this recommendation: "Perhaps the most important thing that a teacher can do is to expect girls to work independently. Teachers should encourage girls to engage in independent learning behavior and praise them for participating in and performing well on high-level cognitive mathematics tasks."[36] This type of encouragement may not be necessary for the typical male student, for whom independence and problem solving have been internalized as part of his role identity.

Although Fennema and Peterson's recommendations focus on mathematics instruction, they seem appropriate to other male-stereotyped subjects, such as the sciences and mechanical trades.

EFFECTIVE CLASSROOM MANAGEMENT

Daniel Duke defined classroom management as "the provisions and procedures necessary to establish and maintain an environment in which instruction and learning can occur."[37] This definition implies that classroom management is not the same thing as teaching, but is a necessary precondition for teaching.

As one would expect, researchers have found that students' academic achievement is higher in well-managed classrooms.[38] This is probably because students are more on task in such classrooms, and their learning processes are better organized.

Many teachers, both preservice and in-service, have difficulty managing their classroom. Their difficulty usually is manifested in two ways: (1) the progression of classroom events is disorganized and frequently interrupted, and (2) many of the students are "off task." The occurrence of these problems is usually distressing for the teacher, as well as for the clinical supervisor. Therefore, supervisors should know effective classroom management practices that can help the teacher bring the class under control.

Carolyn Evertson recently summarized the research that she and her colleagues, and others, have done on classroom management.[39] She identified several practices that effective classroom managers have been observed to use:

1. careful analysis of the rules and procedures that need to be in place so that students can learn effectively in the classroom setting
2. statement of the rules and procedures in simple, clear language so that students can understand them easily
3. systematic teaching of the rules and procedures at the start of the school year, or when beginning a new course with new students
4. continuous monitoring of students' compliance with the rules and procedures, and also careful record keeping of students' academic work

These effective management practices were identified by research in elementary and junior high school classes, but they seem equally applicable to high school classes.

Carefully formulated rules and procedures are at the heart of a good classroom management system. The teacher needs to analyze the instruction in all its complexity, and formulate a rule or procedure to cover each situation. Walter Doyle's comprehensive analysis of classroom management suggests that rules and procedures are needed for the following tasks and situations:

1. seat assignment in the classroom
2. start and end of class (e.g., "Be in your seat and ready to work when the bell rings.")
3. handing in of assignments, materials, etc.
4. permissible activities if a student completes seatwork early
5. leaving the room while class is in session
6. standards for the form and neatness of one's desk, notebooks, assignments, etc.
7. supplies and materials to be brought to class
8. signals for seeking help or indicating a willingness to answer a teacher question addressed to the class as a whole
9. acceptable noise level in the room
10. acceptability of verbal and physical aggression
11. moving around the room to sharpen pencils, get materials, etc.
12. storage of materials, hats, boots, etc., in the classroom
13. consumption of food and gum
14. selection of classroom helpers
15. late assignments and make-up work[40]

The above list demonstrates that managing a classroom is a complex process. It also suggests how a class can easily get out of control if students do not have clear rules and procedures to follow.

In addition to rules and procedures, teachers must consider the physical features of the classroom. Carolyn Evertson found that effective managers arrange their classrooms with three principles in mind:

1. *Visibility.* Students should be able to see the instructional displays. The teacher should have a clear view of instruction areas, students' work areas, and learning centers to facilitate monitoring of students.

2. *Accessibility.* High-traffic areas (areas for group work, pencil sharpener, door to the hall) should be kept clear and separated from each other.
3. *Distractibility.* Arrangements that can compete with the teacher for students' attention (seating students facing the windows to the playground, door to the hall, face to face with each other but away from the teacher) should be minimized.[41]

Effective managers also take care to secure an adequate supply of textbooks and materials for all the students in the classroom.

Another important aspect of classroom management is the teacher's procedures for handling student misbehavior. Common types of misbehavior are: tardiness, cutting class, failure to bring supplies and books to class, inattentiveness, noisiness, callouts, and verbal or physical aggression. Even effective teachers experience student misbehavior, but they manage it differently than less effective teachers. One of their primary techniques is to deal with the misbehavior early before it has a chance to escalate. Another technique is to use an intervention that stops the misbehavior with the least disruption to the ongoing instruction. Eye contact, physical proximity to the misbehaving student, or "the look" are examples of such interventions. In the words of Walter Doyle, "successful interventions tend to have a private and fleeting quality that does not interrupt the flow of events."[42]

Other techniques are also effective in managing student misbehavior. Discussion of these techniques, as well as comprehensive models of classroom discipline, is beyond the scope of this book but is available in other sources.[43]

EFFECTIVE PLANNING AND DECISION MAKING

Madeline Hunter, an influential teacher educator, defined teaching as "the process of making and implementation decisions, before, during, and after instruction, to increase the probability of learning."[44] If this is true, it is important for the clinical supervisor to help teachers make the most effective decisions possible.

Teacher decisions that are made before and after instruction are commonly referred to as teacher planning. This planning is important for the obvious reason that it affects the instruction that students receive in the classroom. For example, Christopher Clark and Penelope Peterson found in their review of research that teachers' plans influence the content of instruction, the sequence in which topics get taught, and the allocation of time to different topics and subjects.[45]

Christopher Clark and Robert Yinger did a research study in which they found that teachers engage in as many as eight different types of planning during the course of a school year.[46] Two of the types—unit planning and lesson planning—involve the content of instruction. The other six types involve planning for different time spans of instruction: daily, weekly, short-range, long-range, term, and yearly. Clark and Yinger also found that planning is not a linear process and that it does not occur at a single point in time. Rather, teachers develop their plans incrementally, starting from a general idea and then gradually elaborating it. The development of their plans is influenced by their reflections on previous plans and experience in the classroom. Clark and Yinger did their study with elementary school teachers, but the findings seem equally applicable to teachers of other grade levels.

Clinical supervisors find that some teachers have difficulty with instruction because they do not plan effectively. One approach to helping these teachers is to ask them to make written lesson plans. However, the research reviewed above suggests that this approach is simplistic, because it does not acknowledge the incremental, cyclical nature of lesson planning or the fact that other types of planning (e.g., unit, weekly) may be more important to a particular teacher. The writing of structured lesson plans may be a useful starting point for the development of planning skills, but it probably should not be the only training focus.

Researchers have not determined whether particular types of planning are more effective than other types in promoting student learning. It seems likely, though, that more effective teachers engage in careful, reflective planning, whereas less effective teachers engage in sporadic or no planning. A clinical supervisor who agrees with this supposition would work with teachers to increase the amount of time they spend planning and help them develop detailed, reflective plans of the various types described above.

We turn now to the decisions that teachers make during the act of instruction. These decisions—sometimes called interactive decisions—involve a deliberate choice to act in a specific way while teaching. Clark and Peterson, in their review of research, found that "on the average, teachers make one interactive decision every 2 minutes."[47] This research finding supports Madeline Hunter's characterization of teaching as a process of decision making.

Researchers have discovered several principles of effective interactive decision making.[48] One of their findings involves teachers' decision making when they judge students' classroom behavior to be unacceptable. Teachers who are prone to consider alternative teaching strategies to handle the problem, but who decide not to implement them, have lower-achieving classes.

Teachers who do not act on alternatives may have a rigid teaching style. Supervisors need to help them learn how to make on-the-spot changes in teaching strategy to accommodate the idiosyncratic, circumstantial nature of student behavior in the classroom.

Another finding is that the decisions of effective teachers are more conceptually based, rapid, and simpler than the decisions of less effective teachers. This finding suggests that clinical supervisors should recommend to teachers that they learn a conceptual model, or models, of teaching. A starting point might be to have teachers study the models presented in this chapter. In addition, the supervisor can recommend that teachers participate in an inservice program where they can learn about Instructional Theory into Practice (ITIP) or other teaching models. It makes sense that these models would facilitate decision making: They simplify the teacher's thinking by focusing attention on salient aspects of instruction; this simplification, in turn, enables quick decisions and changes in actions without disturbing the flow of instruction.

EFFECTIVE IMPLEMENTATION
OF CURRICULUM CHANGE

The school curriculum is constantly changing. The following are just a few examples of curriculum innovations that are currently being introduced into many schools: whole language instruction; instruction in mathematical problem solving; study skills instruction; global studies; thinking skills instruction; instruction in information retrieval using hypercard software. Even the traditional curriculum changes with each new textbook adoption. Some textbook topics are added or given more emphasis, while others are dropped or given less emphasis. The curriculum also is revised to reflect changing perspectives about ethnicity, gender, and other aspects of society.

The manner in which a teacher implements a curriculum change affects students' learning. For example, suppose a school district changes its mathematics curriculum to put more emphasis on problem solving. Teachers who implement the new curriculum fully will give their students more opportunity to learn mathematical problem-solving skills than teachers who implement it halfheartedly or not at all. As would be expected, researchers have found that students' opportunity to learn a curriculum affects how much of the curriculum they actually learn.[49]

The preceding analysis demonstrates that one aspect of effective teaching is implementation of curriculum change. Clinical supervisors should be sensitive to this aspect of teachers' work and help teachers who experience difficulty with it. To do this, supervisors need to be knowledgeable about the process of curriculum implementation and factors that affect it. The following discussion focuses on teacher characteristics that affect curriculum implementation. Research on other factors is reviewed in other sources.[50]

One of the supervisor's first tasks is to assess the teacher's level of implementation of the curriculum change. Gene Hall and his colleagues conducted research that is relevant to this task. They found that there are eight levels at which teachers can implement curriculum change:

Level 0-Non-use. The teacher has no knowledge of or involvement with the new curriculum.

Level I-Orientation. The teacher is acquiring information about the new curriculum.

Level II-Preparation. The teacher is preparing for first use of the new curriculum.

Level III-Mechanical use. The teacher is trying to master the basics of the new curriculum.

Level IVA-Routine. The teacher's use of the new curriculum is stabilized.

Level IVB-Refinement. The teacher varies use of the new curriculum to increase its impact on students.

Level V-Integration. The teacher combines his or her own efforts with those of colleagues to maximize the benefits of the new curriculum for students.

Level VI-Renewal. The teacher modifies the new curriculum in a major way, searches for new alternatives, or sets other goals to further help students.

This model of implementation is applicable to virtually any curriculum change. Hall and his colleagues developed a general interview procedure that supervisors can use to assess the level at which the teacher is implementing a curriculum change.[51]

The supervisor will want to know not only a teacher's level of implementation, but also his concerns about using the new curriculum. Hall found that these concerns follow a predictable progression of stages.[52] The stages are shown in Table 2.1. The first three concerns focus on the self, and are typical of teachers whose use of the new curriculum is at level 0 (non-use) or I (orientation). Management concerns typify teachers at level II (preparation) or III (mechanical use). Finally, impact concerns typify teachers at level IVB (refinement), V (integration), or VI (renewal).

The supervisor can assess the teacher's concerns in the conference phase of the clinical supervision cycle. Another approach is to administer the Stages of Concern Questionnaire (SoCQ), a simple paper-and-pencil instrument consisting of 35 rating items.[53]

Walter Doyle and Gerald Ponder identified additional teacher concerns that affect teachers' implementation of a curriculum change. They found that teachers follow a "practicality ethic" in deciding how much commitment to make to a curriculum change. This means that teachers judge the curriculum change to be practical to the extent that it is (1) stated clearly and specifically, (2) congruent with teachers' existing beliefs and practices, and (3) cost-effective in terms of benefits to students relative to teachers' expenditure of energy. Research by Georgea Mohlman, Theodore Coladarci, and N. L. Gage confirmed the importance of the practicality ethic in determining the extent to which teachers implement a curriculum change.[54]

TABLE 2.1 Stages of concern about implementing a curriculum change

Stages of Concern	Typical Expressions of Concern
Self Concerns	
0. Awareness	I am not concerned about it (the curriculum change).
1. Informational	I would like to know more about it.
2. Personal	How will using it affect me?
Task Concerns	
3. Management	I seem to be spending all my time getting material ready.
Impact	
4. Consequences	How is my use affecting kids?
5. Collaboration	I am concerned about relating what I am doing with what other instructors are doing.
6. Refocusing	I have some ideas about something that would work even better.

SOURCE: Adapted from Shirley M. Hord, William L. Rutherford, Leslie Huling-Austin, and Gene E. Hall, *Taking Charge of Change* (Alexandria, VA: Association for Supervision and Curriculum Development, 1987), p. 31.

To summarize, one indicator of effective teaching is how well the teacher implements a curriculum change. Effective teachers achieve a high level of implementation (levels IVB, V, and VI in Hall's model), whereas ineffective teachers are fixated at lower levels. Their fixation may result from unresolved concerns or perceptions that the new curriculum is impractical. Supervisors can help these teachers by addressing their concerns and perceptions through a clinical supervision process.

TOWARD A DEFINITION OF EFFECTIVE TEACHING

Recent research on teaching suggests the following definition: an effective teacher is one who performs each of the tasks of teaching at a level judged to be at least satisfactory. The tasks of teaching include (1) providing instruction in academic knowledge and skills; (2) providing an instructional climate that helps students develop positive attitudes toward school and self; (3) adjusting instruction in response to students' ability, ethnic identification, home background, and gender; (4) managing the classroom context so that students are engaged in learning; (5) making sound decisions and plans; and (6) implementing curriculum change.

Educators generally agree that these are the major tasks of teaching. The relative importance of the tasks and standards of satisfactory performance are much less clear. This problem and possible solutions are considered in chapter 11.

We reviewed a substantial number of research studies in this chapter. They demonstrate that there is a growing body of research knowledge about teaching practices that can improve teachers' performance of the tasks of teaching. Supervisors and teachers should stay informed about future developments in this field of research. This does not mean, however, that a teacher should abandon the way he teaches and adopt research-validated practices. Rather, these practices should be viewed as possible alternatives to the teacher's current practices. This position follows from our basic premise that clinical supervision is a process of helping the teacher reflect on observational data and other information (including research knowledge) in order to make better teaching decisions and execute them effectively.

CONCLUDING COMMENT

We revisit the effective teaching practices discussed in this chapter in unit III. The overview section of unit III includes a summary list of each practice and a method for observing how well or how frequently the practice is used. We discuss each observational method in detail in chapters 5-8.

NOTES

1. Barak Rosenshine and Norma Furst, "The Use of Direct Observation to Study Teaching," in *Handbook of Research on Teaching*, 2d ed., Robert M. W. Travers (Chicago: Rand McNally, 1973), pp. 122-83.

2. Ned A. Flanders, *Analyzing Teaching Behavior* (Reading, MA: Addison-Wesley, 1970).
3. These studies were reviewed in N. L. Gage, *The Scientific Basis of the Art of Teaching* (New York: Teachers College Press, 1978).
4. Barak V. Rosenshine, "Synthesis of Research on Explicit Teaching," *Educational Leadership* 43, No. 7 (1986): 60–68.
5. List adapted from Rosenshine, "Synthesis," pp. 60–68.
6. Madeline Hunter, "Knowing, Teaching, and Supervising," in *Using What We Know about Teaching*, ed. Philip L. Hosford (Alexandria, VA: Association for Supervision and Curriculum Development, 1984), pp. 169–92.
7. Rosenshine, "Synthesis," p. 60.
8. *Ibid.*, p. 62.
9. Benjamin S. Bloom (ed.), *Taxonomy of Educational Objectives: The Classification of Educational Goals. Handbook 1: Cognitive Domain* (New York: Longman, 1956).
10. Nancy S. Cole, "Conceptions of Educational Achievement," *Educational Researcher* 3 (1990): 2–7.
11. *Ibid.*, p. 2.
12. *Ibid.*, p. 3.
13. See, for example, Richard J. Shavelson, Neil B. Carey, and Noreen M. Webb, "Indicators of Science Achievement: Options for a Powerful Policy Instrument," *Phi Delta Kappan* 71 (1990): 692–97.
14. Joyce P. Gall and Meredith D. Gall, "Outcomes of the Discussion Method," in *Teaching and Learning through Discussion*, ed. William W. Wilen (Springfield, IL: Charles C. Thomas, 1990).
15. Meredith D. Gall and Joyce P. Gall, "The Discussion Method," in *The Psychology of Teaching Methods: The Seventy-Fifth Yearbook of the National Society for the Study of Education*, ed. N. L. Gage (Chicago: University of Chicago Press, 1976), pp. 166–216.
16. Philip H. Winne, "Experiments Relating Teachers' Use of Higher Cognitive Questions to Student Achievement," *Review of Educational Research* 49 (1979): 13–49; Doris L. Redfield and Elaine W. Rousseau, "A Meta-analysis of Experimental Research on Teacher Questioning Behavior," *Review of Educational Research* 51 (1981): 237–45; Barak V. Rosenshine, "Classroom Instruction," in *The Psychology of Teaching Methods: The Seventy-Fifth Yearbook of the National Society for the Study of Education*, ed. N. L. Gage (Chicago: University of Chicago Press, 1976), pp. 335–71.
17. Christiaan Hamaker, "The Effects of Adjunct Questions on Prose Learning," Review of Educational Research 56 (1986): 212–42.
18. David C. Berliner, "Knowledge Is Power: A Talk to Teachers about a Revolution in the Teaching Profession," in *Talks to Teachers*, ed. David C. Berliner and Barak V. Rosenshine (New York: Random House, 1987), pp. 3–33; Walter R. Borg, "Time and School Learning," in *Time to Learn*, ed. Carolyn Denham and Ann Lieberman (Washington, DC: U.S. Department of Education, 1980), pp. 33–72.
19. Charles W. Fisher, David C. Berliner, Nikola N. Filby, Richard Marliave, Leonard S. Cahen, and Marilyn M. Dishaw, "Teaching Behaviors, Academic Learning Time, and Student Achievement: An Overview," in *Time to Learn*, ed. Carolyn Denham and Ann Lieberman (Washington, DC: U.S. Department of Education, 1980), pp. 7–32.
20. Harris Cooper, *Homework* (New York: Longman, 1989).
21. David R. Krathwohl, Benjamin S. Bloom, and B. B. Masia, *Taxonomy of Educational Objectives. Handbook II: Affective Domain* (New York: McKay, 1964).
22. John Dewey, *Experience and Education* (New York: Collier, 1938), p. 48.
23. A. Guy Larkins, C. Warren McKinney, Sally Oldham-Buss, and Allison C. Gilmore, *Teacher*

Enthusiasm: A Critical Review (Hattiesburg, MS: Educational and Psychological Research, University of Southern Mississippi, 1985).

24. Gage, *The Scientific Basis of the Art of Teaching*; Jere Brophy, "Teacher Praise: A Functional Analysis," *Review of Educational Research* 51 (1981): 5-32.

25. Wilbert J. McKeachie and James A. Kulik, "Effective College Teaching," in *Review of Research in Education*, vol. 3, ed. Frederick N. Kerlinger (Itasca, IL: Peabody, 1975), pp. 165-209; J. P. Gall and M. D. Gall, "Outcomes of the Discussion Method."

26. This phenomenon was observed in the following study: Leonard L. Mitnick and Elliott McGinnies, "Influencing Ethnocentrism in Small Discussion Groups through a Film Communication," *Journal of Abnormal and Social Psychology* 56 (1958): 82-90.

27. Robert E. Slavin, "Research on Cooperative Learning: Consensus and Controversy," *Educational Leadership* 47, No. 4 (1989/1990): 52-54.

28. Jere Brophy, "On Motivating Students," in *Talks to Teachers*, ed. David C. Berliner and Barak V. Rosenshine (New York: Random House, 1987), pp. 201-45; *ibid.*, p. 207.

29. Thomas L. Good, "Two Decades of Research on Teacher Expectations: Findings and Future Directions," *Journal of Teacher Education* 38 (1987): 32-47.

30. Gregg Jackson and Cecilia Cosca, "The Inequality of Educational Opportunity in the Southwest: An Observational Study of Ethnically Mixed Classrooms," *American Educational Research Journal* 11 (1974): 219-29. The report of the Jackson and Cosca study used the term Anglo to refer to white persons not of Spanish-speaking background. The term Chicano was used to refer to Mexican Americans.

31. Jackson and Cosca, "Inequality of Educational Opportunity in the Southwest," p. 227; Gall and Gall, "Outcomes of the Discussion Method."

32. James A. Banks, Multiethnic Education: Theory and Practice, 2d ed. (Boston: Allyn and Bacon, 1988).

33. Margaret D. Pusch, H. Ned Seelye, and Jacqueline H. Wasilewski, "Training for Multicultural Education Competencies," in *Multicultural Education: A Cross-Cultural Training Approach*, ed. Margaret D. Pusch (Chicago: Intercultural Network, 1981).

34. Jere E. Brophy, "Interactions of Male and Female Students with Male and Female Teachers," in *Gender Influences in Classroom Interaction*, ed. Louise Cherry Wilkinson and Cora B. Marrett (Orlando, FL: Academic, 1985), pp. 115-42.

35. Elizabeth Fennema and Penelope L. Peterson, "Effective Teaching for Boys and Girls: The Same or Different?" in *Talks to Teachers*, ed. David C. Berliner and Barak V. Rosenshine (New York: Random House, 1987), pp. 111-25.

36. *Ibid.*, p. 124.

37. Daniel L. Duke, "Editor's Preface," in *Classroom Management: The Seventy-Eighth Yearbook of the National Society for the Study of Education, Part 2*), ed. Daniel L. Duke (Chicago: University of Chicago Press, 1979), xi-xv.

38. This research is reviewed in Thomas Good, "Teacher Effectiveness in the Elementary School: What We Know about It Now," *Journal of Teacher Education* 30 (1979): 52-64.

39. Carolyn M. Evertson, "Managing Classrooms: A Framework for Teachers," in *Talks to Teachers*, ed. David C. Berliner and Barak V. Rosenshine (New York: Random House, 1987), 52-74.

40. Walter Doyle, "Classroom Organization and Management," in *Handbook of Research on Teaching*, 3d ed., ed. Merlin C. Wittrock (New York: Macmillan, 1986), 392-431.

41. Evertson, "Managing Classrooms," p. 59.

42. Doyle, "Classroom Organization and Management," p. 421.

43. Examples of such sources are: Carol Cummings, *Managing to Teach* (Edmonds, WA:

Teaching Inc., 1983); C. M. Charles, *Building Classroom Discipline*, 3d ed. (New York: Longman, 1988).

44. Madeline Hunter, "Teaching Is Decision Making," *Educational Leadership* 37, No. 1 (1979): 62–67.

45. Christopher M. Clark and Penelope L. Peterson, "Teachers' Thought Processes," in *Handbook of Research on Teaching*, 3d ed., ed. Merlin C. Wittrock (New York: Macmillan, 1986), 255–96.

46. Christopher M. Clark and Robert J. Yinger, *Three Studies of Teacher Planning* (East Lansing: Michigan State University, 1979, Research Series No. 55).

47. Clark and Peterson, "Teachers' Thought Processes," p. 274.

48. Walter Doyle, "Learning the Classroom Environment: An Ecological Analysis," *Journal of Teacher Education* 28 (1977): 51–55; Greta Morine and E. Vallance, *Special Study B: A Study of Teacher and Pupil Perceptions of Classroom Interaction* (San Francisco: Far West Laboratory, 1975, Tech Rep. No. 75-11-6); Penelope L. Peterson and Christopher M. Clark, "Teachers' Reports of Their Cognitive Processes During Teaching," *American Educational Research Journal* 15 (1978): 555–65.

49. Rosenshine and Furst, "The Use of Direct Observation to Study Teaching."

50. Michael Fullan, *The Meaning of Educational Change* (New York: Teachers College Press, 1982).

51. Gene E. Hall, Susan F. Loucks, William L. Rutherford, and B. Newlove, "Levels of Use of the Innovation: A Framework for Analyzing Innovation Adoption," *Journal of Teacher Education* 24 (1975): 52–56.

52. Gene E. Hall, "The Concerns-based Approach for Facilitating Change," *Educational Horizons* 57 (1979): 202–8.

53. The SoCQ and scoring procedures are reproduced on pp. 47–51 of Shirley M. Hord, William L. Rutherford, Leslie Huling-Austin, and Gene E. Hall, *Taking Charge of Change* (Alexandria, VA: Association for Supervision and Curriculum Development, 1987), p. 31.

54. Walter Doyle and Gerald Ponder, "The Practicality Ethic and Teacher Decision-making," *Interchange* 8, No. 3 (1977): 1–12; Georgea G. Mohlman, Theodore Coladarci, and N. L. Gage, "Comprehension and Attitude as Predictors of Implementation of Teacher Training," *Journal of Teacher Education* 32 (1982): 31–36.

Unit I Exercises

MULTIPLE-CHOICE ITEMS

Answers are on page 255.

1. Clinical supervision includes these sequential stages:
   a. planning conference, feedback conference, classroom observation
   b. classroom observation, feedback conference, planning conference
   c. planning conference, classroom observation, feedback conference
   d. counseling conference, classroom observation, feedback conference
2. Research has shown that teachers
   a. are satisfied with supervision as currently practiced.
   b. believe that supervision plays an important role in their professional lives.
   c. look to supervision primarily for emotional support and reassurance.
   d. hold supervision in low regard.
3. According to the authors, the major purpose of clinical supervision is
   a. to improve the teacher's classroom instruction.
   b. to provide curriculum support to the teacher.
   c. to provide emotional support and reassurance to the teacher.
   d. (b) and (c) are correct.
4. The techniques of clinical supervision
   a. should never be used in teacher evaluation.
   b. can be adapted for use in teacher evaluation.
   c. can be used in teacher evaluation, except for the techniques of the feedback conference.
   d. can be used in teacher evaluation, except for the techniques of the planning conference.

5. Which of the following generalizations is best supported by the available research evidence?
   a. Teachers prefer an indirect supervisory style.
   b. Teachers prefer a direct supervisory style.
   c. Clinical supervision results in improved learning by the teacher's students.
   d. Clinical supervision results in improved teacher retention by school districts.

6. Which of the following indicators has not been found to be a correlate of effective teaching?
   a. teacher warmth
   b. teacher enthusiasm
   c. teacher experience
   d. teacher clarity

7. Of the perspectives for observing what teachers do, which is the most closely associated with the goals of clinical supervision?
   a. observation of the teacher outside the classroom
   b. observation of the teacher's students
   c. observation of the teacher's planning
   d. observation of the teacher's classroom behavior

8. The behaviors of accepting students' feelings, acknowledging student ideas, and praising students are indicators of
   a. teacher task-orientation.
   b. teacher clarity.
   c. academic engaged time.
   d. indirect teaching style.

PROBLEMS

The following problems do not have single correct answers. Possible answers are on page 256. Your answers may differ from ours yet be as good or better.

1. As a clinical supervisor, you are working with a teacher to help develop new skills while making the transition from high school teacher to junior high school teaching. One day the teacher becomes distressed and says she is considering leaving the profession. What do you do in your role as clinical supervisor?

2. You are assigned to be the clinical supervisor of an undergraduate who is just starting a student teaching placement. The undergraduate initiates a conversation with you by asking, "Are you here to evaluate me?" How should you respond?

3. Some educators claim that good teachers are born, not made. Others claim that teaching can never be analyzed because it is an art, not a science. Do you agree or disagree with these claims? Why? Why not?

Techniques of Goal Setting and Planning for Observation

OVERVIEW

There are two parts to the first stage of the clinical supervision process that require planning conferences between the supervisor and the teacher: goal setting and planning for observation. Chapter 3 considers the essentials of an effective goal-setting conference, and chapter 4 describes the elements of a conference in which the supervisor and the teacher plan for an observation. Specific techniques are described with examples of how they can be used to make conferences productive.

OBJECTIVES

The purpose of this unit is to help you develop

Understanding of the basic elements of a positive relationship between the supervisor and the teacher

Specific steps for conducting a conference in which teacher and supervisor plan cooperatively to address specific concerns, observe and record behavior, and work together to improve instruction

Explicit techniques for preparing teachers to seek useful feedback that can aid them in analyzing, interpreting, and modifying their instructional efforts

An approach to supervision consistent in style, strategy, and technique with the purposes set forth in unit I

chapter 3

Goal Setting

If you're not sure where you're going, you're liable to end up someplace else.
Robert Mager

In this chapter we look at goal setting in more detail. Preservice teachers, beginning teachers, and "old pro's" all need to work toward tangible, attainable, important goals. For teachers who are working on growth goals (rather than deficiency needs) the goal-setting conference can be teacher-centered. Teachers who are on plans of assistance may need to have evaluator-centered goal-setting conferences.

Following the goal-setting conference, several cycles of planning, observation, and feedback (as described in the chapters that follow) will take place. If these are conducted by the evaluator, they will result in documentation that will be used in the formal evaluation. If they are carried out by colleagues for formative purposes, it may be left to the teacher, the observer, and the evaluator to decide whether or not data from these observations or conferences will be included in the evaluation.

IDENTIFY THE TEACHER'S CONCERNS
ABOUT INSTRUCTION (TECHNIQUE 1)

The major purpose of clinical supervision is to help teachers improve their classroom instruction. One step toward this goal is to use a goal-setting conference to identify areas of instruction in which a teacher needs improvement.

A supervisor might directly ask a teacher in what ways he or she would like to improve as a teacher, but this is not usually effective. Many teachers have not formulated self-improvement goals and feel put on the spot when asked to do so. A more useful approach initially is to assist the teacher in identifying concerns. A teacher who can identify and verbalize concerns can usually take the next steps of examining the concerns objectively and solving them.

There are a variety of questions that a supervisor might ask to guide the teacher's thinking about concerns. For example: "How has your teaching been going?" "Do you find you are having more success in one area than another?" "Our goal is to help you do the best possible teaching. Are there any aspects of your teaching we should take a look at?"

No one question is better than another. The supervisor should be intent on helping the teacher reveal true concerns without feeling threatened. A threatened teacher is likely to clam up or reveal only "safe" concerns. For example, teachers have told us that "individualization of instruction" is a safe concern, but discipline is not a safe concern. A teacher who mentions discipline problems may be perceived as incompetent, whereas a teacher who mentions individualization is likely to be perceived as well along the road toward being a master teacher.

Some teachers insist that they have no concerns; their class is running beautifully. In some instances this may be an accurate perception by the teacher, but we would suggest that there is always room for improvement in one's teaching. A good teacher can get better. When a teacher insists that he or she has no concerns, the supervisor probably should take the statement at face value. The supervisor might also suggest using a "wide-lens" observation technique such as video recording (see chapter 7), so that they can look together at the teacher's instruction. An appropriate tone can be set by asking, "How about making a videotape of one of your lessons so that we can see what aspects of your teaching please you?" After the video recording has been made and reviewed in the feedback conference, the teacher may become aware of areas for improvement that were not previously apparent.

Sometimes teachers find it helpful to examine a checklist or other instruments that will be used to evaluate their teaching performance. In showing the checklist to a teacher, the supervisor might ask, "Which of these areas do you think you're strong in? Which of these areas do you think we might take a closer look at as areas for improvement?" Frances Fuller did a classic series of investigations at the University of Texas on teachers' concerns during training and in their professional careers.[1] She found that the concerns of preservice teachers and new in-service teachers tend to focus on the self. The concerns of experienced teachers tend to focus on the students. Fuller summarized her findings as follows.

Early Teaching Phase: Concern with Self

Covert Concerns: Where Do I Stand?   When teaching starts, [student] teachers ask themselves, "Where do I stand?" "Is it going to be my class or the teacher's class?" "If I see a child misbehaving in the hall, do I handle it, ignore it, or tell someone else?" These concerns were rarely expressed in either written statements or in routine interviews unless directly elicited.

Overt Concerns: How Adequate Am I?   The concern student teachers feel about class control is no secret. It is a blatant persistent concern of most beginning teachers.

Ability to control the class, however, is apparently just part of a larger concern of the new teacher with his adequacy in the classroom. This larger concern involves abilities to understand subject matter, to know the answers, to say "I don't know," to have the freedom to fail on occasion, to anticipate problems, to mobilize resources and to make changes when failures reoccur. It also involves the ability to cope with evaluation: the willingness to listen for evaluation and to parcel out the biases of evaluators.

Late Concerns: Concern with Pupils

When concerns are "mature," that is, characteristic of experienced, superior teachers, they seem to focus on pupil gain and self-evaluation as opposed to personal gain and evaluation by others. The specific concerns we have observed are concerns about ability to understand pupils' capacities, to specify objectives for them, to assess their gain, to apportion out one's own contributions to pupils' difficulties and gain, and to evaluate oneself in terms of pupil gain.[2]

Frances Fuller's insights suggest the variety of teacher concerns to which the supervisor must remain sensitive. As she notes, some of these concerns are easily verbalized by the teacher. Others must be solicited through careful questioning.

TRANSLATE THE TEACHER'S CONCERNS INTO OBSERVABLE BEHAVIORS (TECHNIQUE 2)

Helping a teacher translate concerns into observable behaviors is one of the most important techniques of clinical supervision. For an analogy, consider the patient who visits a doctor with vague complaints of not feeling well. The doctor's first task is to develop a differentiated picture of the patient's symptoms. The doctor does this by asking such questions as "How long have you felt this way?" "What are the specific problems you've been having?" "What does the discomfort feel like?" These questions are part of a diagnostic process the doctor uses, first to isolate the problem and then to prescribe a treatment.

The clinical supervisor similarly needs to function as a diagnostician in the planning conference. Suppose a student teacher says, "I'm not sure I have the confidence to be a teacher." The teacher's expressed concern is lack of confidence, but the supervisor needs to probe further. Confidence may mean something different to the teacher than it means to the supervisor.

In using the technique of translating concerns, the supervisor needs to listen for the teacher's use of words and phrases that are abstract, ambiguous, or stated at a high level of generality. These typically are concepts that are one level removed from observable behavior. The following are examples of teacher statements that contain abstract or ambiguous words:

"I'm afraid I'm a dictator."

"To me the most important thing is for students to have a healthy self-concept."

"There's just not enough time to cover everything I want to get across."

"Some of my students are just like wild animals."

"I'm afraid I don't project warmth."

"I wonder if I'm too critical of students."

"How do you reach these problem students?"

When you hear a teacher use such terms to refer to a concern, your task is to clarify the terms so that they are stated in observable form. Here are examples of questions that might help the teacher state a concern more concretely:

"Do you know a teacher who projects warmth? What does she do?"

"What kinds of things do you do that make you think you're critical of students?"

"In what ways are these problem students?"

"Can you clarify what you mean by reaching problem students?"

These are not the only kinds of questions that are useful. The supervisor is free to use any questions or other techniques that help the teacher focus on abstract terms and clarify their meaning.

A supervisor can judge success in translating concerns by considering this question: "Do I have enough information so that I can clearly observe the teacher's concern as it is expressed in his/her classroom?" Another good question is "Do the teacher and I mean the same thing when we use the term _____?" If your answer to both questions is a confident yes, this is a good indication that you are using the technique properly.

Several research studies have been done to clarify the meaning of key concepts in teaching. For example, Andrew Bush, John Kennedy, and Donald Cruickshank conducted research to determine the observable referents of teacher clarity.[3] Their approach was to ask students to list five behaviors performed by their clearest teacher. They were able to identify the following observable behaviors underlying the concept of clarity:

- gives examples and explains them
- repeats questions and explanations if students don't understand them
- lets students ask questions
- pronounces words distinctly
- talks only about things related to the topic he is teaching
- uses common words
- writes important things on the blackboard
- relates what he is teaching to real life
- asks questions to find out if students understand what he has told them

Although this list is not exhaustive, it is a great help to teacher and supervisor in their efforts to improve the clarity of the teacher's instruction.

Even a nonverbal concept, such as teacher enthusiasm, can be made observable through careful analysis. Mary Collins identified observable referents for enthusiasm by reviewing previous research on this variable, by her own analysis, and by consulting other teacher educators. Collins's list of observable behaviors is presented below. Using this list as a guide, she was able to train a group of preservice elementary teachers to improve their level of enthusiasm significantly in classroom instruction.[4]

Observable Referents for Enthusiasm
1. *Vocal delivery:* great and sudden changes from rapid excited speech to a whisper; varied, lilting, uplifting intonations; many changes in tone, pitch
2. *Eyes:* dancing, snapping, shining, lighting up, frequently opened wide, eyebrows raised, eye contact with total group
3. *Gestures:* frequent demonstrative movements of body, head, arms, hands, and face; sweeping motions; clapping hands; head nodding rapidly
4. *Movements:* large body movements; swings around, changes pace, bends body
5. *Facial expression:* appears vibrant, demonstrative; changes denoting surprise, sadness, joy, thoughtfulness, awe, excitement
6. *Word selection:* highly descriptive, many adjectives, great variety
7. *Acceptance of ideas and feelings:* accepts ideas and feelings quickly with vigor and animation; ready to accept, praise, encourage, or clarify in a nonthreatening manner; many variations in responding to pupils
8. *Overall energy:* explosive, exuberant; high degree of vitality, drive, and spirit throughout lesson

You will find more examples of observable referents for teacher concerns in chapters 5–8. These chapters present a collection of observation instruments for recording data about many different teacher concerns.

IDENTIFY PROCEDURES FOR IMPROVING THE TEACHER'S INSTRUCTION (TECHNIQUE 3)

The first two techniques are intended to help the teacher identify concerns and translate them into observable behaviors. What happens next?

If the teacher has successfully identified some concerns, the stage is set for thinking about possible changes in instructional behavior. For example, consider a teacher who is worried that he or she comes across as dull and unenthusiastic. As the supervisor helps this teacher identify observable behaviors that comprise enthusiasm, the teacher is likely to ask, "I wonder how I could get myself to do those things?" The supervisor facilitates this process by thinking aloud with the teacher about procedures that can be used to acquire new behaviors.

The simplest procedure, perhaps, is for the teacher to practice the behaviors independently. The supervisor might say, "Why don't you make a list of these enthusiasm behaviors on a five-by-eight-inch card and keep it near you when you teach?

In a week or so, I'll come in and make a video recording so you can see how you're doing."

Sometimes the needed procedures are more involved. For example, one teacher's concern may be how to use learning centers effectively. This involves a whole set of instructional skills. To acquire these skills, the teacher may need to do some reading and to attend workshops on learning centers.

If a teacher's concern is about changing student behavior, a sequence of procedures is needed. To illustrate, suppose the teacher is concerned that students do not pay attention during class discussions. The supervisor first helps the teacher to define "attention" as a set of observable behaviors—answering teacher's questions thoughtfully, looking at other students as they speak, initiating relevant comments and questions, and so forth. The teacher's next task is to develop instructional procedures that will bring about these desired "attending" behaviors. Finally, the teacher will need to practice these instructional procedures until they are mastered.

In brief, three steps are involved in bringing about change in students' behavior:

1. Identify the specific student behaviors you (the teacher) wish your class to use.
2. Identify the instructional procedures you will need to use to bring about the specific student behaviors.
3. Identify a strategy for learning and practicing the instructional procedures.

Bringing about change in student behavior is probably the most difficult goal a teacher can strive for, but it also yields the greatest rewards.

The following is an excerpt from a planning conference in which the goal was change in the behavior of second-grade children:

TEACHER: I'd like you to come in and take a look at Randall and Ronald. They don't do anything but play and talk.

SUPERVISOR: Are Randall and Ronald the only ones you want me to observe?

TEACHER: No. I have a real immature group this year. You might as well observe all of them.

SUPERVISOR: What do you mean by "immature"?

TEACHER: Oh, they have very short attention spans, haven't learned to settle down, and they just talk without permission.

[*At this point, teacher and supervisor decided to focus on one problem behavior—talking without permission. The dialogue continues.*]

SUPERVISOR: Can you give an example of a situation where they talk without permission?

TEACHER: Well, when I have them in a small reading group, and I ask one of them a question, any of them will speak up if they think they have the answer.

Sometimes they don't even listen to the question, they just say what's on their mind. And it doesn't matter whether another child is already talking. They'll just ignore him and speak at the same time.

SUPERVISOR: I think I have a pretty clear idea of what's happening. What do you think you can do so that only the child you call on responds, and so that if another child has something to say, he waits his turn?

TEACHER: I guess I could teach them some rules for participating. Like raising their hands when they wish to speak and remaining quiet when another child is speaking.

Teacher and supervisor proceeded to discuss possible methods of teaching these rules to the children. The teacher took notes on the procedures and agreed to practice them the following week. In addition, the supervisor suggested that the teacher try praising or otherwise rewarding children when they obey participation rules in the reading group. In making this suggestion, the supervisor discovered that the teacher was unfamiliar with the reinforcement principles underlying the use of praise and other rewards in classroom teaching. The supervisor therefore suggested that the teacher might benefit from enrolling in an upcoming workshop on classroom management in which these principles would be discussed.

This example illustrates the three steps in bringing about change in student behavior:

1. Identify the specific student behaviors desired such as students raising hands when they wish to speak and being silent when another child is speaking.
2. Identify instructional procedures such as teaching children the instructional rules and rewarding them for appropriate behavior.
3. Identify a strategy for learning the instructional procedure such as practice in the classroom and attending a workshop.

ASSIST THE TEACHER IN SETTING SELF-IMPROVEMENT GOALS (TECHNIQUE 4)

If the supervisor has used the first three techniques effectively, it should be relatively easy to help the teacher take the next step: setting personal goals for improvement of instruction.

Some supervisors and teachers may feel this step is superfluous. In discussing the previous technique, we presented the example of a teacher concerned about students speaking out of turn. The supervisor helped the teacher identify several observable behaviors of students that reflected this concern and also helped the teacher identify procedures for changing these behaviors. It seems apparent that the teacher's goal is to improve students' verbal participation behaviors in reading groups. The clinical supervision process is facilitated by making this goal explicit. By doing so, teacher and supervisor both develop a clear understanding of the direction toward which the clinical supervision process is headed. It also prevents a state of confusion, with the teacher thinking, "I wonder what the supervisor expects me to be doing?"

The supervisor or the teacher can state the goal, but whoever does so should check that the other person has the same understanding of the goal and agrees with it. In the example we have been considering, the goal formulation process might occur as follows:

SUPERVISOR: To review, then, one of the things you're concerned about is students' speaking out of turn. You've picked out a number of behaviors you'd like to see your students engage in. Given that, is there a goal you would set for yourself?

TEACHER: Yes. My first goal is to reduce the incidence of students' speaking out of turn. My other goal is to have my students engage in more positive behaviors, like listening to one another and raising their hands when they have something to say.

SUPERVISOR: Those are worthwhile goals, and I'll do what I can to help you with them.

This interchange between teacher and supervisor, if done naturally and genuinely, gives structure and focus to the planning conference.

NOTES

1. Frances F. Fuller, "Concerns of Teachers: A Developmental Conceptualization," *American Educational Research Journal* 6 (1969): 207-26.
2. *Ibid.*, pp. 220-21.
3. Andrew J. Bush, John J. Kennedy, and Donald R. Cruickshank, "An Empirical Investigation of Teacher Clarity," *Journal of Teacher Education* 28 (1977): 53-58.
4. Mary L. Collins, "Effects of Enthusiasm Training on Preservice Elementary Teachers," *Journal of Teacher Education* 29 (1978): 53-57. Other studies agree with Collins's findings. See Edward Bettencourt, "Effects of Training Teachers in Enthusiasm on Student Achievement and Attitudes" (Ph.D. diss., University of Oregon, 1979); Maxwell Gillett, "Effects of Teacher Enthusiasm on At-Task Behavior of Students in Elementary Classes" (Ph.D. diss., University of Oregon, 1980).

chapter 4

The Planning Conference

The most important link between a teacher and his supervisor is effective com-
munication. . . . The principal must set the stage for open communication.
Teachers see the justification for supervision and evaluation programs, but
they want to be a partner in the process.
   Robert L. Hershberger and James M. Young, Jr., "Teacher Perceptions
             of Supervision and Evaluation"

The planning conference sets the stage for effective clinical supervision. It provides
the teacher and supervisor with an opportunity to identify teacher concerns and
translate them into observable behaviors. Another outcome of the planning conference is a decision about the kinds of instructional data that will be recorded during
classroom observation, which is the next phase of the supervisory cycle.

  The planning conference is organized around an agenda that calls for the identification of teacher concerns, possible solutions to these concerns, and observation
techniques. Less obvious but no less important are certain processes that occur in
the conference. For example, during the planning conference, the teacher may decide how much trust to place in the supervisor. Trust refers to the teacher's confidence that the supervisor has the teacher's interests at heart and will not use data
that emerge during supervision against the teacher. Supervisors may be technically
proficient, but unless they also instill trust, their supervision is likely to be ineffi-
cient. We have more to say about trust-instilling behaviors in chapters 9 and 10.

  A basic purpose of the planning conference is to provide an opportunity for the
teacher to communicate with a fellow educator about a unique classroom situation
and style of teaching. Many teachers feel isolated in their work because they usually
teach alone in a self-contained classroom. By periodically observing the teacher's
classroom, the supervisor or consultant builds a set of shared experiences that su-

pervisor and teacher can discuss together in their conferences. These conferences are especially important to the student teacher who may have no one in the school other than the supervisor with whom to share concerns and perceptions.

Planning conferences need not be long. As a supervisor, you might allow 20 to 30 minutes for the first planning conference unless the teacher has a particularly difficult problem to discuss. Later planning conferences might require only five to ten minutes, especially if there has been no change in the teacher's goals for improvement since the preceding clinical supervision cycle of planning-observation-feedback.

Planning conferences probably are best held on neutral territory (e.g., the school cafeteria, if it is free) or in the teacher's classroom. Going into a supervisor's office for a conference may be perceived by the teacher as being "called on the carpet."

This chapter presents several techniques to use in the planning conference. These techniques constitute an agenda for the conference. In fact, you should consider using them in the order in which they are presented.

These techniques are important for a successful planning conference, yet we also acknowledge their limitations. A supervisor may use all these techniques and still not have a satisfactory conference because some other element (e.g., teacher's trust) is missing. There may be conference techniques that we have overlooked. Also, the techniques presented here are not highly specific prescriptions. You will need to use judgment in incorporating them into your supervisory behavior and in applying them to a particular supervisory situation. Our only claim is that judicious use of these techniques provides a sound base for conducting a planning conference. What you as a person contribute to this base is critical for success.

ARRANGE A TIME FOR CLASSROOM
OBSERVATION (TECHNIQUE 5)

The first four techniques involved the teacher and supervisor talking about the teacher's instruction and setting goals. Now it is time to plan for observing the instruction firsthand.

The first step in planning for observation is to arrange a mutually convenient time for the supervisor to visit the classroom. For one reason or another, there may be certain lessons the teacher does not wish you to observe or you are unable to observe because of time conflicts. The major criterion for selecting a lesson is that it should present opportunities for the teacher's concerns and solutions to those concerns. If the teacher's concern is students' responses to discussion questions, there is no point in observing a lesson in which students are engaged in independent learning projects.

Arranging a mutually convenient time for classroom observation is important for another reason. Teachers are resentful when supervisors come to their room unannounced. Teachers need to feel that the supervisor respects them as professionals and as people with first-line responsibility for their classrooms. They are not likely to feel this way if a supervisor pops in anytime he or she wishes to do so.

The technique of arranging a mutually convenient time is important when supervising experienced teachers, but it is equally important when working with student teachers. They can be put into a state of constant tension if they are led to think the supervisor can enter their class anytime unannounced. Arranging a time beforehand enables the student teacher to prepare instructionally (and emotionally) for the supervisor's visit. It also gives the student teacher a feeling of some control over the supervisory process. A student teacher who has this feeling of control is likely to use supervision for self-improvement rather than to feel used by it.

SELECT AN OBSERVATION INSTRUMENT AND BEHAVIORS TO BE RECORDED (TECHNIQUE 6)

The planning conference is based on the teacher's perceptions of what occurs in the classroom. These perceptions may coincide or differ substantially from what actually occurs. Observational data are needed to provide an objective check on the teacher's perceptions and also to record instructional phenomena that may have escaped the teacher's attention. Therefore, an important step in the planning conference is for supervisor and teacher to decide what kinds of observational data might be worth collecting.

A wide range of observation instruments are presented in unit III. You will need to become familiar with them in order to help the teacher select an observation instrument appropriate for his or her instructional concerns.

The observation instrument should be matched carefully with the teacher's particular instructional concerns. For example, if a teacher is concerned about nonverbal behavior, a video recording (technique 15) might be appropriate. If the concern is about a problem child in the classroom, an anecdotal record (technique 14) would be helpful. Or if a teacher is concerned about the level of commotion in his classroom, a record of students' movement patterns (technique 13) could be made.

The selection of an observation instrument helps sharpen a teacher's thinking about instruction. If teacher and supervisor use the conference only to talk about instruction, the conversation may drift off into vague generalities and abstractions. Selecting an observation instrument brings the teacher "down to earth" by focusing attention on the observable realities of classroom instruction.

Either the supervisor or the teacher can suggest appropriate observation instruments and behaviors to be recorded on them. If the teacher is unfamiliar with methods of classroom observation, the supervisor may need to initiate suggestions. Once teachers become familiar with the range of instruments, however, they should be encouraged to initiate their own suggestions.

In discussing observation instruments with teachers, you may wish to stress their nonevaluative nature. These instruments are designed to collect nonevaluative, objective data that teachers can inspect in the feedback conference and from which they can form their own judgments about the effectiveness of their teaching. The teacher should be able to

1. describe the lesson to be observed.
2. describe what he or she will be doing during the lesson.
3. describe expected student behaviors.

4. predict problems, "rough spots," concerns.
5. agree upon the observer's role (what will be observed and what data will be collected).

During the planning conference, the teacher-supervisor team can get the teacher to describe lesson objectives (student outcomes), to consider options among two or more teaching strategies, and to plan to use specific techniques that make up the strategy. This will help to clarify what the teacher intends to do and will also give ideas on what you can plan to observe. Once the teacher states what the students are to learn from the lesson, you have a basis for deciding what instructional approaches will aid that learning and what observational methods may be appropriate.

CLARIFY THE INSTRUCTIONAL CONTEXT IN WHICH DATA WILL BE RECORDED (TECHNIQUE 7)

Throughout this book we emphasize the importance of focusing on one or two areas of concern at a time. A teacher who is asked to look at too many aspects of instruction at once is likely to become confused. Your classroom observation might focus on the teacher's enthusiasm or discipline technique or on the task behavior of students. However, there is a risk that the recording of observational data will be oversimplified. Instructional behaviors do not occur in a vacuum. They occur in a context that must be understood if the target behaviors are to be interpreted properly.

In short, the supervisor cannot walk into a teacher's classroom "cold" and expect to understand what is happening. Therefore, an effective technique is to ask the teacher a few questions about the instructional context of the behaviors to be recorded. Since the usual instructional context is a lesson that the teacher plans to teach, you may wish to ask the teacher such questions as:

"What is the lesson that I'll be observing about?"
"What do you expect the students to learn in this lesson?"
"What strategy[1] will you be using?"
"Is there anything I should be aware of as you teach this lesson?"

Asking these questions indicates to the teacher that you wish to understand the teacher's "world" from his or her perspective. Your presence in the classroom during the lesson will be tolerated better because the teacher and you have a shared understanding of what the lesson is about.

You need to know various observation techniques and other means of data collection in order to carry out this step. In the planning conference, both you and the teacher contribute information and ideas to figure out what you ought to look for in the observation, how you can record what happens, when you should observe, and what the two of you will do with the results.

Constraints

It's important to be realistic about the number of contacts that you can have with a particular teacher. If your schedule limits you to two sessions per month, for example, you may not be able to include a cycle in which your observation and discussions would be needed for three consecutive days. The kinds and intervals of participation that are feasible should be understood by both the supervisor and the teacher before making plans.

Getting Started

How do you find out what to look at? One of the ways is to use the technique we call "Translate abstract concerns into observable behaviors." In your early contacts with a teacher, however, you may want to limit your attention to concrete behaviors. After a few observations, both you and the teacher will be able to explore together even complex abstractions and devise observational methods for collecting pertinent information.

NOTE

1. A strategy is an overall approach to an instructional session. A technique is a specific behavior or skill that the teacher performs while implementing the strategy. In football, a pass play or a running play is strategy; blocking, running, tackling, and throwing are skills or techniques.

Unit II Exercises

MULTIPLE-CHOICE ITEMS

Answers are on page 255.

1. General areas of agreement that should be established between teacher and supervisor are
    a. teacher's goals for the year.
    b. mutual concerns.
    c. common rationale.
    d. teaching strategies to be considered.
    e. all of the above.
2. Goals written by teachers for their personal development and as the basis for annual evaluation may be
    a. trivial.
    b. idiosyncratic.
    c. vague.
    d. abstract.
    e. all of the above.
3. Which of the following assumptions about teachers are not compatible with the authors' view? Most teachers have
    a. reasonable goals.
    b. access to alternative strategies.
    c. little need for improvement.
    d. preference for democratic supervision.
    e. adequate information and perspective on their own.

4. Which of the following topics should not be part of a conference to plan for an observation?
   a. problems or concerns
   b. selection of data to collect
   c. selection of observation instruments
   d. identifying what teacher and students will be doing
   e. suggesting solutions for the teacher's problems

PROBLEMS

Answers are discussed on page 256.

1. Think of a teacher you have known who had a severe deficiency in the techniques of teaching. Write a goal for that teacher.
2. Think of the best teacher you can remember. Write a goal for that teacher.
3. Assume you are the teacher in either problem 1 or 2 above. You are in a conference with your supervisor planning for an observation of a lesson you have prepared. What should you and the supervisor discuss?

Techniques of Classroom Observation

OVERVIEW

In order to have persuasive data available for feedback conferences, the supervisor needs a wide range of observation techniques and recording devices, such as the VCR and laptop computer. These are described in this unit. Most of them are easily understood and can be used effectively after a little practice. Also, most of the techniques and devices can be used to observe either a whole class, a group of students, or an individual student. The information they provide the teacher and supervisor is a central element of the clinical cycle.

OBJECTIVES

The purpose of this unit is to help you develop

A repertoire of data-recording techniques

Skill in selecting an appropriate observation method for a given teaching practice

Understanding of the strengths and limitations of different observation methods

An appreciation of the need for regular, systematic observation in doing clinical supervision

SUMMARY OF METHODS FOR OBSERVING
EFFECTIVE TEACHING PRACTICES

In chapter 2 we reviewed teaching practices that research has found to be effective. These practices are listed in the left column of the following list. The right column lists methods for collecting observational data on how frequently or how well the teacher uses each practice. These methods are described in more detail in the chapters of this unit: chapter 5 (selective verbatim); chapter 6 (seating charts); chapter 7 (wide lens); and chapter 8 (checklists and timeline coding).

Most of the effective teaching practices can be observed using methods other than those listed here. In fact, virtually any observation method can be adapted to observe virtually any teaching practice. This list only includes the method that we believe is most convenient and appropriate for each practice.

Effective Teaching Practices and Methods for Observing Them

Effective Teaching Practice	*Method(s) of Observation*
1. Clarity	Wide lens (audio recording)
2. Variety	Wide lens (audio recording)
3. Enthusiasm	Wide lens (video recording)
4. Task-oriented approach	Wide lens (video recording)
5. Avoidance of harsh criticism	Selective verbatim (teacher feedback)
6. Indirect teaching style	Timeline coding (Interaction Analysis)
7. Teaching content covered on criterion test	Wide lens (anecdotal record)
8. Structuring statements	Selective verbatim (teacher directions and structuring statements)
9. Questions at multiple cognitive levels	Selective verbatim (teacher questions)
10. Praise and encouragement	Selective verbatim (teacher feedback)
11. Explicit teaching model	Wide lens (anecdotal record)
12. Discussion method	Checklist
13. Allocated time	Timeline coding (Stallings Observation System)
14. Student at-task behavior	Seating chart (at task)

Effective Teaching Practice	*Method(s) of Observation*
15. Homework	Wide lens (anecdotal record)
16. Cooperative learning method	Seating chart (at task; movement patterns)
17. Use of value statements and success to motivate students	Wide lens (anecdotal records; reflective journal)
18. Equitable treatment of students varying in achievement, ethnicity, and gender	Seating chart (verbal flow)
19. Classroom management	Selective verbatim (classroom management statements)
20. Changing strategy based on decisions while teaching	Wide lens (video recording)
21. Curriculum implementation	Wide lens (reflective journal)

chapter **5**

Selective Verbatim

Except in special instances in which some quality of timing or of sound or of sight evolved as a salient supervisory issue, written data have proven most useful and most wieldy to clinical supervisors. Perhaps the greatest advantage of a written record ... is that Teacher and Supervisor can assimilate it most rapidly and most easily; the eye can incorporate, almost instantaneously, evidence that took a relatively long time to unfold in the lesson.

Robert Goldhammer

The learning process is heavily influenced by how teachers and students talk to each other. Therefore, teachers can learn how to improve their instruction by a careful analysis of their communication patterns. This analysis is made possible by an observation technique called selective verbatim.

Selective verbatim requires the supervisor to make a written record of exactly what is said, that is, a verbatim transcript. Not all verbal communication is recorded, however. The supervisor and teacher select beforehand the particular types of verbal events to be transcribed; it is in this sense that the verbatim record is "selective." In this chapter we identify verbal events that reflect effective or ineffective teaching and that are amenable to the selective verbatim technique.

A selective verbatim is usually made while the teacher's class is in progress, but this is not a requirement. If an audio or video recording of a class session is available (see chapter 7), the selective verbatim can be made from the recording.

The selective verbatim should be word-for-word. For example, suppose the supervisor is recording a teacher's questions, and the teacher asks, "What do we call animals that live exclusively off plants ... you know, we have a certain name for these animals ... does anyone know it?" If the supervisor writes, "What is the name of animals that live exclusively off plants?" this is not a verbatim transcription.

Selective verbatim has several advantages as a classroom observation technique. We mention four of them here. First, providing teachers with a selective verbatim transcript focuses their attention on what they say to students or on what students say to them. In this way they become sensitized to the verbal process in teaching. All other levels of communication are screened out by the transcript.

Another advantage of a selective verbatim, compared to a complete transcript, is that it focuses teachers' attention on just a few verbal behaviors. Teachers who are trying to improve their instruction are more successful if they do not try to change many aspects of behavior at once. Changing a few behaviors at a time encourages further changes. For example, we have witnessed the feeling of accomplishment teachers get when they realize they habitually use an annoying verbal mannerism, such as "you know" or "uh," and then achieve control over it. This feeling of control and change further motivates more substantial changes in teaching behavior.

The third advantage of selective verbatim is that it provides an objective, non-judgmental record of the teacher's behavior. While in the act of teaching, many teachers get so caught up in the process that they do not listen to what they are saying. Even if they do listen, the verbal events are so fleeting that they are unable to reflect on the impact of what they said. Selective verbatim overcomes this problem by holding up a "verbal" mirror to teachers, which can be analyzed at their convenience.

Finally, selective verbatim has the advantage of being simple to use. All that the supervisor needs is a pencil and pad of paper. Also, the verbatim transcript can be made while the supervisor is observing the teacher's classroom. There is no need for additional transcription work after the observation period.

Selective verbatim is clearly a powerful tool for observation, but some problems can occur in using it. A teacher who knows in advance what verbal behaviors will be recorded may become self-conscious in using them. For example, just knowing that a supervisor will observe verbal praise may increase a teacher's use of this behavior. Even if this happens, the teacher may gradually internalize the technique of verbal praise and use it even when the supervisor is not around.

We find in practice that teachers generally do not become self-conscious when selective verbatim is used. As teachers realize the impact of their verbal behavior on students, they usually want to cooperate with the supervisor to learn more about what they and their students say.

Another problem with selective verbatim arises from its "selectivity." The larger context of classroom interaction is lost if teacher and supervisor focus too narrowly on verbal behavior. For example, a teacher may look at a selective verbatim of praise statements and dismiss them with, "Oh, I see I used verbal praise ten times. I guess that's pretty good." The analysis needs to go further to explore such questions as whether the praise was given to students who deserved it and whether it was not used when it should have been. In-depth analysis of this kind requires that the supervisor record, at least mentally, the entire flow of the lesson. A skillful supervisor is one who simplifies the teaching process by focusing the teacher's attention on a few aspects of teaching, yet relates these aspects to the total context in which the behaviors occurred.

Still another problem with selective verbatim is that the teacher or supervisor may select trivial behaviors for observation. To avoid this problem, the supervisor and teacher should explore why each identified verbal behavior is worth recording and analyzing. If a satisfactory rationale cannot be given, they must consider whether scarce supervisory time should be used to record the particular verbal behavior.

Supervisors occasionally find that they cannot keep up with the flow of verbal interactions. It simply goes by too fast to record. In this situation we recommend that supervisors use a symbol, such as a line, to indicate where they stopped recording temporarily. It is generally better to record a few verbal statements word for word than to paraphrase or shorten what was said.

TEACHER QUESTIONS (TECHNIQUE 8)

Question-asking is one of the most important aspects of teaching. This is what educator Mary Jane Aschner had in mind when she called the teacher a "professional question maker."[1]

Researchers have found that teachers rely on question-asking as a staple of their teaching repertoire. More than 80 years ago, R. Stevens discovered that high school teachers asked almost 400 questions during an average school day. Unbelievable as this figure may seem, it also has been observed in studies of more recent vintage. More recently, William Floyd found that a sample of primary school teachers asked an average of 348 questions each during a school day, and John Moyer found elementary school teachers asking an average of 180 questions in a science lesson. In Joan Schreiber's study, fifth-grade teachers asked an average of 64 questions in a 30-minute social studies lesson. At the high school level, Arno Bellack and his colleagues found that "the core of the teaching sequence found in the classrooms studied is a teacher's question, a pupil's response, and, more often than not, a teacher's reaction to that response."[2]

These findings lead us to recommend that if a teacher and a supervisor can observe only a single aspect of classroom interaction, it should be the teacher's question-asking behavior.

Technique

The supervisor's task is to make a written record of each question asked by the teacher. (Another approach is to use a checklist, such as that shown in Figure 8.3 in chapter 8.) Because teachers typically ask many questions, the supervisor might ask the teacher to estimate the length of the lesson. Then the supervisor can use time sampling, which means that the supervisor observes samples of the lesson (e.g., the first 3 minutes of the lesson, 5 minutes in the middle of the lesson, and 3 minutes at the end of the lesson). Obviously, if you are planning to observe the teacher's use of questions, you will want to select a lesson in which this verbal behavior occurs with some frequency.

It seems a simple matter to decide what is or is not a question. "How many kilometers in a mile?" is obviously a question. But how about "Johnny gave a good answer, didn't he?" or "Sue, won't you stop fidgeting in your seat?" or "I'd like someone to tell me how many kilometers there are in a mile." The latter example is a declarative statement, not an interrogative, yet it clearly has the intent of a question.

To avoid confusion, we suggest a simple rule. If the teacher's statement is asked in a questioning manner or has the intent of a question, include it in the transcript. There is no harm in including ambiguous examples, but omitting them may cause a teacher to overlook a significant aspect of his question-asking behavior.

Figure 5.1 shows selective verbatims based on observation of two fifth-grade teachers. The teachers assigned students to read the same brief handout on the behavior patterns and environment of the wolf, followed by a question-and-answer session to help the students review and think about what they had just read.

Data Analysis

When teachers examine selective verbatims of their questions, they often observe the behaviors described below.

Cognitive Level of Question.   Teachers' questions can be classified into two categories: "fact" and "higher cognitive." Fact questions require students to recall facts or information stated in the curriculum materials. Higher cognitive questions (also called "thought" questions), in contrast, require students to think about the information they have studied and to state their own ideas. Questions can be analyzed into additional categories using Bloom's taxonomy or other question classification system,[3] but the two levels of "fact" and "higher cognitive" are satisfactory for most purposes.

The research we reviewed in chapter 2 does not demonstrate unequivocally that higher cognitive questions are superior to fact questions. On the basis of the available evidence, it seems reasonable to conclude that an emphasis on either type of question can be effective depending on the teacher's objectives for the lesson. If the lesson's purpose is to teach or review facts and routine skills, an emphasis on fact questions probably will be effective. If the purpose is to develop students' ability to think, the emphasis probably should be on higher cognitive questions.

Fact questions and higher cognitive questions are not always easy to distinguish from one another. For example, a student may be asked to recall a fact stated in the assigned reading. The student may not be able to recall the fact but can deduce it, using higher cognitive processes and other information he or she knows. A question that is higher cognitive in form (e.g., a "why?" question) may actually be a "fact" question if the student simply repeats an idea heard or read elsewhere.

It is apparent that the first teacher in Figure 5.1 is emphasizing fact questions as indicated by phrases like "What do we know about . . . ?" "Who said that?" and "Did you have a chance to look at that last night?" In contrast, the second teacher focuses on higher cognitive processes, as indicated by phrases like "What would lead you to believe. . . ?" "Why. . . ?" and "Does anyone have another idea?" One of these

Teacher 1

1. Now, what do we know about this animal? What do you know about the wolf? You can refer back to this little ditto, if you'd like. Jeff?
2. Next?
3. Mike?
4. Heather?
5. Now Jeff just said that sometimes livestock . . . people or farmers hate them because they kill their livestock. Would livestock be small animals? What do you think?
6. Terry?
7. John?
8. Mike?
9. Terry, again?
10. Jeff?
11. Jerry?
12. Who said that, Jerry? Was there a quote or something in that article?
13. Do you remember the man's name?
14. Do you know something? Last night, after we read this article, after school, Jeff said, "Gee Mr. Edwards, I think I've seen that name, or something." He went right down to the library and brought back this book, and it's by the same man. Jeff, did you have a chance to look at that last night?
15. Jeff, does it just concern itself with the wolf?
16. Does anyone have anything else to say about what we already know?

Teacher 2

1. What do you know about the Arctic and that kind of area that would lead you to believe that a dog would have to be more strong there than he would have to be, say, here? Dana?
2. Pam?
3. What kind of work does he have to do?
4. Terry?
5. Karen?
6. Why do the dogs work harder in the north than they work here? John?
7. Why don't our dogs have to work?
8. What don't we need done here?
9. Allen?
10. Doug?
11. Why do you suppose the Eskimos don't have machines? Joey?
12. Do you think so? Does anyone have another idea about why they don't, 'cause there's probably more than one idea?
13. Why would they be primitive? Pam?
14. Wanda?
15. It mentioned in the stories that wolves traveled in packs, in groups. Why do you suppose they do? What do you suppose is their reason for doing this? Joe?

FIGURE 5.1 Selective verbatims of fifth-grade teachers' questions.

teachers is not necessarily more effective than the other. The first teacher may have had good reasons to emphasize fact questions, and the second teacher may have had equally good reasons to emphasize higher cognitive questions. The supervisor can identify these reasons by conferencing with the teachers about the thinking that went into their lessons.

Amount of Information.   Fact questions can be classified further into "narrow" and "broad," depending on the amount of information called for in the question. For example, the first teacher in Figure 5.1 asked, "What do you know about the wolf?" This is an example of a broad fact question. "Do you remember the man's name?" is an example of a narrow fact question because it asks for only one bit of information. Teachers sometimes ask a series of narrow fact questions—a teacher-centered practice that uses up much class time—when one broad question might be sufficient.

Redirection.   Teachers can call on one student to answer each question, or they can ask several students to respond. That is, they can "redirect" the question. Redirection is a useful technique for increasing student participation and eliciting a variety of ideas for students to consider. Higher cognitive questions are redirected more easily than fact questions, because the former usually do not have a single correct answer.

Both teachers in Figure 5.1 used the technique of redirection by naming the student they wished to respond. Redirection also can occur by nonverbal acknowledgement of a student who has his hand raised or by establishing eye contact with a student. These instances of redirection will not show up in a selective verbatim. If the supervisor wishes to record these instances, he or she can do so by writing an R or other symbol whenever they occur. The names of the students can be recorded, instead, if the supervisor knows them.

Probing Questions.   These are "follow-up" questions designed to help students improve or elaborate on their initial response to the teacher question. They are not easy to detect in a selective verbatim, unless the supervisor makes special note of them, such as by placing a P beside each one. The following is a complete verbatim of the events that transpired when the second teacher in Figure 5.1 asked questions 6 and 7.

TEACHER: Why do the dogs work harder in the north than they work here? John?

JOHN: Well, most of the dogs here don't really have to work hard.

TEACHER: Why don't our dogs have to work?

JOHN: They're house pets, and we do most of the work ourselves, and we don't need stuff like they do up there.

TEACHER: What don't we need done here?

JOHN: We don't need dogs to pull things here. We have cars, but the Eskimos don't, so they use dogs.

The teacher's two probing questions helped John give a more complete and specific answer to the initial question.

Teachers sometimes are unaware that they accept or overlook poor responses to their questions. A record of their probing questions provides one indication of whether this is happening. An absence of probing questions suggests lack of attention to student responses, whereas liberal use of this technique suggests that the teacher is listening carefully to what students say and is challenging them to do their best work.

Multiple Questions.   The practice of asking several questions in a row can be spotted easily in a selective verbatim. Note that the first teacher begins his lesson by asking two questions in succession: "Now, what do we know about this animal? What do you know about the wolf?" The same teacher also asks multiple questions in the fifth and twelfth recorded statements. The second teacher asks multiple questions in the twelfth and fifteenth recorded statements.

Teachers usually engage in this behavior when they are "thinking on their feet." They may try various phrasings and ideas before they hit upon the question they want to ask. If this is a teacher's habitual practice, he should reflect on whether it is distracting or confusing to students. The teacher can avoid asking multiple questions by preparing questions in advance of the actual lesson.

Teachers also engage in multiple question-asking when they literally repeat their question. They do this because they think students did not hear them the first time they asked the question. The problem is that repeating the question may condition students not to listen carefully to the teacher the first time he or she asks a question.

TEACHER FEEDBACK (TECHNIQUE 9)

Researchers have found that teacher feedback affects the learning process (see chapter 2). This research finding makes sense. If we are learning a new skill, we need feedback to know how well we are performing the skill. Without feedback, we may simply practice bad habits or terminate training too soon. It is probably for this reason that "correction and feedback" is an important component of the research-based "explicit teaching model" shown in Figure 2.1 of chapter 2.

Praise and negative remarks are a particular form of feedback. They can have a strong effect on student behavior, especially their motivation to learn. Praise encourages students to learn and to keep trying if obstacles arise. Harsh criticism has just the opposite effect.

Technique

As the supervisor, you need to arrange with the teacher to observe a sample of classroom instruction in which there is ample opportunity for verbal interchange between teacher and students. During instruction, you record the teacher's verbal feedback statements. It also may be useful to record the immediately preceding student remark or action that prompted the feedback. Another option is to make note of the affective context: Was the verbal feedback hostile in tone? Enthusiastic? Automatic?

As with question classification, it is not always an easy matter to decide whether a particular teacher remark is an instance of verbal feedback. You will need to rely on your judgment to determine whether the remark is likely to be perceived by a student as feedback on his or her behavior. Thus, the supervisor needs to be a close observer of students' reactions and the total instructional context when making the selective verbatim.

Figure 5.2 presents a selective verbatim of a junior high school teacher's feedback statements and the context in which they occurred. The lesson was organized around an article about population explosion that the students had been asked to read.

You may wonder whether to include probing questions, which we described earlier in the chapter, as instances of teacher feedback. Consider, for example, the second and third teacher utterances in Figure 5.2. We classified them as probing questions because they were intended to elicit a more specific answer from the student. At the same time, the fact that the teacher asked the questions is feedback to the students that the answer can be improved. That, at least, is our view of the situation. As an observer of classroom instruction, you will need to make your own judgment about whether to include probing questions in a selective verbatim of teacher feedback.

Data Analysis

The teacher and supervisor can examine a selective verbatim of feedback comments from several perspectives, including:

Amount.   The simplest analysis you can make of the selective verbatim is to determine the frequency with which the teacher provides feedback. You may observe teachers who provide little or no feedback to their students. These teachers tend to use a very directive style of instruction; their primary concern is to impart knowledge (perhaps with too little concern about whether students are "receiving" the knowledge). Other teachers make extensive use of feedback. They tend to be more responsive to students and to encourage teacher-student interaction. In Figure 5.2, we counted ten instances of teacher feedback—a fairly high frequency for this quantity of transcription.

Variety.   Of concern here is whether teachers rely on a few limited forms of feedback or whether they provide a variety of feedback. John Zahorik, in his study of classroom feedback behavior of teachers, found that teachers' verbal feedback tends to be constricted.[4] Only a few kinds of feedback are used regularly. Zahorik found that the most frequent form of feedback to students was simply to repeat the student's answer to a question. An illustration of this practice is the seventh teacher utterance in Figure 5.2.

T: All right. Could someone tell me what the report was about? Ann?

S: Well, it was about birth control.

T: Birth control?

S: Uh, population explosion.

. . .

S: It was about the population explosion, but it was also about limits. It made a lot of predictions, like we won't have room to get around, and there's not going to be any room to plant crops.

T: I'm glad you remembered that the author said that these were "predictions." Why do you think I'm glad you remembered that the author used the word "predictions?"

. . .

S: I also heard that they're going to have a farm under the sea, for sea-farming.

T: Who's "they"?

S: Well . . . the scientists.

. . .

S: And as the years go by, cars will get better and better.

T: Are you sure?

S: Well, I'm not certain, but pretty sure.

T: Pretty sure. This is kind of what I wanted you to get out of this article. These are your opinions, your predictions of what might happen. And they sound pretty good to me, and I'll bank on them to a certain extent, but something might happen to the automobile industry so that your predictions wouldn't come true.

. . .

T: Who made that statement that was quoted in the article?

S: Professor Kenneth E. F. Watt.

T: Professor Kenneth E. F. Watt is saying it. Do we know that what he's saying is worthwhile?

S: Well, Professor Kenneth E. F. Watt isn't the only one that is making these predictions. There's probably thousands of people making these predictions.

T: Yes, that's a good point, Rodney. We can have some faith in what he's predicting because others are making similar predictions.

. . .

T: Why, throughout the whole world, are there so many people having so many children? Did you ever stop to think about it? Steve?

S: When the children grow up, they want children. Then when those children grow up, then they get more children, and that goes on and on.

T: Steve, I'm not sure I'm following you. Could you clarify your idea a bit? Why do people want to have so many children?

. . .

T: (concluding remark) I thought the ideas you had to contribute were a lot more interesting than the article itself.

FIGURE 5.2 Selective verbatim of teacher feedback.

Ned Flanders found that a particularly effective form of feedback is to ac-knowledge students' ideas by building on them.[5] (You will recall from chapter 2 that this practice is an important element of Flanders's model of indirect teaching.) He identified the following ways in which to build upon student ideas:

1. *Modifying* the idea by rephrasing or conceptualizing it in the teacher's own words
2. *Applying* the idea by using it to reach an inference or take the next step in a logical analysis of a problem
3. *Comparing* the idea with other ideas expressed earlier by the students or the teacher
4. *Summarizing* what was said by an individual student or group of students

The sixth teacher utterance in Figure 5.2 is an example of acknowledgment by ap-plying students' ideas to reach an inference.

Teacher verbal feedback also can be analyzed to determine whether there is va-riety in the teacher's use of praise and critical remarks.

Another perspective for analyzing variety of teacher feedback is to determine the nature of the student responses that elicited the feedback statement. Does the teacher limit feedback to the information contained in the student's answer? Or does the teacher extend feedback to include the student's behavior and feelings? Research conducted by Flanders and others indicates that teachers seldom acknowledge stu-dents' feelings, even though most educators would agree that feelings—and other aspects of the affective domain—are an important part of the instructional process.

Specificity.   Teachers tend to give simple, nonspecific forms of feedback, such as, "Good," "Uh-huh," or "OK." Jere Brophy, among other educators, suggests that teach-ers should develop the habit of making their praise or criticism more specific. Below is a list of guidelines that he developed for this purpose.[6] The guidelines are for praise statements, but they can be applied also to criticism and other forms of feed-back (rewards, assignments to remediate academic weaknesses, etc.). You will note that Brophy's guidelines concern not just the phrasing of the praise statement, but also the characteristics of students, especially their motivational state.

Effective Praise
1. is delivered contingently.
2. specifies the particulars of the accomplishment.
3. shows spontaneity, variety, and other signs of credibility; suggests clear attention to the student's accomplishment.
4. rewards attainment of specified performance criteria (which can include effort criteria, however).
5. provides information to students about their competence or the value of their accomplishments.
6. orients students towards better appreciation of their own task-related be-havior and thinking about problem solving.

7. uses students' own prior accomplishments as a context for describing present accomplishments.
8. is given in recognition of noteworthy effort or success at difficult (for this student) tasks.
9. attributes success to effort and ability, implying that similar successes can be expected in the future.
10. fosters endogenous attributions (students believe that they expend effort on the task because they enjoy the task and/or want to develop task-relevant skills).
11. focuses students' attention on their own task-relevant behavior.
12. fosters appreciation of and desirable attributions about task relevant behavior after the process is completed.

Ineffective Praise
1. is delivered randomly or unsystematically.
2. is restricted to global positive reactions.
3. shows a bland uniformity, which suggests a conditioned response made with minimal attention.
4. rewards mere participation, without consideration of performance processes or outcomes.
5. provides no information at all or gives students information about their status.
6. orients students toward comparing themselves with others and thinking about competing.
7. uses the accomplishments of peers as the context for describing students' present accomplishments.
8. is given without regard to the effort expended or the meaning of the accomplishment (for this student).
9. attributes success to ability alone or to external factors, such as luck or easy task.
10. fosters exogenous attributions (students believe that they expend effort on the task for external reasons—to please the teacher, win a competition or reward, etc.).
11. focuses students' attention on the teacher as an external authority figure who is manipulating them.
12. intrudes into the ongoing process, distracting attention from task-relevant behavior.

TEACHER STRUCTURING STATEMENTS AND CLASSROOM MANAGEMENT (TECHNIQUE 10)

In chapter 2 we reviewed nine characteristics of effective teaching that were identified in Rosenshine and Furst's review of research. One of these characteristics is the use of structuring statements, which are teacher utterances that help students focus their attention on the lesson's purpose, organization, and key points. Common types of structuring statements are:

- previews of what will happen in the lesson
- summaries of what did happen
- comments that signal transitions in the lesson
- nonverbal cues that emphasize key points in the lesson

Rosenshine and Furst found consistent research evidence that students whose teachers make structuring statements have better academic achievement. Also, several components of Madeline Hunter's model of effective teaching (discussed in chapter 2) directly involve the use of structuring statements, namely: anticipatory set, stating of objectives, and closure.[7] Structuring statements also can be incorporated into teachers' use of other components of Hunter's model.

As we discussed in chapter 2, classroom management has two major aspects: (1) ensuring that students learn and follow classroom rules and procedures; and (2) handling student misbehavior, which can be viewed as noncompliance with classroom rules and procedures. One way in which teachers get students to follow rules and procedures is by giving directions during the lesson. Directions are similar to structuring statements in that they focus students' attention and organize their learning. Teacher statements when students misbehave also can serve these purposes. For example, "desist" statements (e.g., "Jonnie, stop talking to Bill and get back to your worksheet") serve to refocus the student's attention on the learning task to be performed.

Technique

It is probably best to observe a teacher's statements involving structuring, directions, and classroom discipline in the context of a complete lesson. Therefore, as the supervisor, you need to speak beforehand with the teacher to determine when to begin observing and approximately how long the lesson will last. Then, during the lesson, you will make a selective verbatim of each set of directions, structuring statements, and classroom discipline statements made by the teacher. (Of course, you can limit the selective verbatim to just one or two of these types of statements.) Most such statements occur at the beginning and end of the lesson, so you need to be especially observant at these times.

Figure 5.3 presents a composite of lessons in which teachers gave directions and made structuring and disciplinary comments. We used this approach, rather than presenting the selective verbatim of one teacher, to show the variety of forms that these verbal comments can take.

Data Analysis

As with teacher feedback, the teacher and supervisor can observe the amount, variety and specificity of statements involving directions, structuring, and discipline. In addition, it is helpful to observe whether the statements are clear, that is, whether they tell the student precisely what to do or precisely what is happening in the lesson.

Structuring Statements

1. OK. Most of you have finished. We will go on to the next poem.
2. The report we're going to read today is about apartheid in South Africa.
3. The film we just saw on how glass is made illustrates very well some of the points that were covered in the book we're using in this course.
4. Yes, electric cars are one of the really important ways we might be able to control air pollution in the future. You might want to remember that when you write your science-fiction stories.
5. OK. Today I've shown you three different ways you can do calculations. First, we have the slide rule. Second, you can use the desk calculator. And third–does anyone remember what the third method is?

Directions

1. Make sure you write this down in your notebook.
2. Would someone please read the introduction?
3. Class, let's have an orderly discussion today. When you want to talk, please raise your hand and I'll call on you.
4. Hand in your papers from the back to the front of the room.
5. Please take out your homework.

Disciplinary Statements

1. Jimmy, stop talking to Jason and get back to your work.
2. Shut up! I can't hear myself think.
3. Katrin, I thought I told you to clean out your binder. It's a mess.
4. If you don't settle down by the count of three, you won't get to see the film.
5. Jeremy, you blew it. I'm giving you a referral to the principal's office.

FIGURE 5.3   Examples of teacher statements involving structuring, directions, and classroom discipline.

As we stated above, structuring comments can take a variety of forms, for example:

1. an overview of the lesson about to be taught
2. the objectives and purpose of the lesson
3. cueing remarks that focus the student's attention on key points in the lesson
4. a summary of what was covered in the lesson
5. statements that relate the lesson to curriculum content previously covered or to events outside the classroom
6. reinforcement of key structuring comments by repeating them in another format (e.g., through a handout, on a blackboard, or by an overhead projector)

You and the teacher can review the selective verbatim to determine the presence of these types of structuring comments, and whether the lesson could have been improved by including some of them.

The teacher's directions in a lesson reflect his rules and procedures. If the rules and procedures have been taught well at the beginning of the school year or course, the directions can be briefly stated. Also, it probably is not necessary to give many directions. This is because most rules and procedures apply from one lesson to the next. This point is illustrated in chapter 2 in Walter's Doyle's list of 18 tasks and situations for which rules and procedures are necessary.[8] For example, item 11 on Doyle's list concerns moving around the classroom for such purposes as pencil-sharpening and getting materials. If students have been taught rules for moving around the classroom, the teacher should not need to repeat them during the lesson.

Classroom discipline statements also can be viewed as a reflection of how well rules and procedures have been taught. In a well-managed classroom, there should be relatively few statements of this sort. It is unlikely that there will be no such statements, however, because some students will misbehave for reasons that have nothing to do with the teacher's instruction.

Classroom discipline statements can be analyzed for their severity. As we discussed in chapter 2, effective classroom managers try to use mild interventions that accomplish their purpose without disrupting the class. The first statement in the list of disciplinary statements in Figure 5.3 seems fairly mild. The second statement is severe. Teachers can analyze their disciplinary statements to determine their level of severity and whether they were effective in accomplishing their purpose. In chapter 2 we reviewed research that found that effective teachers teach classroom rules and procedures systematically, monitor their use continually, and correct misbehavior unobtrusively and before it has a chance to escalate.

An important aspect of teacher structuring statements and directions is their clarity. Students may get off task and misbehave simply because they do not understand what the teacher is saying to them about classroom rules and procedures. Not surprisingly, Rosenshine and Furst found in their review of research (see chapter 2) that students learn better when they have teachers who make clear verbal statements.[9]

Teachers can make their own judgments about the clarity of the statements recorded in the selective verbatim. This process is facilitated if the selective verbatim is reviewed fairly quickly after the lesson, while the teacher can still recall whether the statements were clearly understood by the students. If clarity is a concern, this can become the focus of subsequent clinical supervision. Procedures for observing and analyzing clarity in teaching are described in chapter 7.

NOTES

1. Mary Jane Aschner, "Asking Questions to Trigger Thinking," *NEA Journal* 50 (1961): 44–46.
2. R. Stevens, "The Question as a Measure of Efficiency in Instruction: A Critical Study of Classroom Practice," *Teachers College Contributions to Education* 48 (1912); William D.

Floyd, "An Analysis of the Oral Questioning Activity in Selected Colorado Primary Classrooms" (Ph.D. diss., Colorado State College, 1960); John R. Moyer, "An Exploratory Study of Questioning in the Instructional Processes in Selected Elementary Schools" (Ph.D. diss., Columbia University, 1966); Joan E. Schreiber, "Teachers' Question-Asking Techniques in Social Studies" (Ph.D. diss., University of Iowa, 1967); Arno Bellack, Herbert Kliebard, Ronald Hyman, and Frank L. Smith, Jr., *The Language of the Classroom* (New York: Teachers College Press, 1966).

3. Benjamin S. Bloom (ed.), *Taxonomy of Educational Objectives: The Classification of Educational Goals. Handbook 1: Cognitive Domain* (New York: McKay, 1956).

4. John A. Zahorik, "Classroom Feedback Behavior of Teachers," *Journal of Educational Research* 62 (1968): 147–50.

5. Ned A. Flanders, *Analyzing Teaching Behavior* (Reading, MA: Addison-Wesley, 1970).

6. Jere Brophy, "Teacher Praise: A Functional Analysis," *Review of Educational Research* 51, No. 1; chart from p. 26. Copyright © 1981 by the American Educational Research Association. Reprinted by permission of the Publisher.

7. Barak Rosenshine and Norma Furst, "The Use of Direct Observation to Study Teaching," in *Handbook of Research on Teaching*, 2d ed., ed. Robert M. W. Travers (Chicago: Rand McNally, 1973), pp. 122–83. Madeline Hunter, "Teaching Is Decision Making," *Educational Leadership* 37, No. 1 (1979): 62–67.

8. Walter Doyle, "Classroom Organization and Management," in *Handbook of Research on Teaching*, 3d ed., ed. Merlin C. Wittrock (New York: Macmillan, 1986), 392–431.

9. Rosenshine and Furst, "The Use of Direct Observation."

chapter 6

Observational Records Based on Seating Charts

These seating chart techniques look simple, but they're not. True, all the supervisor gives you to look at is a seating chart with lines and arrows all over it. But they tell you a lot about what happened in your lesson. You can see that your teaching is following a definite pattern. Then the question you need to ask yourself is, Is this a good or a bad pattern, something I want to change or something I want to keep on doing?

Comment of a high school teacher

Several techniques for observing teacher and student behavior make use of seating charts. For this reason we call these techniques Seating Chart Observation Records (SCORE).

One of the main advantages of SCORE techniques is that they are based on classroom seating charts. Because teachers use seating charts in their daily work, they find it easy to interpret SCORE data.

SCORE techniques have several other advantages. They enable the supervisor to condense a large amount of information about classroom behavior on a single sheet of paper. They can be created on the spot to suit the individual teacher's concerns. They are easy to use and interpret. Moreover, they record important aspects of classroom behavior, such as students' level of attentiveness and how teachers distribute their time among students in the class. A special benefit of SCORE techniques is that they enable the teacher and supervisor to spotlight individual students in the class, at the same time observing what the class as a whole is doing. An example of this use of SCORE techniques is provided by Jane Stallings and her colleagues.[1]

SCORE techniques have a few limitations. They simplify the teaching process by isolating certain behaviors for observation, but unless these behaviors are related to the total teaching-learning context, the teacher may draw simplistic conclusions from the data. Another hazard is that teacher or supervisor may select trivial behaviors for observation. Another problem is that classroom behavior occasionally will "speed up" or become chaotic. In this situation, you may need to modify or temporarily abandon the data collection process.

AT TASK (TECHNIQUE 11)

The at-task technique was developed in the 1960s by Frank MacGraw at Stanford University.[2] MacGraw devised a system of classroom observation that used a 35 mm camera, remotely controlled. From the front corner of the room the camera took a picture of the total class every 90 seconds, using a wide-angle lens. The photos were developed and enlarged. The observer was then provided with a set of pictures of a classroom during a given time period (e.g., 20 pictures to represent a 30-minute lesson).

A variety of results were obtained. Some looked like the films formerly shown in nickelodeons, where the students gradually move from a position of sitting erect at their desks to a position of sleeping with their heads on their desks, back to a position of sitting and looking attentive. Other collections of pictures showed students working feverishly on matters that had nothing to do with the task at hand, or vacant from their seats talking to their neighbors, or engaged in a variety of actions the teacher regarded as inappropriate.

The data obtained from the pictures were valuable for the teacher in understanding individual students. But the method of collecting data was so demanding, expensive, and time-consuming that experiments were conducted using alternative methods. Ultimately a paper-and-pencil technique was developed to provide much the same data as the 35 mm camera. This paper-and-pencil technique has come to be known as an "at-task" analysis. A completed at-task chart is shown in Figure 6.1.

As we discussed in chapter 2, researchers have found a strong link between students' at-task behavior and their learning. In other words, when students are at task during much or most of a lesson, they are likely to learn more than when they are at task during only some or little of the lesson. Because student at-task behavior is so clearly linked to learning, the at-task observational technique is probably the most important of the SCORE procedures.

Technique

The intent of at-task observation is to provide data on whether individual students during a classroom activity are engaged in the task or tasks that the teacher indicates are appropriate. Therefore, before an observer can use this technique, he or she must be acquainted with what the teacher expects the students to be doing during a given classroom period. In other words, the teacher rather than the supervisor defines what constitutes at-task behavior.

Typical at-task behaviors are reading, listening, answering questions, doing seatwork, and working cooperatively to complete a group project. Lessons in which one task is expected of all students usually present no problem. However, in lessons in

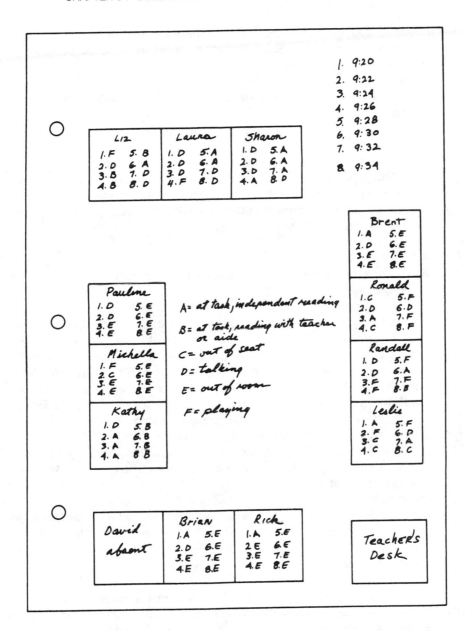

FIGURE 6.1   At-task seating chart.

which students are able to do a variety of tasks, some preparation is necessary before the supervisor can use the at-task technique. If the variety of tasks is too complex, the teacher and supervisor may choose to limit the observation to one group or section of the classroom.

A record of students' at-task behavior can be made in several ways, including the procedure described by Jane Stallings and her colleagues.[3] In the procedure we use, the supervisor completes the following seven steps:

1. Stations herself in a section of the room where she is able to observe all students.
2. Constructs a chart that resembles a seating pattern of the students in the room that day.
3. Indicates on the chart the gender or some other characteristic of each student. The purpose is to guide subsequent analysis of the data to determine whether certain types of students act or are treated differently.
4. Creates a legend to represent at-task behavior and each type of inappropriate behavior observed. A typical legend might be:
   A: At task
   S: Stalling
   R-: Schoolwork other than that requested by the teacher
   O: Out of seat
   T: Talking to neighbors
5. Systematically examines the behavior of each student for a few seconds in order to determine whether the student is at task, that is, doing what the teacher considers appropriate. If so, indicates this by marking a 1A in the box on the seating chart meant to represent the student. Figure 6.1 indicates that this is the first observation; the letter A refers to at-task behavior. If the student is not at task, the observer indicates this by recording 1S, 1R-, 1O, or 1T (using the legend created in step 4).
6. Repeats step 5 at 3- or 4-minute intervals for the duration of lesson using the same letter legend to indicate observed behavior but changing the number to indicate the sequence of observations. For example, 3A in a box indicates that the student was at task during the supervisor's third observation.
7. Indicates time of each set of observations. This is marked somewhere on the chart (e.g., see upper right-hand corner of Figure 6.1). The observer also may find it helpful to record the classroom activity that the teacher was conducting at each time of observation.

You are advised to follow a few precautions in using the at-task technique. First, avoid forming too many categories for observation. Step 4 (above) lists five categories—at task, stalling, other schoolwork than that requested by the teacher, out of seat, and talking to neighbor—which is probably as many categories as you would want to form. Adding more categories complicates the observation process greatly, and it becomes increasingly difficult for the teacher to interpret the resulting data. In many classroom observations, two categories are sufficient: at task and off task.

In using the at-task technique, supervisors sometimes become overly concerned about the accuracy of their observations. This can be avoided by keeping in mind that observation of at-task behavior requires a moderate degree of inference. The expression on a child's face may be interpreted as thoughtful reflection about what the teacher is saying or as daydreaming. We suggest you think probabilistically. If you think it is more likely that the child is engaged in thoughtful reflection than in daydreaming, use the at-task category. If you think it is more probable that the child is daydreaming, indicate this by using one of your off-task codes. You may wish to tell the teacher that the completed chart is, to an extent, subjective. Thus the teacher should look for general patterns rather than question the accuracy of a few isolated observations.

The at-task chart in Figure 6.1 has one box for each student in the class. The students are identified by name on the chart. If the feedback conference occurs fairly soon after the observation, the teacher should have no difficulty matching students with the boxes even without names. However, if the feedback conference is delayed, you should consider putting students' names in the appropriate boxes of the seating chart. This creates a problem if the teacher does not have a prepared seating chart to assist you and if you don't know the students' names. A simple solution is for the teacher to have students say their names aloud at the beginning of the class period while you jot them down; the student's first or last name should be sufficient.

You may wish to use several different colored pencils or pens to record at-task data. The seating chart can be one color, and the at-task observations can be a different color. This procedure results in a visually pleasing display for the teacher to study and interpret.

Example

An elementary school principal observed a first-grade teacher's reading class. The decision to do an at-task seating chart grew out of a planning conference between the teacher and the principal. Part of this conference is reproduced below:

TEACHER: Would you come in and do an at task in my classroom? Randall and Ronald do nothing but play and talk. I would like to see just how much they really work.

PRINCIPAL: Are Randall and Ronald the only ones you want me to observe?

TEACHER: No. I have a real immature group this year. You might as well observe all of them.

PRINCIPAL: What do you mean by "immature"?

TEACHER: Oh, they have short attention spans, haven't learned to settle down, and they are all talking without permission. In other words, this first grade doesn't really know how to settle down and do some work.

PRINCIPAL: Do they seem to understand what you have planned for them?

TEACHER: Yes, but they have a hard time settling down to work. Ronald moans and groans most of the time or plays.

PRINCIPAL: What kinds of behavior should I observe for the at task? What categories should I use?

TEACHER: Before I forget, remember some of my children are out of the room for music at the time you're coming.

PRINCIPAL: That's right. I'll put it on my checklist so I won't forget it.

TEACHER: Check to see if they're out of their seats, talking, playing, or at task. They will also be reading to my aide or to me.

PRINCIPAL: I'll make a note of the reading aide, and I'll see you tomorrow.

For the purpose of this observation, at-task behavior was defined as independent reading in a workbook at one's seat (A) or as reading with the teacher or aide (R). The principal also recorded several other categories of behavior: out of seat (S), talking (T), out of room (O), playing (P). The categories are shown in the legend in Figure 6.1, together with the completed at-task seating chart.

Data Analysis

Figure 6.2 provides a convenient summary of the observations recorded on the seating chart (Figure 6.1). The teacher can see at a glance how many children were engaged in each category of behavior—either at a particular point in time or summed across all the time samples. The last column indicates the average percentage of students who engaged in each category of behavior during the class period. For example, 6 percent of the children were out of their seat on average during the lesson. The numerator used to derive this percentage is the total of 6 children (see total column) who were out of their seat across the 8 observations that were made of the lesson. The denominator (96) is the 8 observations multiplied by the 12 children in the class. Dividing the numerator (6) by the denominator (96) gives the average percent (6 percent).

FIGURE 6.2   Summary of at-task data from Figure 6.1.

BEHAVIOR	9:20	9.22	9:24	9:26	9:28	9:30	9:32	9:34	Total	%
A. At task independent work	4	1	2	2	2	4	2	0	17	18%
B. At task reading with Teacher or aide	0	0	1	1	2	1	1	2	8	8%
C. Out of seat	1	1	1	2	0	0	0	1	6	6%
D. Talking	5	8	2	0	0	2	2	3	22	23%
E. Out of room	0	1	5	5	5	5	5	5	31	32%
F. Playing	2	1	1	2	3	0	2	1	12	13%

Analysis of at-task is illustrated nicely by the feedback conference that occurred between the principal and the first-grade teacher. Part of this conference is reproduced below:

TEACHER: Let's see. Randall was at task once. Ronald was, too. Here is a shocker! Liz, Laura, and Sharon do a lot of visiting. I can see where I need to do some changes in the seating.

PRINCIPAL: That may solve some of your talking and visiting problems.

TEACHER: Boy, from 9:20 to 9:36, five of my students are out to music. This only leaves seven to work with. Gee, I only worked with two children, and the aide worked with one.

PRINCIPAL: It seems as though quite a few of your students are gone at one time.

TEACHER: Yes, I should try to work with these students before they go to music.

PRINCIPAL: That's a good idea! In that way you can usually have them read to you every day.

TEACHER: Maybe I could ask the aide to have Kathy only read a few pages and then listen to someone else.

PRINCIPAL: That sounds great!

TEACHER: This doesn't solve my problem with Randall and Ronald. Since Brian and Rick go to music, maybe I could put Ronald at Rick's desk. This way I can get a direct view of him. This also would separate the two boys.

PRINCIPAL: This sounds like a good step. Maybe you'll want to keep the boys apart permanently in the classroom.

TEACHER: I sure hope this works. If not, I'll find something else.

PRINCIPAL: I'm sure you will. You seem to have some good ideas already.

TEACHER: I could even have the aide work with Ronald and Randall in reading and have her play some phonics games with them. This would help expand their attention span, too.

PRINCIPAL: You're really getting some good ideas. It will be interesting to see how they work out. Maybe I could come back and do an at task again.

TEACHER: Yes, I'd like to see if some of my ideas will help the children settle down, especially Ronald and Randall.

This interaction between principal and teacher illustrates the importance of at-task data in clinical supervision. The data focus the teacher's attention directly on the extent to which students are engaged in productive classroom behavior. If students are not at task, the teacher knows that there is a problem that needs correction. As illustrated in the above conference excerpt, the teacher and supervisor can develop solutions once the problem has been diagnosed.

In inspecting Figures 6.1 and 6.2, you might have noted how much the students' at-task behavior changed from one observation to the next. This is characteristic of young children. Except for those who left the room, the children were likely to change from one category of behavior to another with each observation. For example, Leslie varied back and forth among behavior categories A, C, D, and F within the 14-minute (9:20 to 9:34) period of observation.

VERBAL FLOW (TECHNIQUE 12)

Verbal flow is primarily a technique for recording who is talking to whom. It also is useful for recording categories of verbal interaction—for example, teacher question, student answer, teacher praise, student question. Verbal flow is similar to the technique of selective verbatim (see chapter 7) in that both techniques deal with classroom verbal behavior. Selective verbatim is concerned more with actual content of the verbal communication, whereas verbal flow identifies the initiators and recipients of the verbal communication and the kind of communication in which they are engaged.

We reviewed in chapter 2 a study by Gregg Jackson and Cecilia Cosca, who found that teachers in the Southwest directed significantly more verbal behavior toward Anglo students than toward Chicano students. Research has identified other forms of bias in teacher verbal behaviors as well. Michael Dunkin and Bruce Biddle reached the following conclusions about one such bias in their review of research:

> The majority of both emitters and targets [of verbal behavior]—whether they be teachers or pupils—are located front and center in the classroom. Thus, pupils who are located around the periphery of the classroom are more likely to be spectators than actors in the classroom drama. It could be, then, that if the teacher wants to encourage participation on the part of a quiet pupil or silence on the part of someone who is noisy, she need merely move the pupil to another location in the room![4]

Although teachers tend to talk more to students seated closest to them, other "location" biases can occur. For example, one teacher found that he had a tendency to acknowledge more questions from students seated to his right than from students seated to his left. After learning of this tendency, the teacher realized that, in talking to a class, he usually looked to the right side of the classroom. Thus, students seated to this side were in the teacher's central line of vision, whereas students to the left were in his peripheral vision. It occurred to the teacher how frustrated students to his left might be if they had questions but could not ask them because they were out of his line of sight. With this new awareness, the teacher made a conscious effort to distribute eye contact equally to all parts of the classroom. This led to a more equal distribution of verbal behaviors.

Verbal flow is a valuable supervisory technique because it helps teachers discover (1) biases in their own verbal behavior, and (2) differences between students in verbal participation. Verbal flow is particularly appropriate when the lesson involves discussion, question-and-answer recitation, or other methods that require many verbal interchanges between teacher and students. It is not appropriate for observing instruction low in verbal interaction (e.g., lecture and independent study).

Technique

As with other SCORE observational instruments, the first step in doing a verbal flow is to make a classroom seating chart. Because of the many seating patterns that can occur in classrooms, we suggest that you not make a standard form; rather, create the seating chart on a blank sheet of paper.

A box is used to represent each student. You can put the students' names in the appropriate boxes, or if you wish to focus on a particular characteristic, you can just indicate the characteristic. For example, the teacher may suggest in the planning conference that you label each student as male or female; characteristically verbal or nonverbal; high-achieving, average, or low-achieving. Of course, the teacher will need to tell you the labels that apply to each child. The advantage of this kind of chart is that teachers can more easily determine whether they respond differentially to students who vary in these characteristics. Arrows are used to indicate the flow of verbal interaction. The base of the arrow indicates the person who initiates a verbal interaction, and the head of the arrow indicates the person to whom the comment is directed.

The teacher is an exception to this procedure. Because the teacher usually initiates most of the verbal interactions, it would be awkward to have an arrow leading from the box that designates the teacher to each student to whom a comment is directed. Arrows would be crisscrossing one another as they made their way from the teacher's box to boxes situated at diverse points on the seating chart. This problem is avoided by placing the arrow completely within the student's box. The base of the arrow should come from the general direction of the teacher. This means that the teacher made these statements directed toward this student.

One way to keep a verbal flow chart visually simple is to use notches in an arrow to indicate repeated interactions of the same kind. (See Figure 6.3.) For example, in box A a separate arrow is used to record each interaction. Analysis of these data indicates that the teacher directed four comments to this student, and the student directed two comments back to the teacher. The same data are recorded in box B by two arrows. The arrow indicating the teacher-initiated comment has three notches on it. The arrow indicates one comment, and each notch represents a comment, for a total of four teacher-initiated comments. Similarly, box B indicates a total of two student-initiated comments.

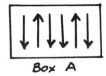

Box A

Box B

FIGURE 6.3 Verbal flow chart.

The standard verbal flow chart can be elaborated by using additional categories of observation. The following are possible teacher categories:

$\rightarrow$ +   teacher praise or encouraging remark
$\rightarrow$ −   teacher criticism or reprimand
$\rightarrow$ F?   teacher fact question
$\rightarrow$ T?   teacher thought question

Student verbal behaviors also can be differentiated, for example:

$\rightarrow$ @   student volunteered a relevant or correct response
$\rightarrow$ *   student volunteered an irrelevant or incorrect response
$\rightarrow$?   student question
$\rightarrow$ }   student comment directed to the class as a whole

The teacher should participate during the planning conference in deciding what categories are to be observed. It is advisable to form no more than a few categories. Otherwise the recording and interpretation of verbal flow data become unwieldy.

Some supervisors prefer to use an alphabetic notation system rather than arrows. Letters of the alphabet indicate discrete categories of verbal interaction, for example:

Q   teacher question
P   teacher praise
C   teacher criticism
r   student volunteered a relevant or correct response
x   student volunteered an irrelevant or incorrect response
q   student question

Teacher and student behaviors are easily distinguished by the use of uppercase and lowercase letters.

Either arrows or alphabetic notation will get the job done. The choice of one or the other is a matter of preference.

Example

The assistant principal of a high school, one of whose responsibilities is teacher supervision, was asked by a first-year English teacher to determine which students were contributing to classroom and small-group discussions. The teacher's purpose was not to use the supervisor's data to evaluate the students, but to learn whether she was influencing students' participation and how nonparticipating students could be encouraged to join the discussion.

The teacher and supervisor agreed that a verbal flow chart was an appropriate technique for collecting the data. The supervisor arranged to visit the teacher's class at a time when a discussion was scheduled.

The verbal flow chart made by the supervisor is shown in Figure 6.4. Horizontal lines are used to indicate empty desks. Students' gender is indicated by an M or F. The supervisor recorded verbal flow data into four categories: teacher questions, student response, teacher positive response, and teacher negative response. Because some students talked among themselves, the supervisor decided to record this behavior by drawing an arrow between the students engaged in such talk. The period of observation was 22 minutes.

Data Analysis

Verbal flow data can be analyzed from various perspectives. They include, but are not limited, to the following:

Seat-Location Preferences. As we mentioned, some teachers direct more of their attention to students seated in a certain part of the room. This is quite apparent in the teacher's verbal flow chart. As she herself noted, she suffers from tunnel vision. You can see in Figure 6.4 that she asked most of her questions of students seated directly in her line of sight. Students on either side of her line of sight were ignored. This is a common pattern even among experienced teachers. You also may have noted that comments among students, while the lesson was in progress, occurred only at the periphery of the seating arrangement.

On seeing the verbal flow chart, the teacher commented that she might solve the problem of tunnel vision by seating students closer together, using the available empty seats. Another suggestion is to place students in a circular seating arrangement so that everyone can have eye contact with one another.

Student Preferences. In Figure 6.4 students are identified by gender. One can ask whether the teacher interacted equally with boys and girls, and whether she used each category of verbal behavior equally with them.

The verbal flow chart indicates that 13 girls and 11 boys were present for the lesson. Of the 20 questions asked by the teacher, 12 (60 percent) were directed to boys, and 8 (40 percent) were directed to girls. Of the 12 positive responses by the teacher, 8 (66 percent) were directed to boys and 4 (33 percent) were directed to girls. The 2 negative responses by the teacher were both directed to girls. Nine of the 13 girls (70 percent) and 4 (36 percent) of the 11 boys did not participate in the lesson. These data suggest a gender bias favoring boys.

You might also note in Figure 6.4 that two students, a boy and a girl, dominated the participation. (The supervisor needed to create additional boxes to contain their data.) Thirty percent of the total number of questions asked by the teacher were directed to these two students. Moreover, these two students accounted for nearly half the student responses.

Verbal Behavior Preferences. Verbal flow charts can be inspected to determine how frequently teachers and students use certain behaviors and whether they em-

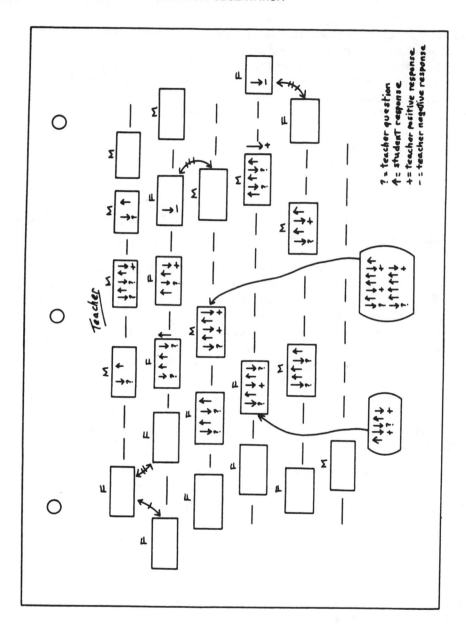

FIGURE 6.4 Supervisor's verbal flow chart.

phasize certain behaviors more than others. One contrast of interest in Figure 6.4 is the teacher's use of positive response behavior compared with her use of negative response behavior. Of the teacher's fourteen responses, all but two of them were positive responses. The two negative responses were directed toward girls near the periphery of the classroom. Another possible comparison in Figure 6.4 is the number of student responses followed by a teacher positive response versus the number of student responses not followed by a teacher positive response. There were 32 student responses in the lesson. Of these, 12 (38 percent) were accompanied by a teacher positive response. This is a relatively high percentage, compared with teachers' usual practice.

MOVEMENT PATTERNS (TECHNIQUE 13)

Another use of seating charts is to record the movements of teacher and students during a class lesson. We call this SCORE technique "movement patterns." The supervisor's task is to record how the teacher and individual students walk from one section of the room to another during a given time interval. This focus on movement differentiates movement patterns from the other SCORE techniques presented in this chapter: at task, which focuses on students' level of attentiveness and engagement in classroom tasks; and verbal flow, which focuses on the nature and direction of verbal communication in the classroom.

Many teaching situations, especially in primary and elementary school, require teachers to make decisions about where to position themselves in the classroom. For example, as students file into class after recess, the teacher needs to decide whether to stand by the door, at the desk, or elsewhere. When students are engaged in seatwork or group projects, the teacher must decide whether to stay at the desk or move around the room checking on students' work.

The nature of the teacher's movement patterns may affect classroom control and student attentiveness. The teacher who "hides" behind a desk may have more discipline problems than the teacher who checks on students as they work at their desks. The teacher who always stands in one position while speaking to the class may not hold students' attention as effectively as the teacher who moves about for dramatic emphasis or to illustrate a concept on the blackboard or chart.

Teachers may reveal a persistent bias in their movement patterns. Some prefer one part of the classroom over another, perhaps because certain students are seated here. Others tend to stand some distance away from students' seats while speaking to the class. This may create difficulties for students who do not see or hear well, and it may provide an excuse for some students to engage in off-task behavior ("the teacher can't see what I'm doing").

Students' movement patterns can reveal whether they are at task. Sometimes it is necessary for students to move about the classroom to complete an assigned activity. At other times students move about to avoid an assigned task or because they have no assigned task. The latter situation often occurs when students finish their work early in the class period; they mill around to find a classmate to engage in conversation or to find another activity.

Movement patterns can be recorded during any lesson, but the technique is most useful when the teaching situation contains the potential for movement about the classroom. For example, seatwork and group projects provide situations where the teacher needs to move about, and where students do move about even when they don't need to. On the other hand, the showing of a film or a question-and-answer recitation places many constraints on teacher and student movement. There is not likely to be much movement behavior to record.

Technique

The seating charts used in other SCORE instruments often consist of interconnected boxes, as in Figure 6.1. To record movement patterns, each student and the teacher should be represented by self-contained boxes. Also, the seating chart should represent the physical layout of the classroom, including aisles and desks or tables where students might congregate.

FIGURE 6.5   Physical movement.

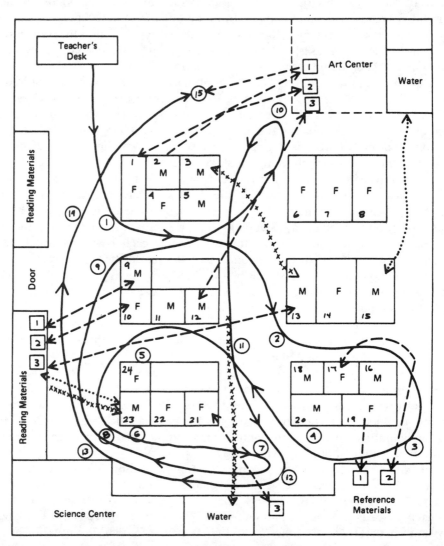

Figures 6.5 and 6.6 show seating charts used to record movement pattern data. Teacher or student movement from one point in the room to another is indicated by a continuous line. The line for each person originates at the point where that person was located in the room when the supervisor began observing. The teacher and students are likely to move from one point to another, stop for a while, then move to another. Each stopping point should be represented by an indicator—for

FIGURE 6.6 Movement pattern chart.

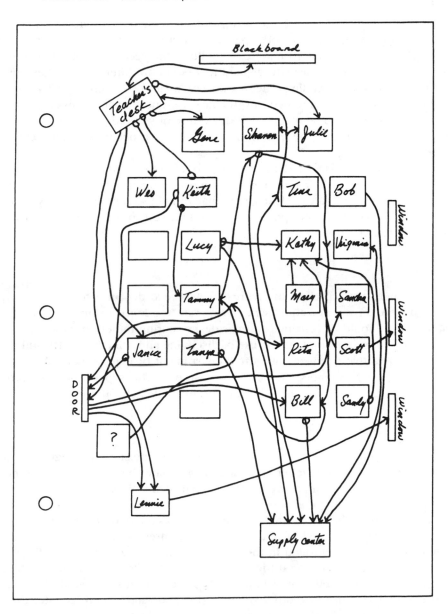

example, an arrow (——>—), a circle (——⊖——), or x (——✗——). Figure 6.5 uses circled numbers to indicate stopping points. This physical movement chart shows that the teacher started the lesson standing at the front of the classroom, next moved to the student designated by box 1, and then proceeded to student 13.

A single line with a different symbol at each end can be used when a person goes from his desk to another location and then returns to his desk. For example, in Figure 6.5 the teacher went from her desk (designated by ○) to Wes's desk and then returned to her desk. In contrast, Keith went from his desk to the teacher's desk and then returned.

You may wish to indicate the pattern of movement at different points in the lesson. A supply of different colored pencils is useful for this purpose. For example, you might record the first 10 minutes in yellow, the second 10 minutes in green, and so on. If the teacher plans to divide the lesson into different activities, this can form the basis for color coding. The first activity might be direction giving, followed by small-group projects, followed by whole-class question-and-answer. Movement during each activity can be recorded with a different colored pencil. This technique helps the teacher analyze the pattern of movement that occurred at different stages of the lesson.

Occasionally so many students will mill about in the classroom that you will not be able to record all their movements. When this occurs, you can suspend data recording for a few minutes. (Make a note that you did so somewhere on your movement pattern chart.) Another possibility is to limit your observation to only certain students in the classroom.

Example

The movement pattern chart in Figure 6.6 was recorded in a high school typing class. The teacher worried about whether he ran "too loose a ship." He didn't think that students should be "chained to their desks" during the entire class period, yet he wanted to instill in students a sense of discipline and self-control. He and the supervisor agreed that a movement pattern chart might be a good method for recording the extent of order-disorder in the classroom. The supervisor observed and recorded the class's movement behavior for approximately 30 minutes.

Data Analysis

At first glance a movement pattern chart such as the one shown in Figure 6.6 looks like a hopeless maze. If teacher and supervisor isolate the behavior of one person or one section of the room, however, they usually can make helpful inferences from the chart.

The first thing that caught the teacher's eye was the door leading into the classroom. Six students entered or left the classroom after the lesson had begun. One student who was not enrolled in the class (indicated by a "?") apparently entered the classroom, talked to several friends and then left. The teacher thought that the mystery student probably was wandering about during his free study period. The chart also indicates that two other students (Bill and Sandra) entered late. Two students (Janice and Keith) left the class while it was in session and then returned. The teacher did not realize this had happened.

After inspecting these data, the teacher decided he needed to monitor students' entry and exit behavior more closely. Also included in this resolution to himself was the decision to give students some ground rules about leaving class while it is in session. The teacher then focused his attention on his own movement behavior. He recalled that he had gone to the blackboard at the start of the lesson to write down key terms relating to typing business letters. Keith then came to his desk to ask a question. Next the teacher decided to check on students' progress, so he visited a few students (Lennie, Wes, Gene, and Julie), each time returning to his desk to catch up on some paperwork. Finally, he decided he should circulate a bit; this is reflected in a large loop starting and ending at his desk. Although he did not stop at every student's desk, he felt he got to each area of the classroom so that if a student desired to speak with him, the student could get his attention easily. The teacher generally felt satisfied with his movement pattern in this lesson.

He and the supervisor next turned their attention to the supply center. Six students (Tanya, Lucy, Sharon, Bill, Virginia, and Bob) went to the center for supplies during the observed part of the lesson. After seeing these data, the teacher wondered whether he should ask students to get any necessary materials at the start of the lesson. This procedure might create a more orderly class and might help students become more organized and systematic in their approach to typing. The supervisor suggested that the teacher experiment with this procedure and see for himself whether it produced the desired effects.

Finally, the teacher looked at other student behavior. He noted that several students had visited with each other, and in fact four of them (Lucy, Mary, Scott, and Sandy) had congregated around Kathy's desk. Two students (Scott and Lennie) had gone to the window to see what was happening outside. The supervisor told the teacher that most of this kind of classroom movement occurred near the end of the observation period. The teacher realized then that he had an activity planned for students who finished early but had forgotten to relay it to them because he was preoccupied about some paperwork he wanted to complete during the lesson. Summing up his inferences from the movement chart data, the teacher felt that he might make a few changes that would create a more orderly class without losing the relaxed atmosphere he valued.

NOTES

1. See pp. 140–45 of Jane Stallings, Margaret Needels, and Georgea Mohlman Sparks, "Observation for the Improvement of Classroom Learning," in *Talks to Teachers*, ed. David C. Berliner and Barak V. Rosenshine (New York: Random House, 1987), 129–58.
2. Frank MacGraw, Jr., "The Use of 35-mm Time-Lapse Photography as a Feedback and Observation Instrument in Teacher Education" (Ann Arbor, MI: University Microfilms, No. 66-2516, 1966).
3. Stallings, Needels, and Sparks, "Observation."
4. Michael J. Dunkin and Bruce J. Biddle, *The Study of Teaching* (New York: Holt, Rinehart and Winston, 1974), p. 226.

chapter 7

Wide-Lens Techniques

It was a shock to listen to the audiotape of my lesson. I never knew before how I sounded when talking to students. The idea of audiotaping lessons is good. After all, students have to hear you talk, so you might as well know how you sound to them. Just listening for a few minutes to the audiotape helped me learn quite a few things about how I communicate. I'm ready now to have myself videotaped. I want to see what that's like!

Comment of a preservice secondary teacher

The advantage of the observation techniques described in chapters 5 and 6—selective verbatim and observational records using seating charts—is that they enable the teacher and supervisor to focus on a few teaching behaviors. Other classroom "noise" is screened out. But sometimes it is the "noise" (i.e., what you didn't plan to observe) that's most interesting. For example, an unanticipated teaching event might occur and strike you as noteworthy, because of its effect on the class. Or perhaps the teacher does something that makes you wonder, "Why did he do that?" Another possibility is that the teacher has nothing that he particularly wishes to focus on in the supervisory process.

In each of these instances, wide-lens techniques may be the most appropriate method of observation. We characterize these techniques as "wide lens," because they capture and record a large number of teaching phenomena. By contrast, selective verbatim and observational records using seating charts can be characterized as "narrow lens."

Wide-lens techniques make few prior assumptions about what is important or effective in teaching. For this reason, they provide a good starting point in supervising teachers who are defensive or who are not yet ready to select particular teaching behaviors for improvement. After reviewing wide-lens data, these teachers may be more ready to reflect on their teaching, identify specific teaching behaviors for focused observations, and set self-improvement goals.

ANECDOTAL RECORDS AND SCRIPT TAPING (TECHNIQUE 14)

Anecdotal records are an easy way to record classroom interaction using a wide lens. The basic technique is to make brief notes of events as they occur in the classroom. This is a favorite technique of anthropologists, who are highly trained in the process of making notes (called ethnographies) that describe what happens in a culture. In fact, the process of making good anecdotal records in supervisory observations is similar to the process of preparing ethnographies because a teacher's classroom and his students constitute a culture of sorts.

We use the term *anecdotal record* to describe this technique because it suggests informality and reminds the teacher and supervisor that the record is not complete. Like any other classroom observation technique, the anecdotal record provides a selective set of data for the teacher to examine.

Madeline Hunter, the developer of the teaching model called Instructional Theory into Practice (see chapter 2), developed a similar note-taking method for recording classroom observations. She called her method script taping.[1] A script tape is essentially the same thing as what we refer to as an anecdotal record. It is the supervisor's set of notes of what happened and what was said during the lesson.

Hunter claimed seven advantages for the use of script taping in the supervision process:

1. The only materials required are paper and pencil.
2. It can be used to record virtually anything that occurs in a classroom.
3. Events are recorded in a temporal order, making it easy to determine how teacher behavior affects student behavior, and vice versa.
4. It is relatively unbiased, if used by a trained observer.
5. The script tape can be "played back" to the teacher in any location and at any time following the observation.
6. The script tape can be scanned quickly to find any part of the lesson.
7. Script tapes are easily stored.

Videotapes and audiotapes (see technique 15) also have advantages. They provide a more compelling and complete record of a lesson, but they are not as easy to make and use in a postconference as a script tape.

Technique

Making an anecdotal record or script tape is a good technique to use when the teacher cannot think of specific behaviors that should be observed. This situation is most likely to occur in the beginning stages of supervision; that is, when the teacher is first learning about the supervisory cycle of planning conference-classroom observation-feedback conference. The teacher may comment, "I guess I'd just like a general idea of what I'm like as a teacher." In response, you can suggest the anecdotal record as a wide-lens technique for collecting descriptive data about teacher and student behavior. Audio and video recordings, discussed later in the chapter, are other possibilities.

The anecdotal record has a wide focus, but you and the teacher will need to decide just how wide to open the lens. You can make anecdotal observations of the teacher, one student, one group of students, the whole class of students, or everyone in the class (teacher, students, teacher aides, etc.). The wider the lens, the more behaviors can be observed. As you narrow the lens, you will have a narrower set of behaviors to observe, but you will also have the opportunity to make more intensive descriptions of these behaviors.

The anecdotal record usually consists of short descriptive sentences. Each sentence summarizes a discrete observation. You may wish to start each sentence on a separate line and every so often record the time that an observation was made. Thus the teacher can get a sense of the temporal flow of the events that were recorded.

The sentences should be as objective and nonevaluative as possible. Instead of writing "Students are bored," you might note "Several students yawn; Jane looks out window." Instead of writing "Teacher does good job of giving directions," you might note "Teacher gives directions. Asks if students understand. Most of class nod or say yes." If you make evaluative comments in your anecdotal record, the teacher is likely to react to the evaluation rather than to what occurred. If your comments are descriptive and neutral, the teacher can more easily form conclusions about the effectiveness of the lesson.

Teacher and student behaviors are not the only events to observe and describe in the anecdotal record. You should be alert also to the context of the teacher's lesson, for example:

"The room is warm; wall thermometer reads 78 degrees."

"Teacher shows map to class. Map is faded. Names of countries are difficult to read."

"Lesson is interrupted by announcement over intercom."

"One of the fluorescent lights starts to hum loudly."

An anecdotal record of these contextual phenomena can help the teacher interpret certain behaviors of students (or of the teacher) that occurred during the lesson.

The anecdotal record consists of handwritten notes made by the supervisor as he or she sits unobtrusively somewhere in the classroom. Anthropologists often make handwritten ethnographic notes, too, but they have the option of using a portable audiotape recorder. As they make each observation, they simply make an audio-recorded description on the spot. This option is not usually available to supervisors because they and their audio-recorder are usually situated too far from the teacher and students.

Unless you have good handwriting, the anecdotal record will be difficult for the teacher to read and study. The preferred practice is to have your notes typed, so that the teacher has a neatly typed transcript to reflect upon in the feedback conference. Also, a typed transcript has a more objective, neutral appearance than a set of handwritten notes.

Example

Madeline Hunter provided the following example of a script tape:

> Opn p. 43 I'm ask ver hd-use mark to find ans whn fnd sho me w/ sig who has lots of pets Every had mark on rt ans Who can't see Mr. Sleeper (wrong ans) that rt if askd who sees but can't see. Now just rt.[2]

In unabbreviated form, the script tape recorded the following teacher statement:

> Open your book to page 43. I'm going to ask some very hard questions. Use your marker to find the answer. When you have found the answer, show me with the signal (thumbs up). Who has lots of pets? Everyone had the marker on the right answer. Who can't see Mr. Sleeper? (A girl gave the wrong answer.) That would be right if I asked who sees Mr. Sleeper, but I asked who can't see Mr. Sleeper? (Same child responds correctly.) Now you're just right![3]

This example illustrates Hunter's preference for abbreviations as a way to record as much as possible of what happens in a classroom. Of course, the disadvantage is that only the observer can make sense of the script tape, and so the observer must read back parts of the lesson on which he or she wishes the teacher to focus.

In our experience, we have found it possible to record at least the main events of a lesson in neat handwriting and with only minor abbreviations. The advantage is that the teacher can read the script tape without assistance. This allows the teacher to get an overview of the entire lesson and to share control of the feedback conference by initiating comments and questions based on the script tape.

Jane Stallings, Margaret Needels, and Georgea Sparks provide an example of an anecdotal record that resulted from observing a child who was proving to be a management problem for the teacher being supervised.[4] The supervisor made 60 pages (!) of handwritten notes about the child recorded over a 2-day period. The following is a summary of the information contained in the notes:

> On the first day, Billy had wandered about the room 57 times. Since the school day was 5 hours long, this was about 10 times an hour. Billy had fallen off his chair 14 times, picked his nose 17 times, rubbed his eyes 23 times, received 13 smiles and 27 reprimands—mostly to stop falling off his chair and pay attention. Billy had initiated conversations with other children 44 times, but the interactions were only 1 or 2 sentences long. Billy spoke to everyone who passed his seat, tried to trip 3 people, succeeding

twice. Billy was rejected 15 times by other children who were involved in some activity and was physically pushed away from a group of 3 who were working on a mural. During recess, he put a blanket over his desk, took his reading workbook and disappeared underneath. He stayed there for 5 minutes.[5]

The second day's observations were similar, and the picture that emerged was one of a hyperactive, highly distractible child who needed help in screening out the myriad distractions in the classroom.

This information was useful in working with the child's parents, reading specialist, and school psychologist to plan an educational program for the child.

Figure 7.1 presents a sample of an ethnographic protocol made by a professionally trained ethnographer. It represents the rich description possible with this method. Anecdotal records made by clinical supervisors do not usually have the same amount of detail, although this is possible if the supervisor becomes proficient in quick note taking.

You will observe in Figure 7.1 that the ethnographer does not focus on any particular child or type of teacher behavior. The ethnographer instead records any salient event as it occurs. In this particular protocol the salient events seem to relate to the teacher's management and direction-giving techniques. The teacher can review the protocol to determine whether he or she wishes to maintain or change these techniques.

VIDEO AND AUDIO RECORDINGS (TECHNIQUE 15)

Video and audio recordings are among the most objective observation techniques. They allow teachers to see themselves as students see them. Another advantage of recordings is that they have a wide focus. They can pick up a great deal of what teachers and students are doing and saying. A good recording captures the "feel" of classroom interaction.

Not too many years ago video and audio recorders were expensive and bulky. Their cost is now well within the reach of most schools. Unfortunately, they are used infrequently in teacher supervision even when the equipment is available. Video recorders are much more likely to be used in the coaching of school sports. Athletes and their coaches spend hours analyzing film or video recordings of games and individual player actions. Shouldn't we spend a fraction of our supervisory time with teachers reviewing recordings of their classroom interaction?

The portable video recorder is often an integral component of the microteaching method.[6] Microteaching, which was developed at Stanford University in the 1960s, is widely considered to be an important innovation in the training of teachers. In microteaching the teacher practices a few specific teaching skills in a scaled-down teaching situation involving a 10- or 15-minute lesson with five or so students. The microteaching lesson is videotaped and played back to the teacher so that her teaching performance, especially the use of target skills, can be analyzed.

Teachers almost invariably find that the video recording, whether made in a microteach situation or regular classroom, provides an important self-learning experi-

2nd Grade Class. Open
1. Classroom, with two team teacher
2. and two other adults.
3. This is a joint observation with
4. Elizabeth. I will be observing two
5. reading groups today, simultan-
6. eously, including 9 children. Out of
7. the nine children, 2 are girls, 7 are
8. boys.

8:30 Noise level 2
10. At 8:30 the noise level is 2. The
11. children have just been let into the
12. classroom, taking their coats off
13. and wandering around the room.
14. Several boys are in the corner
15. fighting, and some girls are sitting
16. on the floor playing a puzzle. The
17. teacher is walking back and forth in
18. the back of the classroom not at-
19. tending the children. The noise
20. continues and the children are run-
21. ning around. There is much con-
22. fusion in the room. Two teachers
8:35 23. stand at the desk talking to one
24. another. At 8:35, Mrs. Tyler
25. leaves the room. The team teach-
26. er stays seated behind the class-
27. room at her desk. At 8:40 Mrs.

28. Tyler comes back into the room.
29. She walks to the desk at the far
30. left hand side of the classroom,
31. which is a round table, and sits
32. on the edge. She says "Blue
33. Group, get your folders and go up
34. in the front. Green Group, come
35. here." Noise levels drop to 1, and
36. the children begin to follow her
37. orders. She says, "Anybody lose
38. a quarter?" No one responds, and
39. she repeats the question again
40. with irritation in her voice. She
41. says I know someone found.
42. someone lost a quarter because
43. it was found in the coat room.
44. Look in your pockets and see."
45. No one says anything.
46. She now stands up and pulls a
47. pile of workbooks from across
48. the table over to her. They are
49. the ___ reading workbooks.
50. She opens one of them on the
51. top and says, "Ah Daniel!" She
52. says this with a loud sharp voice.
53. She continues, "Your work yes-
54. terday was not too bad but you
55. need some work. Evidently there
56. are still some words you don't
57. understand." She thumbs through
58. the rest of his lesson. Danny is
59. standing at the outside of the cir-
60. cle around her, not listening to

61. what she is saying. Mrs. Tyler
62. now stands and gives instructions
63. to the Green Group. She tells
64. them to go through 8 through 13,
65. reading the two stories between
66. those pages and to go over the
67. work in the workbooks that she is
68. about to give back. She tells them
69. that they may seat any place but
70. not together and she says, "And I
71. don't want any funny business."
72. She now opens the next work-
73. book which is Nicole's. She tells
74. Nicole that she is having the
75. same problem that Danny is hav-
76. ing without specifying further.
77. Nicole looks up at her with an ex-
78. pectant look on her face. She
79. then looks at a third book and
80. says "Michelle, you're having the
81. same problem." She says,
82. "Snatch means to grab. Beach.
83. what does it mean?" Michelle
84. doesn't answer. She has her fin-
85. ger in her mouth and looks anx-
86. ious. The teacher closes the
87. workbook and pushes it to
88. Michelle. Michelle takes it and
89. walks away, with Nicole. Teacher
90. then opens the next workbook
91. and says, "Mike, I don't appreci-
92. ate all these circles. She points

FIGURE 7.1 A sample protocol.

SOURCE: Adapted from David C. Berliner and William J. Tikunoff, "The California Beginning Teacher Evaluation Study: Overview of the Ethnographic Study," *Journal of Teacher Education* 27 (1976): 24–30.

ence. Nevertheless, there are several problems to avoid. First, supervisors must be careful to arrange the video recording equipment so that it does not interfere with the lesson. This is best done by setting up the equipment ahead of time, before the students enter the classroom. Second, our experience indicates that teachers, when first exposed to a videotape of themselves, tend to focus on the "cosmetics" of their performance (e.g., physical appearance, clothes, and voice quality). In fact, a study by Gavriel Salomon and Fred McDonald revealed that in a videotape replay situation, 58 percent of teachers' self-observations were concerned with physical appearance, and only 18 percent were focused on teaching behavior.[7] This is a natural reaction. Ways to deal with it are suggested later in this section.

Another problem is that some teachers initially are anxious about the prospect of being videotaped. This problem can be alleviated by allowing teachers to experiment with the equipment before the classroom lesson is to be videotaped. Another helpful procedure is to allow teachers to keep their own videotape or show them how to erase it. This calms any fear that the video recording might get into the "wrong hands."

Although video recordings appear to be a more powerful observational tool than audio recordings, this may not be so. Teachers sometimes are captivated by the image on the TV screen and do not listen to what is being said. Audio recordings have fewer distracting cues, and so it is easier for teachers to concentrate on the verbal interaction. Research has shown that video and audio feedback are equally effective in helping teachers improve their use of verbal teaching skills.[8]

Technique

The first step in making audio or video recordings is to obtain equipment that is in good working order. The portable videocassette recorder (VCR) typically includes a TV camera with a built-in microphone and viewer, a recorder, and cables for connecting the various components of the system. In addition, a supply of videotapes and television for playback viewing are needed.

We suggest you find a free room where the equipment can be used and stored, especially if more than one teacher's classroom is to be videotaped. Perhaps later the same day, or the next day, each teacher can use the room to view the videotape replay.

Audio recorders are much simpler than VCRs to set up and operate. Many self-contained models of audio recorders include a built-in microphone, and operate on batteries.

The recording process becomes more complicated as the size of the class increases. If you plan to record a regular classroom situation, it is a good idea to experiment beforehand with various camera and microphone placements in the classroom to get the best sound and camera angle. You are likely to find that the microphone for your audio or video recorder has a small pick-up range. As the focus of supervision is usually the teacher, we suggest that you place the microphone fairly close to the teacher. By doing so, you are likely to record everything the teacher says and some of what students say.

Teachers can learn to make their own video recordings, but in many situations it is more helpful if you, the supervisor, are present to make the recording. You may find it best to set up the camera on a stationary base; then, change the lens focus and turn the camera to follow the teacher as the lesson proceeds. Cameras with a zoom lens allow you to make close-up recordings of events that interest you or the teacher.

A 30-minute recording is usually more than adequate. It will try the teacher's patience and yours to play back a recording that is any longer than this. You can record continuously for 30 minutes, or stop and start the recording depending on what is happening in the lesson.

An efficient procedure is to have teachers play back the entire recording for themselves. They can share insights about their teaching performance with you during the feedback conference. At this time you can select a short segment of the recording (perhaps 3 to 5 minutes) for more intensive analysis. You will find that even a brief segment can yield many insights into the teacher's skill level and teaching style.

The wide focus of video or audio recordings is both a strength and weakness. The insightful teacher will be able to observe many different aspects of teacher behavior and student behavior. Some teachers will notice only a few aspects, however, and may focus on the "cosmetic" features mentioned earlier. Your role in the feedback conference is to guide the teacher's observations, encouraging the teacher to draw inferences whenever possible, but also drawing the teacher's attention to significant classroom phenomena if they are being overlooked.

Example

At many universities and colleges Teaching Strategies is a required course in the secondary education program. Often, one requirement of the course is for students to attend microteaching sessions in which they practice several different teaching methods. Students audio-record their lessons for later analysis. They may also be required to make a transcript covering several minutes of the audio recording. This procedure ensures that students listen carefully to what was said.

Figure 7.2 presents a partial transcript made by a student who had done a poetry lesson using the lecture method. This example shows that an audio recording and transcript made from it provided a rich source of feedback to the student on his teaching behavior.

Students are also asked to write an analysis of their lesson based on the transcript and other feedback data. Figure 7.3 (p. 116) presents the first part of an analysis written by the student who gave the poetry lesson, accompanied by the instructor's comments in the margin. It illustrates that the process of teaching a lesson and audio-recording it for later analysis is a powerful technique for helping the student see areas for instructional improvement.

Preservice teachers, including the one discussed here, tend to criticize themselves too severely in their initial encounters with an audio recording of their teaching performance. The supervisor can ameliorate this problem by reassuring students that flaws noted in their teaching performance are commonplace and can be eliminated with practice.

CI 314

0:00	OK, um, what I want to talk about is, uh, a poem by Denise Levertov, called "Living." (pause) And the reason I wanted to talk about this is because I think it's something that I can cover in 10 minutes, and uh, well, not in, not entirely but it's short enough to go over the basics, and, uh, Denise Levertov I, I think is, is . . . one of the
0:30	greatest of living poets, and not, not as well known as she should be. This poem in particular I think is, is, uh, one of her greatest poems, and it's not as well known as many, many poems that aren't nearly as good. (pause) Um, what I want to do is, is, is approach the poem in
1:00	terms of how it's organized . . . 'cause that's one way to get a grip, a grasp on a poem and Uh, not so much talk about what it says as, as the way it's, the way it's set up, um, and I, I don't think that's the only way to read a poem, in fact I don't think it's a very complete way but it's, um, it can lead you farther into a poem sometimes than
1:30	just talking about what it's about. And so let me just start with the way it sounds to me: "The fire in leaf and grass/ so green it seems/ each summer the last summer.// The wind blowing, the leaves/ shivering in the sun,/ each day the last day.// A red salamander/ so cold and so/ easy to catch, dreamily// moves his delicate feet/ and long tail. I hold/ my hand open for him to go.// Each minute the last minute."
2:00	(Pause) OK, um, it seems to me that that poem holds together very well. It's, it's a very tightly knit poem. Um. But it's not held together in any of the, the traditional ways: it's not, it doesn't have a rhyme scheme, there's no beat or rhythm that carries you along.
2:30	And so if you look at it – Well, does everybody agree that, that, it doesn't, it doesn't seem like a fragmented poem? It goes, it goes along, and I think it builds, builds very strongly towards its conclusion. Um . . . to start with, to start with the smallest units, just to
3:00	look at the sounds of the poem, and the way it . . . the way the sounds hold together – Starting in the first line: the, the first significant word is "fire." And you see that the "f" sound is repeated immediately in "leaf." And the "r" sound in "fire" carries forward into "grass," which then carries you forward into "green" again, and then down to the
3:30	"r" ending in "summer" and "summer" which is repeated. And then you see these, the "r" sound particularly you find again down in the poem down in the the uh, in "shivering" which repeats the "er" sound from "summer"--and that turns up again in "salamander" in the last, next to last triplet. And then the, when you get into "leaf" the, the
4:00	"ea" sound from "leaf" is repeated twice in the next line in "green" and in "seems"--and in "each" and in "leaves" in the next, the next stanza, and then, then you hear it again in "each"--in "easy"--in "dreamily"--in "feet"--and then again in "each" in the last line.
4:30	(Pause) And, um . . . these, these sounds (pause) are, um--well, the, uh, the tying together of the, of the poem through the, through the, uh, the sounds in the words goes on throughout the poem. For instance: if you look for the "o" sound, you don't see it until you get into the poem, but it turns up towards the end. If you move down
5:00	toward, to the third verse, it starts coming in very strongly, in this in a line "so cold and so/ easy to catch"--then it turns up again in "I hold my hand open for him to go." And these, these are, these are, these are the significant sounds in the poem. And this, this technique that Levertov relies on very, very strongly in a lot of her writing is called "assonance." Um, I--does, everyone know
5:30	what the meaning of assonance is? There's, there's two, uh, basic techniques used, but a lot of modern poets--assonance

FIGURE 7.2 Transcript of lecture microlesson.

JOURNAL WRITING (TECHNIQUE 16)

We discussed in chapter 1 that reflective teaching is an important recent development in teacher education and clinical supervision. The reflective teacher, among other things, is aware of the dilemmas inherent in teaching, is aware of his or her belief systems and feelings and how they affect his or her teaching, considers choices among instructional strategies, and evaluates the effects of those choices.[9] Reflection

It wasn't a disaster. I think the students in the group and I learned some things about poetry from it. ↓

I would rate this lecture <u>as a disaster</u>, and this
for two main reasons which are not unrelated:
nervousness and poor organization. A sudden attack
of stage fright was for some reason quite
unexpected, and because I hadn't anticipated it I
hadn't written out any more than a general outline
of the points I wanted to cover. This, as it turned
out, was not enough to see me through. Some of the
faults in this lecture, such as the astonishing
number of "um's," "uh's," and stuttering repetitions
(e.g., "What I want to do is, is, is approach the
poem . . .") are simply signs of nervous excitement;
having heard tapes of myself in conversation, I know
these mannerisms are not always present, at least
not to this degree. These I can only expect to
correct by calming down a bit, but this I think I
will be able to do if I correct some of the more
fundamental mistakes I made this time around.
   The most important thing missing from this lecture
is an introduction. Immediately upon hearing the
first questions after I finished, I was made aware
that I had left out the necessary background for
reading the poem. And even though biographical
information about the author, for instance, was not
what I was mainly concerned with, it would have
given students <u>some</u> context, which is a necessary
preliminary to any appreciation. A preliminary
statement of what the poem is <u>about, or perhaps
simply some lead-in remarks about summer days and
why some moments seem more alive than others, would
have been very useful</u>. And although before the
lecture I had wanted not to seem too schematic,
afterwards I realized that I needn't have worried:
and I now regret not having outlined ahead of time
the areas I was going to cover.

Yes. This would help. A good Technique! →

   It now seems to me, also, that I went at the poem
exactly backwards: for some reason I began with the
smallest details, the sounds of the poem, and went
on to its larger structure before talking about its
over-all theme. This is absolutely perverse; it is
almost as if I had been trying to keep the main point
a secret until the last possible moment. Clearly, it
would have been better to begin with the most
general statements, and to proceed to the more
particular ones only after these landmarks had been
mapped out.
   I feel that, even so, using a blackboard would have
improved things immeasurably. Not only could I have
communicated better by writing down a few terms like
"assonance" and by marking the repetitions of sounds
rather than simply listing them; but also I think it
would have helped simply to get everyone's eyes and
attention (not least of all my own) away from the
handout sheet <u>and out into a more central meeting
place</u>. I even think that just having something to do
with my hands would have put me more at ease.

nice phrase →

   I only asked questions twice in the course of the
lecture, and both questions were almost rhetorical,
being put in such a way as to actually discourage a
response: the first one beginning "does everyone
agree . . ." and the second one beginning "does
everyone know . . ." There were several other places
in the lecture where a question would have been in
order: and all of the questions should have been
less leading, more open to genuine answers. This
constricted questioning is, again, at least partly a
function of nervousness; as is the fact that I
forgot to ask for questions at the end.

on teaching can be the primary focus of clinical supervision, or it can complement a focus on actual teaching behavior.

Journal writing is an effective supervisory technique for encouraging the development of reflectivity in teachers. The technique simply involves having teachers keep a regular journal in which they record their teaching experiences and raise questions about their teaching. Just as a video tape records the external reality of teaching, so can journals record the internal reality of teaching. Although teachers can be asked to limit their journal entries to certain kinds of perceptions, they generally are left free to record whatever they wish. For this reason we classify journal writing as a wide-lens technique.

Journal writing has been used primarily to date in preservice clinical supervision. In that context, researchers have found that this technique helps prospective teachers become more reflective and less custodial in their attitudes toward students.[10] It seems likely that journal writing would have similarly positive effects in in-service clinical supervision.

Technique

Willis Copeland suggested that the effectiveness of journal writing depends upon two factors.[11] First, teachers need to be taught explicitly how to keep a reflective journal. Simply telling them to keep a journal is not sufficient. Second, teachers need to receive thoughtful feedback about the content of their journal entries from their supervisor.

With respect to the first element, teachers need guidance about the kinds of content to include in their journal entries. One approach is to tell teachers to record problems and dilemmas that occur in their day-to-day teaching. Teachers also can be asked to report attempts to solve the problem or dilemma, and the effectiveness of their solutions. These journal entries can provide the basis for discussion in supervisory conferences.

Another approach to journal writing is for teachers to focus on a particular teaching strategy or curriculum. For example, teachers can be asked to record their experiences in implementing a teaching method (e.g., cooperative learning) or a new curriculum adopted by the school district.

Whatever the content focus of the journal, teachers should be allowed to describe relevant contextual factors. This means that the teacher is not limited to what happens in his classroom. He can reflect on what is happening in the school, community, or the students' family that affects instruction.

All the other observation techniques described in this unit of the book stress objectivity on the part of the observer. The technique of journal writing is an exception. Teachers should be encouraged to record not only what happened in the classroom, but also their beliefs, feelings, insights, and evolving philosophy of education. This inner reality is important to understanding a teacher's behavior in the classroom.

FIGURE 7.3 (opposite) Lecture microlesson evaluation.

The confidentiality of the journal will certainly influence what teachers are willing to record in it. Therefore, the supervisor should make explicit whether the journal is the property of the teacher, and whether its contents will be shared with persons other than the supervisor.

The scope of the journal should be negotiated with teachers. For how long a period of time is the journal to be kept? Are entries to be made daily, weekly, or whenever the teacher wishes? Should entries be made for each class period during the school day, or just for selected periods? Journal writing requires effort, and so the teacher and supervisor should decide on a scope that is appropriate to, but does not exceed, the goals of clinical supervision for the particular teacher.

It is common practice in preservice education for the supervisor to write comments on the margins of teachers' journal entries. It seems unlikely that supervisors of in-service teachers would follow this procedure, though, because it puts teachers too much in a student role. Instead, the supervisor can read the journal and mark entries, or make notes about entries that he wishes to discuss with the teacher during a supervisory conference. Another option is for only the teacher to read the journal, and for the teacher to decide which parts of the journal he or she wishes to talk about during the conference.

We can imagine a supervision process that is built entirely around the teacher's journal writing. The teacher and supervisor discuss what the content of the journal entries should be; the teacher makes journal entries; and the teacher and supervisor meet periodically to discuss problems, insights, beliefs, and feelings recorded in the entries.

This approach undoubtedly has value, but also the limitation that it may not correspond to what is actually happening in the teacher's classroom. Therefore, we recommend a process in which journal writing and direct classroom observation complement each other. For example, a journal entry can reveal a concern (see technique 1 in chapter 3) that leads to direct classroom observation by the supervisor. Discussion of the observational data in a postconference can stimulate the teacher to engage in reflection, which he records in his journal. In this way, the supervisory process is informed by the objectivity of observational data and by the personal meaningfulness of recorded reflections.

Example

Frances Bolin presented examples of journal writing by a student teacher in the preservice program in Childhood Education at Teachers College, Columbia University.[12] The teacher, assigned the pseudonym Lou, kept a daily journal in which he reflected on his student teaching experiences and also a weekly journal in which he recorded reflections about his student teaching, his supervision, and the total preservice program. Lou's supervisor read the journal entries, wrote responses to them, and referred to them in supervisory conferences.

One of Lou's journal entries concerned classroom management:

> Sometimes I am not sure how "strict" I should be with the kids as a student teacher. Max [Lou's cooperating teacher] said he wants me not to be

so timid. My timidness comes from not knowing the disciplinary boundaries at [the school]. Since I didn't know, I didn't really react. I am by no means timid, as the kids [I have worked with every summer] will attest. Now that I know what the system of discipline is I can implement it.[13]

The supervisor might help Lou with his management concerns by collecting data on students' at-task behavior (see technique 11) while Lou is teaching them. The data might indicate that his management style is fine as it is. If modification is needed, Lou can try different (possibly "stricter") management techniques, and the supervisor can collect more at-task data, which will provide Lou with feedback on the techniques' effectiveness.

Another of Lou's journal entries concerns creativity in teaching at the open space school where he is student teaching and creativity in a traditional school, which he prefers:

Maybe I am just old fashioned [sic]. I guess it depends on the kids and the school. Who said that a teacher in a typical, traditional school can't be creative and try new things. I hope that no matter what type school I work in I will be creative and not fall into a mold.[14]

In this journal entry and others, Lou expresses the view that creative teaching is important to him. The supervisor can respond to these entries by helping Lou clarify what he means by creative teaching (see technique 2 in chapter 5). The supervisor then can collect observational data on Lou's use of creative teaching behaviors in the setting of the open space school. In the postconference, Lou and the supervisor can review the data and consider whether the same creative teaching patterns would be possible in a traditional school.

NOTES

1. Madeline Hunter, "Script-Taping: An Essential Supervisory Tool," *Educational Leadership* 41, No. 3 (1983): 43.
2. *Ibid.*
3. *Ibid.*
4. Jane Stallings, Margaret Needels, and Georgea Mohlman Sparks, "Observation for the Improvement of Classroom Learning," in *Talks to Teachers*, ed. David C. Berliner and Barak V. Rosenshine (New York: Random House, 1987), pp. 129–58.
5. *Ibid.*, p. 144.
6. Dwight W. Allen and Kevin Ryan, *Microteaching* (Reading, MA: Addison-Wesley, 1969).
7. Gavriel Salomon and Fred J. McDonald, "Pre- and Posttest Reactions to Self-Viewing One's Performance on Videotape" (paper presented at the annual meeting of the American Psychological Association, 1968).
8. Meredith D. Gall, Helen Dell, Barbara B. Dunning, and John Galassi, "Improving Teachers' Mathematics Tutoring Skills through Microteaching: A Comparison of Videotape and Audiotape Feedback" (paper presented at the annual meeting of the American Educational Research Association, 1971).

9. Virginia Richardson, "The Evolution of Reflective Teaching and Teacher Education," in *Encouraging Reflective Practice in Education*, ed. Renee T. Clift, W. Robert Houston, and Marleen C. Pugach (New York: Teachers College Press, 1990), pp. 3–19.

10. B. J. Benham, "The Effect of Reflective Writing on Identifying Maintenance in Student Teachers" (paper presented at the annual meeting of the American Educational Research Association, 1979); Kenneth M. Zeichner and Daniel P. Liston, "Teaching Student Teachers to Reflect," *Harvard Educational Review* 57 (1987): 23–48.

11. Willis D. Copeland, "The RITE Framework for Teacher Education: Preservice Applications," in *Reality and Reform in Clinical Teacher Education*, ed. J. V. Hoffman and S. A. Edwards (New York: Random House, 1986), pp. 25–44.

12. Frances S. Bolin, "Helping Student Teachers Think about Teaching," *Journal of Teacher Education* 39 (1988): 48–54.

13. *Ibid.*, p. 50.

14. *Ibid.*, p. 51.

chapter 8

Checklists and Timeline Coding

To be useful, observations must be reliable and credible.
Jane Stallings

The observation instruments described in the previous chapters are relatively unstructured. In using selective verbatim, the SCORE techniques, anecdotal records, or video and audio recordings, the teacher and supervisor jointly decide the categories of behavior to be observed. There may be occasions, though, when you will want to use a more highly structured instrument to observe behavior. This type of instrument has predetermined categories that may be well suited to the objectives that your teacher and you wish to pursue.

This chapter presents a sampling of these instruments.[1] Some are checklists that students complete to give feedback to their teachers, whereas others are checklists that the supervisor completes while observing the teacher's classroom behavior.

STUDENT CHECKLISTS

In the process of attending class, students have the opportunity to make extensive observations of their teacher's behavior. Summary data on the students' observations can be useful in clinical supervision because teachers often are very concerned about how their students perceive them (even more than they are concerned about how supervisors perceive them!).

Pupil Observation Survey (Technique 17)

The Pupil Observation Survey is a student-administered checklist that was developed in the 1960s, but it is still useful in clinical supervision.[2] It measures the extent to which the teacher

1. is friendly, cheerful, admired.
2. is knowledgeable, poised.
3. is interesting and preferred to other teachers.
4. uses strict control.
5. uses democratic procedures.

These five dimensions are measured by 38 items that should be comprehensible to students in fifth grade and higher.

A short version of this instrument, the Student Evaluation of Teaching form, is available. It is shown in Figure 8.1. The first five items measure, in order, the five dimensions listed above. The second five items also measure, in order, the same dimensions. For example, the first item ("is always friendly toward students") and sixth item ("is usually cheerful and optimistic") measure the first dimension listed above ("is friendly, cheerful, admired").

One way to summarize the data yielded by the Student Evaluation of Teaching form is to count the number of students in the class who circled each response option (F   f   t   T) in each question. Another way is to score each item (for example, F = 0, f = 1, t = 2, T = 3) and then compute the mean score for each pair of items that measure the same dimension.

IDEA H Questionnaire (Technique 18)

The IDEA H questionnaire, shown in Figure 8.2 (p. 124), was developed by Judith Aubrecht and Gerald Hanna at Kansas State University.[3] It is designed for use with secondary school students, and it provides a comprehensive picture of the teacher's instruction. An interesting feature of the questionnaire is that teachers can complete part of it (items 1–9) to indicate the relative importance of each item to their course goals (items 1–9). The forms are scored electronically, taking into account the teacher's priorities. The items were selected, modified, and validated through field testing, and norms were established based on a sample of more than 1,000 representative classrooms.

IDEA H avoids a common fault of many student reaction forms, that is, forcing all teachers into a Procrustean bed regardless of whether they are attempting to be didactic or heuristic, factual or conceptual, behavioral or humanistic. The feedback from the scoring center tells the teacher what items (behaviors) to emphasize or continue to use given the teacher's preferences as expressed in marking which of the first nine items are essential, important, or not so important to this teacher.

STUDENT EVALUATION OF TEACHING

D. J. VELDMAN and R. F. PECK

TEACHER'S LAST NAME: _____

SUBJECT: _____

SCHOOL: _____

CIRCLE THE RIGHT CHOICES BELOW

Teacher's Sex: M   F

My Sex: M   F

My Grade Level:

  3   4   5   6   7   8   9   10   11   12

DO NOT USE

CIRCLE **ONE** OF THE FOUR CHOICES IN FRONT OF EACH STATEMENT.
THE FOUR CHOICES MEAN:

F = Very Much False
f = More False Than True
t = More True Than False
T = Very Much True

This Teacher:

F f t T   is always friendly toward students.

F f t T   knows a lot about the subject.

F f t T   is never dull or boring.

F f t T   expects a lot from students.

F f t T   asks for students' opinions before making decisions.

F f t T   is usually cheerful and optimistic.

F f t T   is not confused by unexpected questions.

F f t T   makes learning more like fun than work.

F f t T   doesn't let students get away with anything.

F f t T   often gives students a choice in assignments.

FIGURE 8.1   Pupil observation survey.

SOURCE: Research and Development Center for Teacher Education, The University of
Texas, 1967.

123

iDEA ═══ STUDENT REACTION TO COURSE AND TEACHER: IDEA FORM H

Your honest and thoughtful answers to the questions on this form can help your teacher improve this course and his/her teaching methods. Record all your responses on the separate answer card. Do not write your name on either this form or on the answer card. Your teacher will receive a summary of the responses of all students in your class, but should not know how any individual person answered.

Part I. Some of the things that students learn in school are listed below. For each, rate the amount of progress you have made in this course by marking the numeral of the most suitable response.

1 = None	4 = Much
2 = Little	5 = Great
3 = Medium	

1. Gaining factual information (such as learning definitions, dates, vocabulary).
2. Understanding and applying principles, ideas, and theories.
3. Improving my learning skills (such as listening, reading, note-taking).
4. Improving my writing skills.
5. Improving my speaking skills.
6. Gaining skills and habits useful in everyday life or on a job.
7. Developing good feelings about myself (more acceptance of myself, more self-confidence).
8. Discovering or realizing my own interests, aptitudes, beliefs, and values.
9. Getting along with most other people.

Part II. For each of the following features of the course, fill in the numeral that best describes your reaction.

1 = Definitely not enough	4 = Too much
2 = Not enough	5 = Definitely too
3 = About right	much

10. Amount of homework.
11. Number of tests.
12. Difficulty of reading.
13. Difficulty of course.

Part III. Describe your attitudes, feelings, and behaviors by filling in the appropriate numeral for each of the following statements.

1 = Definitely False	4 = More True than False
2 = More False than True	5 = Definitely True
3 = In Between	

14. In general, I like my school teachers.
15. I am very glad it was this teacher who taught this course.
16. I try very hard to learn in all of my courses.
17. As a result of taking this course, I like this subject more.
18. I really wanted to take this course regardless of who taught it.

© Center for Faculty Evaluation and Development, 1981

Part IV. Indicate how well each of the following statements describes the students in this class by blackening the proper numeral.

1 = Definitely False	4 = More True than False
2 = More False than True	5 = Definitely True
3 = In Between	

The students in this class:

19. Enjoy working together.
20. Are angry about grades.
21. Use their mistakes as opportunities to learn.
22. Take responsibility for their own learning.
23. Think they are wasting their time.
24. Are bored.
25. Have interesting and useful discussions.
26. Are rude and out of control.

Part V. Indicate how well each of the following statements describes your teacher by blackening the most suitable numeral.

1 = Definitely False	4 = More True than False
2 = More False than True	5 = Definitely True
3 = In Between	

This teacher:

27. Understands student ideas and questions.
28. Expresses interesting and challenging ideas about the subject.
29. Uses tests, papers, projects, etc., that closely relate to the course purposes.
30. Cares about students as people.
31. Gives understandable explanations of course materials.
32. Asks interesting and stimulating questions.
33. Gives tests, projects, etc., that cover the important points of the course.
34. Shows interest in student ideas.
35. Speaks in an understandable voice.
36. Suggests clearer ways for students to express their ideas.
37. Gives quizzes, papers, projects, etc., that help students to learn.
38. Makes helpful comments about student work.
39. Reviews material in ways that help students remember it.
40. Gives projects, tests, or assignments that require original or creative thinking.
41. Creates opportunities for students to use the material they learn.
42. Makes helpful suggestions about what kinds of things to study for a test.
43. Shows how the subject relates to other areas of knowledge.
44. Speaks with expressiveness and variety.
45. Is sensitive to student feelings about the subject.
46. Provides helpful instructional materials (such as worksheets, study questions, unit objectives).
47. Identifies strong points of student work.
48. Uses good examples and illustrations.
49. Tries different ways of teaching when students have trouble learning.
50. Seems to enjoy teaching.

FIGURE 8.2 The IDEA H questionnaire.

SOURCE: Judith Aubrecht and Gerald Hanna, IDEA H Questionnaire, Kansas State University, Center for Faculty Education and Development.

OBSERVER-ADMINISTERED CHECKLISTS

Clinical supervisors sometimes construct their own checklist for recording observations of classroom behavior. For example, the following are descriptions of several checklists that we constructed for our own use in supervision. You are invited to use them as is or to adapt them to your particular purpose.

Question-and-Answer Teaching (Technique 19)

Question-asking sometimes occurs when the teacher is introducing a new topic, but it is most often used to review curriculum material that students have just finished reading or seeing. For example, question-asking may occur after students have read a chapter in a book, seen a film, completed a science experiment, or participated in a role-playing exercise.

The question-and-answer checklist shown in Figure 8.3 is organized around three types of teacher behavior. The research basis for these behaviors is discussed in chapter 2 and also in the sections on techniques 8 (Teacher Questions) and 9 (Teacher Feedback) in chapter 5. You will note that techniques 8 and 9 are selective verbatim procedures, whereas Figure 8.3 is a checklist. The advantage of the checklist is that it is fairly easy to use, and a substantial number of teacher behaviors can be recorded in observing one lesson. The advantage of the selective verbatim procedures is that, although fewer questioning behaviors are observed, they are recorded more completely.

The first set of teacher questioning behaviors in Figure 8.3 is important because these behaviors usually lead to increased student participation in the lesson. For example, the first behavior in the checklist is calling on nonvolunteers to respond.

FIGURE 8.3   Checklist for question-and-answer teaching.

```
Behaviors That Increase Student
Participation
1. Calls on nonvolunteers
2. Redirects question
3. Praises student responses
4. Invites student-initiated questions

Behaviors That Elicit Thoughtful Responses
1. Asks higher cognitive questions
2. Pauses 3-5 seconds after asking a
   question
3. Asks follow-up questions to an initial
   response

Negative Behaviors
1. Reacts negatively to student response
2. Repeats own question
3. Asks multiple questions
4. Answers own questions
5. Repeats student's answer

Strong Points of Lesson

Suggestions for Improvement
```

Teachers are likely to call on students who raise their hands and who customarily give good answers to their questions. Yet nonvolunteers often make good contributions if the teacher takes the initiative by calling on them.

Student participation also can be increased by redirecting the same question to several students. The teacher may invite additional responses to a question by a nod acknowledging a particular student or by a statement such as "Does anyone have a different idea?" or "Would someone like to add to what Susie said?" Praising answers is a technique that helps students feel that their answers are worthwhile; as a result, they are encouraged to speak up when other questions are asked. Another good technique is to ask students if they have any questions of their own about the lesson content. The teacher may choose to answer these student-initiated questions directly or may call on other students to answer them.

The second category in the Question-and-Answer Checklist refers to the cognitive level of the teacher's lesson. Educators generally agree that students should not just recite back the facts they have learned. (This is done by asking simple fact questions of Who, What, Where, When variety.) Students also should be encouraged to think about the curriculum content. This goal is accomplished by asking higher cognitive questions, which are questions that cannot be answered simply by looking in the textbook. The student must think and formulate an original response. Higher cognitive questions may require the student to compare and contrast, state possible motives or causes for observed phenomena, draw conclusions, provide evidence, make predictions, solve problems, make judgments, or offer opinions.

Asking a higher cognitive question may not be sufficient to elicit a thoughtful response. One helpful behavior is to pause several seconds before calling on a student to respond. This gives students time to think. It also encourages all students in the class to generate an answer, because they do not know whom the teacher will call on to respond. The third technique for eliciting thoughtful responses on the checklist is to ask follow-up questions after the student has given an initial answer to a question. For example, the teacher might ask, "Did you agree with the jury's verdict?" and the student might respond, "No, I didn't." The teacher can follow up by asking the student to support his position (e.g., "Why didn't you agree?"). Follow-up questions also can be used to encourage a student to clarify a vague answer (e.g., "I'm not sure I understood what you said. Can you restate your answer?"), to generate additional ideas (e.g., "Can you think of other ways of solving the energy crisis?"), or to challenge the student (e.g., "That's a good idea, but have you considered possible adverse consequences that might occur if your idea were put into practice?"). Follow-up questions can be used, too, to prompt a student who is unable to respond to the initial question.

The first two categories of behavior in the checklist in Figure 8.3 refer to the "do's" of question asking. The third category refers to the "don'ts." Teachers avoid reacting negatively to student responses by making critical remarks (e.g., "That doesn't make any sense at all") or by showing annoyance. Critical behavior only increases the likelihood that the student will volunteer no response in the future. The second negative behavior, repeating one's question, is to be avoided because it wastes class time and encourages students not to listen carefully the first time the teacher asks a question. The third "don't," asking multiple questions, refers to the practice of asking several questions in a row before settling on a question to which a response is invited. Teachers tend to do this when they are unsure of the lesson content or if they are inclined to think aloud. Multiple questions also waste class time, and they are likely to confuse students. The final "don't" is repeating student answers verbatim. A better practice is to praise the answer, extend the answer by adding new information, or invite another student to build on the answer.

The bottom two headings of the checklist provide an open-ended opportunity for the observer to comment on strong points of the lesson and areas in which the teacher may need to improve.

Lecture-Explanation Teaching (Technique 20)

Researchers have found that teachers on average do two-thirds of the talking in elementary and secondary classrooms.[4] The percentage is probably higher in some settings (e.g., college teaching) and lower in others. Much of this "talk time" is spent in presenting new concepts and information to students, or in explaining difficult parts of the curriculum. We have found that many teachers say they rarely use lecture as a teaching strategy when, in fact, much of their time is spent talking to students—presenting new curriculum content or explaining ideas and procedures.

The checklist shown in Figure 8.4 is designed for analyzing various aspects of the teacher's lecture-explanation behavior. Research evidence supporting the effectiveness of these behaviors is presented in chapter 2.

You will note that the checklist is in two parts. The first part includes behaviors that can be tallied each time they occur. The tallies are counted to determine how often the teacher used a particular lecture-explanation behavior during the lesson. Some of these behaviors are techniques for increasing the meaningfulness of the curriculum content, for example, the technique of giving examples to illustrate a concept. Other behaviors are techniques for involving students so that they do not sit passively through the entire lecture-explanation. Asking students if they have questions about the lesson is an example of a technique that usually creates student involvement.

The second part of the checklist is a list of teacher behaviors rated by the observer. Some of the rated behaviors concern how well the teacher organizes the lecture content. For example, repeating key points and summarizing them at the end of the lesson is a technique that helps students organize the various ideas in the lecture as "more important" or "less important."

The largest category of behaviors in the checklist relates to the teacher's skill in delivery. Speech is the primary medium in this type of teaching, and so the teacher's mastery of oral delivery determines in large part how well the curriculum content is conveyed to students. The enthusiasm in the teacher's voice, the clarity of the teacher's remarks, the avoidance of nervous gestures and filler phrases—all contribute to the effectiveness of the lesson.

As in the Question-and-Answer Checklist (Figure 8.3), this checklist can be augmented by including space for additional comments about the strong points of the lesson and suggestions for improvement.

BEHAVIORS TO BE TALLIED

Meaningful Content
1. Relates lecture content to content already familiar to students
2. Gives example to illustrate concept
3. Gives explanation for generalization or opinion

Student Involvement
1. Asks students if they have questions
2. Directs question to students
3. Has students engage in activity

BEHAVIORS TO BE RATED

Organization

	good			needs improvement	
1. Lecture has clear organization and sequence	5	4	3	2	1
2. Uses blackboard, handout, etc., to show organization of lecture	5	4	3	2	1
3. Tells students what (s)he expects students to remember from lecture	5	4	3	2	1
4. Repeats key points and summarizes them at end	5	4	3	2	1
5. Avoids digressions	5	4	3	2	1

Delivery

	good			needs improvement	
1. Speaks slowly and clearly	5	4	3	2	1
2. Conveys enthusiasm	5	4	3	2	1
3. Avoids reading from lecture notes	5	4	3	2	1
4. Avoids filler phrases such as "you know"	5	4	3	2	1
5. Avoids nervous gestures	5	4	3	2	1
6. Maintains eye contact with students	5	4	3	2	1
7. Uses humor	5	4	3	2	1

FIGURE 8.4 Checklist for lecture-explanation teaching.

Other Checklists

We presented checklists for observing two general strategies of teaching: question-and-answer and lecture-explanation. Other checklists are available for observing other teaching strategies. For example, Bruce Joyce and his colleagues present rating checklists for observing teaching strategies organized into three models: information processing, social interaction, and personal.[5]

THE FLANDERS INTERACTION ANALYSIS SYSTEM (TECHNIQUE 21)

The Interaction Analysis System developed by Ned Flanders is one of the best-known techniques of classroom observation. It was widely used in teacher training and in research during the 1960s and 1970s.[6] Less use of it is made now as other conceptualizations of effective teaching have become popular. Nonetheless, the Interaction Analysis System records important aspects of teaching that are not included in other observation systems. Therefore, clinical supervisors should consider learning how to use the system. An adaptation can be found in the ASCD videotape, "Another Set of Eyes; Techniques of Classroom Observation."

The Flanders Interaction Analysis System has two principal features: (1) verbal-interaction categories; and (2) procedures for using the categories to make classroom observations. The verbal interaction categories are shown in Figure 8.5. You will note that, with the exception of category 10 (silence or confusion), all categories pertain to a specific type of verbal behavior. Any verbal statement that might be made by a teacher or student can be classified into one of the ten categories. This is true irrespective of grade level, subject area being taught, or personal characteristics of the teacher and students. Indeed, one of the major appeals of Interaction Analysis to educators is its universality. The ten categories can be applied to virtually any teaching situation. For example, a first-grade reading group and a graduate-level seminar could be compared for similarities and differences using the system.[7]

You will note in Figure 8.5 that there are three kinds of categories. Some verbal behaviors are responses, either made by a teacher to a student (categories 1, 2, and 3) or made by a student to a teacher (category 8). Other verbal behaviors are intended to initiate communication. Either a student (category 9) or the teacher (categories 5, 6, and 7) can play the role of initiator. Categories 4 and 10 are neutral. They reflect neither response nor initiation.

Another way of grouping the ten categories into larger units is to consider who is the speaker during a particular verbal interchange. In a classroom situation, the speaker is either the teacher or a student.[8] Figure 8.5 shows that the first seven categories are used to code teacher statements. Categories 8 and 9 are for coding student talk. Category 10 reflects confusion or the fact that no one is speaking at a particular point in time.

The most critical distinction in Flanders's system is between response and initiation. If you think about the way in which you communicate with others, you will realize that you do one of two things: (1) respond to what someone else has said by listening or by offering a comment that directly relates to the other's communication, or (2) take the initiative by such means as putting forth an idea, giving a direction, or criticizing what someone else has said or done.

When teachers make a responsive comment (categories 1, 2, or 3), they are said

Teacher Talk	Response	1. <u>Accepts feeling</u>. Accepts and clarifies an attitude or the feeling tone of a student in a nonthreatening manner. Feelings may be positive or negative. Predicting and recalling feelings are included. 2. <u>Praises or encourages</u>. Praises or encourages students; says "um hum" or "go on"; makes jokes that release tension, but not at the expense of a student. 3. <u>Accepts or uses ideas of students</u>. Acknowledges student talk. Clarifies, builds on, or asks questions based on student ideas.
		4. <u>Asks questions</u>. Asks questions about content or procedure, based on teacher ideas, with the intent that a student will answer.
	Initiation	5. <u>Lectures</u>. Offers facts or opinions about content or procedures; expresses his own ideas, gives *his own* explanation, or cites an authority other than a student. 6. <u>Gives directions</u>. Gives directions, commands, or orders with which a student is expected to comply. 7. <u>Criticizes student or justifies authority</u>. Makes statements intended to change student behavior from nonacceptable to acceptable patterns; arbitrarily corrects student answers; bawls someone out. Or states why the teacher is doing what he is doing; uses extreme self-reference.
Student Talk	Response	8. <u>Student talk—response</u>. Student talk in response to a teacher contact that structures or limits the situation. Freedom to express own ideas is limited.
	Initiation	9. <u>Student talk—initiation</u>. Student initiates or expresses his own ideas, either spontaneously or in response to the teacher's solicitation. Freedom to develop opinions and a line of thought; going beyond existing structure.
Silence		10. <u>Silence or confusion</u>. Pauses, short periods of silence, and periods of confusion in which communication cannot be understood by the observer.

*Based on Ned A. Flanders, *Analyzing Teaching Behavior,* 1970. No scale is implied by these numbers. Each number is classificatory; it designates a particular kind of communication event. To write these numbers down during observation is to enumerate, not to judge, a position on a scale.

FIGURE 8.5 Flanders interaction analysis categories* (FIAC).

to be using an "indirect" style of teaching. You will note that these indirect behaviors are also associated with positive affect—accepting feelings, praising, and acknowledging students' ideas. When teachers initiate a verbal interchange (categories 5, 6, or 7), they are said to be using a "direct" style of teaching. According to Flanders, a teacher question can be either direct, as in a narrow or specific question, or indirect, as in a broad or open question.

Student verbal behavior is summarized in two categories. Students are either responding in a narrow way to the teacher (category 8), or they are expressing personal ideas and opinions (category 9). Flanders and other researchers have found consistently that teacher's use of an indirect style of teaching (categories 1, 2, 3) encourages students to offer their own ideas and opinions (category 9). In contrast, a teacher's use of a directive style (categories 5, 6, 7) has been found consistently to channel students' ideas and behavior to meet teacher expectations (category 8).

This brief glimpse into Interaction Analysis reveals that it is both simple and complex. All classroom communication is coded into ten categories, yet the resulting data can lead to complex analyses of the teacher's behavior. The intent of a teacher's communication can change from one second to another; these changes can form patterns that reveal a teacher's characteristic way of interacting with students. For example, one teacher's routine may be to ask a question (category 4), elicit a narrow student response (category 8), and respond in turn by asking a new question (category 4). This is a 4-8-4 pattern. Another teacher may be in the habit of asking a question, eliciting an open-ended student answer; then the teacher praises the student for the quality of the answer, builds on what the student has said, and initiates a new question. This is a 4-9-2-3-4 pattern.

As teachers are exposed to Interaction Analysis data on their classroom teaching, their verbal behavior patterns are likely to become more complex and varied. They also become more aware of how their verbal behavior affects student learning.

At this point you have probably asked yourself, "Which is better—an indirect or a direct teaching style?" As we discussed in chapter 2, research on Interaction Analysis suggests that use of an indirect teaching style is associated with more positive student attitudes and higher student achievement. But this does not mean that a direct style is necessarily poor teaching. Flanders suggests that there are occasions when the teacher needs to be direct, as in presenting new content to students and giving directions. When using direct teaching, though, there is opportunity to use some indirect verbal behaviors. For example, the teacher may be giving an extended series of directions for doing an experiment (category 6). While doing this, the teacher might consider pausing to praise or encourage the students for their efforts and success in following directions (category 2).

A similar situation can occur in indirect teaching. For example, the teacher may be moderating a discussion in which students are encouraged to state their own opinions on an issue (category 9). The teacher may acknowledge students' ideas (category 3), encourage silent students to talk (category 2), and verbalize awareness of the feelings that underlie students' opinions (category 1). All these are indirect verbal behaviors. At some point in the discussion, though, the teacher may discover that students are misinformed about a particular issue and so decide to interrupt the discussion temporarily to provide information (category 5) and direct students to do homework reading (category 6). Thus, the teacher has interspersed direct teaching into a predominantly indirect, student-centered lesson.

This is only a brief introduction to the Flanders Interaction Analysis System. We trust that it is enough to help you understand why these classroom observation categories have captured the attention of educators worldwide and why the system has been used extensively in teacher supervision.

TIMELINE CODING (TECHNIQUE 22)

In describing Interaction Analysis, we stated that it has two main features. The preceding section discussed the first feature, namely, the ten categories for coding verbal behaviors. The other distinguishing feature is the way in which the behaviors are coded by the observer.

Figure 8.6 presents several examples of timelines used in conjunction with the Flanders Interaction Analysis System.[9] The first thing to notice about a timeline is its columns. Each column represents a 3-second interval. The 3-second interval is long enough that the observer need not become preoccupied with recording data. In most lessons there usually are several periods of time lasting a minute or more when only one interaction category is being used. (These are usually categories 4, 5, or 6.) The observer can relax during these time intervals until the pace of interaction increases again.[10]

The timelines shown in Figure 8.6 have 30 columns for recording 30 discrete observations. Because an observation is made every 3 seconds, each timeline covers about $1^1/_2$ minutes of classroom interaction.

The other salient feature of an Interaction Analysis timeline is the rows. Each row represents one or two categories. The middle row is for the teacher questions (category 4), which often are a stimulus for a series of interactions between teacher and students. Categories reflecting an indirect teaching style (1, 2, and 3) are above the middle row, as is the category reflecting open, student-initiated responses (category 9). Categories that indicate a direct teaching style (5, 6, and 7) are below the line, as is the category for structured, restricted student responses (category 8).

Category 10 (silence or confusion) is not represented by a discrete row. Tallies for this category are made below the timeline. Several categories (1 and 2, 6 and 7) share the same row in order to conserve space. Observers can use different tallies in the cells to differentiate 1 from 2 or 6 from 7, or they can simply change the timeline form by adding two rows so each category has its own row.

The organization of the Interaction Analysis categories on the timeline helps the supervisor and teacher detect verbal patterns that occurred during the lesson. For example, a majority of tallies above the middle row indicates that the lesson was indirect in style. A majority of tallies below the middle row indicates the lesson was direct in style. These patterns can be detected much more quickly than by playing back a video or audio recording of a lesson. A timeline usually can be interpreted in less than 2 minutes, whereas the time required to interpret a video or audio record-ing of a lesson will take longer than the elapsed time of the lesson.

The first timeline in Figure 8.6 is characterized by alternating 4s and 8s. This pattern suggests that the teacher was engaged in a rapid question-and-answer inter-change with students, with the level of discourse probably focused on fact recall.

The second timeline in Figure 8.6 suggests a richer, more indirect dialogue. The

FIGURE 8.6 Timelines.

SOURCE: Copyright 1974, Far West Laboratory for Educational Research and Development, San Francisco, California. Published by Paul S. Amidon & Associates, Inc., 4329 Nicollet Avenue South, Minneapolis, Minnesota 55409.

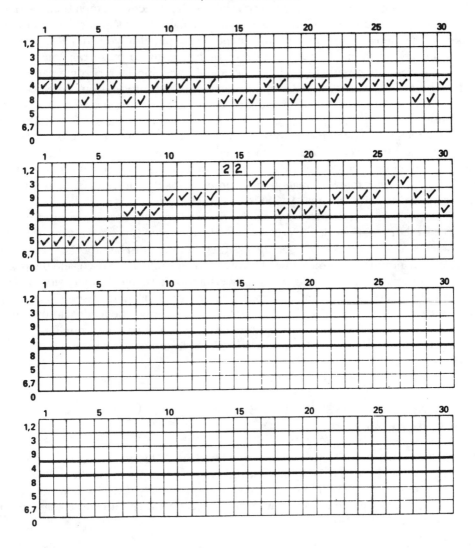

teacher starts by giving some information on a curriculum topic. Then students are invited to offer their own ideas on the topic. After each student response, the teacher takes care to acknowledge the student's idea and, in some cases, to praise it.

When teachers first become exposed to Interaction Analysis, they typically find that they use a few simple patterns in interacting with their students. As they see these patterns recorded on a timeline, they are likely to become dissatisfied and want to explore how they can become more flexible in their use of verbal behavior. Sometimes, but not always, this involves a shift from a more direct to a more indirect style of teaching.

Our discussion of timelines has focused on its application to Flanders Interaction Analysis categories. Timelines are a generic recording device, however. With a bit of creativity on your part, you can imagine other behaviors that can be inserted in place of the Interaction Analysis categories. Also, the 3-second interval represented by the columns of the timeline can be varied. You may want a shorter or longer time interval depending on the observation categories included in your timeline system.

Computer technology has been developed recently to make timeline coding more efficient. The observer uses a pen-like device and special recording paper that contains a bar code for each interaction category and also for designated classroom participants, if that is desired. By moving the "pen" across the appropriate bar codes, the observer can record how long the teacher or student engaged in a particular type of interaction. Following the observation period, the observer inserts the "pen" in a computer interface device, which stores the information in a data file. A computer program has been developed to create printouts that display the information in the data file in various formats (e.g., a timeline display or a list of each interaction category and the amount of time it was used in the lesson).

The process described above is similar to that currently used by many stores. A clerk passes a pen-like device over the bar code imprinted on each product that the customer is purchasing. A device on the cash register then displays for the customer's benefit such information as the name of the item, the quantity purchased, and the price.

Computerized timeline coding is a powerful tool for clinical supervision. It simplifies the process of collecting and analyzing observational data. Also, it speeds up the process of getting feedback to the teacher, and it allows the feedback to be presented in a variety of formats. Clinical supervisors who use timeline coding routinely are advised to learn more about this technique from its developers—Innovative Assessment LTD.[11]

THE STALLINGS OBSERVATION SYSTEM (TECHNIQUE 23)

The Stallings Observation System, developed by Jane Stallings and her colleagues, is one of the most important classroom instruments to come into use in the past decade. It has been used in research,[12] in-service education,[13] and preservice education.[14] It can be used at any grade level and with any subject area, and it can be adapted for observing special situations.

This instrument is similar to the Flanders Interaction Analysis System in its coding procedure and emphasis on observable classroom behaviors. However, the Stallings system is more sophisticated. Whereas the Flanders system measures ten aspects of teacher and student behavior, the Stallings system measures 64. Another difference is that the Flanders system is based on group-process theory and research, whereas the Stallings system is based on research on effective teaching of academic knowledge and skills. (See chapter 2 for a review of this research.)

The Stallings Observation System has two components: (1) the classroom snapshot, and (2) the Five-Minute Interaction (FMI). The snapshot data show how the teacher and students spend their time during a lesson and the types of activities in which they engage. The FMI data show how the teacher and student verbally interact with each other during a lesson. Together the snapshot and the FMI provide a comprehensive picture of what happened during the lesson.

Snapshot data are collected at five evenly spaced intervals during a lesson, and FMI data are collected at another five evenly spaced intervals during the same lesson. It is recommended that three lessons be observed to get a stable picture of the teacher's instruction, but one lesson—if it is typical—should be sufficient for the purposes of clinical supervision.

In collecting snapshot data, the observer takes a sweep of the classroom and quickly marks the categories that correspond to what he sees on a scantron sheet. (The scantron sheet is a special type of checklist that can be scored mechanically.)

When the next interval for collecting snapshot data occurs, this process is repeated. In effect, the observer has taken a series of "snapshots" of the teacher's lesson. Instead of scantron sheets, the observer has the option of using a laptop computer with a software program that allows easy keyboard entry and processing of the snapshot data.

An example of a teacher profile that can be created from snapshot data is shown in Table 8.1 (p. 136). The left column lists the aspects of instruction that are observed by the snapshot. The "criterion" column lists the optimal amount of time that should be spent on each aspect of instruction, as determined by research on effective teaching.[15] Because these criterion percentages are not always appropriate for every age and subject, they may be adjusted as the situation requires. The third column shows the actual percentage of observed time that the teacher (Betty) and her students spent on each aspect of instruction.

To understand Table 8.1 better, let us consider how the teacher, Betty, spent her time monitoring student work. This aspect of instruction is reflected in the top two rows, "Monitoring Silent Reading" and "Monitoring Written Work." Looking at the two columns of time-use percentages, we find that Betty used less time (0%) than considered optimal (15%) in monitoring silent reading, but more time (36%) than considered optimal in monitoring written work (20%). Looking now at the student activity rows, we find that students read silently (2%), less than considered optimal (15%), and they spent much more time doing written assignments (55%) than considered optimal (20%). We also note that students spent 55 percent of their time on written assignments, but Betty only spent 36% of her time monitoring them. This is probably because she spent a substantial amount of her time working by herself (18%—see the row labeled "Organizing—teacher alone").

TABLE 8.1 Snapshot profile of a teacher lesson

Observation Variables	Percent of Time Spent	
	Criterion	Betty's Class
Teacher Involved In		
Monitoring silent reading	15.00	.00
Monitoring written work	20.00	36.00
Reading aloud	6.00	.00
Instruction or explanation	25.00	10.00
Discussion or review assignments	10.00	13.00
Practice drill	4.00	.00
Taking test or quiz	5.00	.00
Classroom management with students	2.50	.00
Making assignments	10.00	20.00
Organizing—teacher alone	2.50	18.00
Social interacting with students	.00	.00
Student uninvolved	.00	.00
Providing discipline	.00	3.00
Students Involved In		
Reading silently	15.00	2.00
Written assignments	20.00	55.00
Reading aloud	6.00	.00
Receiving instruction or explanations	25.00	26.00
Discussion or review	10.00	12.00
Practice drill	4.00	7.00
Taking test or quiz	5.00	6.00
Social interaction	.00	14.00
Student uninvolved	.00	12.00
Being disciplined	.00	3.00
Classroom management	5.00	.00
Receiving assignments	10.00	10.00

SOURCE: Adapted from Figure 2.4 in *Improving Teaching* (1986 ASCD Yearbook), ed. Karen K. Zumwalt (Alexandria, VA: Association for Supervision and Curriculum Development, 1986), p. 24.

These data suggest two goals for instructional improvement as part of the clinical supervision process. First, the teacher should consider providing more interactive instruction and spending less time working alone. Second, she should consider assigning more silent reading and less written work.

The FMI involves a different data collection procedure than the classroom snapshot. The codes of the FMI were based on naturalistic observations in classrooms. Frequently occurring behaviors were identified and developed as codes for the system. The observer records all teacher and student verbal communications that occur during a 5-minute period. The data can be recorded on a scantron sheet or on the laptop computer described above.

The scantron sheet consists of a series of rectangular boxes, as illustrated in Figure 8.7. In the first column of each box, the observer fills a bubble to indicate whether the communication was in a language other than English (NE); it was a repeat of the same communication pattern as recorded in the preceding box (R); or the observer made an error and wishes to cancel what he coded in the box (Ca). The other parts of the box are used to code who was talking (e.g., teacher, student, visitor, aide); to whom the person talked; what the person said (e.g., a command, literal question, response to a question or command); and how the communication related to the lesson (e.g., academic, organizing, behavior management).

An FMI box is coded approximately every 5 seconds during the 5-minute period, and there are five such time periods during the lesson. Therefore, a typical FMI for a lesson consists of 300 coded boxes (12 codings per minute × 5 minutes × 5 time periods).

You will note that the FMI method of coding is similar to the timeline coding in the Flanders system in two ways. First, the emphasis is on teacher and student communication behaviors. Second, the observer does not need to write her observations. All observations are in the form of filling in bubbles on the scantron sheet or typing a single letter code on the computer.

FIGURE 8.7 FMI scantron sheet.

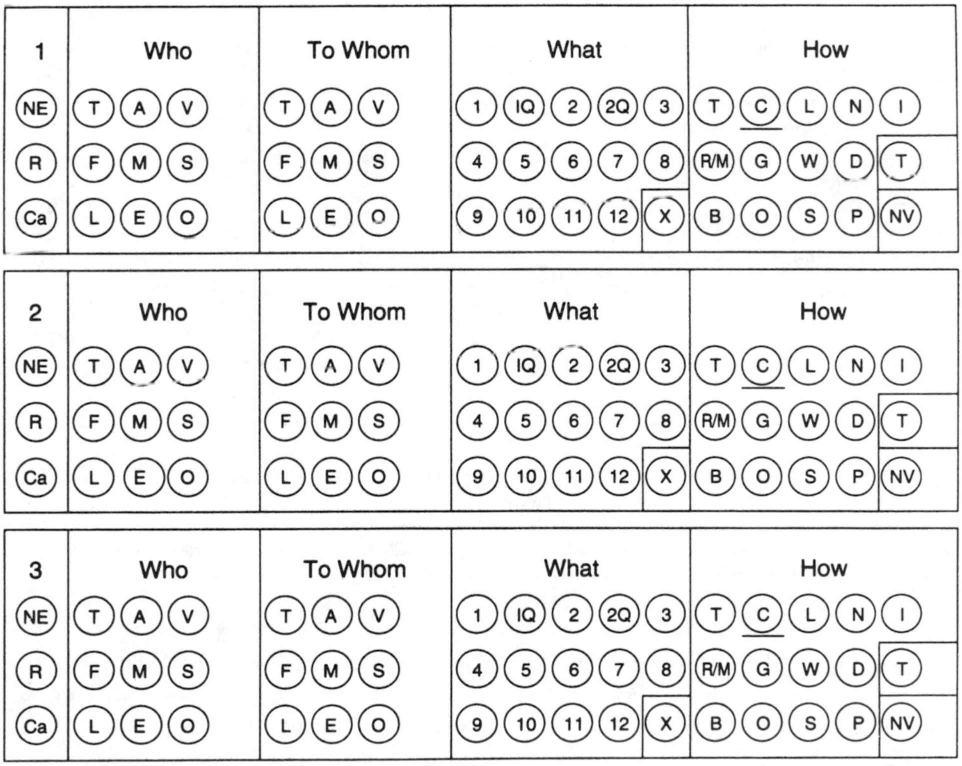

TABLE 8.2 Five-minute interaction (FMI) profile of a teacher's lesson

		Percentage of Time Spent	
	Observation Variables	Criterion	Betty's Class
001	All academic statements	80.00	65.28
002	All organizing or management statements	15.00	30.76
003	All behavior statements	3.00	3.83
004	All social statements	2.00	.00
005	Total for discrete variables	100.00	100.00
006	Teacher instructs or explains	12.00	15.45
007	Teacher asks direct questions or commands	10.00	4.00
008	Teacher asks clarifying questions	3.00	.13
009	Teacher asks open-ended questions	3.00	.79
010	Student asks academic questions	2.00	1.32
011	Teacher calls upon new students (academic)	6.00	5.02
012	Students respond academically	15.00	5.00
013	Student shouts-out or initiates remarks	.00	7.39
014	Student doesn't know answer	1.00	.13
015	Student refuses to answer	.00	.00
016	All praise	8.00	2.00
017	Teacher praises or supports academic responses	6.00	2.00
018	Teacher praises behavior	2.00	.00
019	Teacher corrects academic responses	6.00	4.35
020	Teacher corrects with guidance	4.00	.00
021	Teacher corrects behavior	2.00	3.03
022	Teacher monitoring academic work	6.00	10.96
023	All written work	.00	.00
024	Students read aloud	10.00	4.62
025	Teacher reads aloud	1.00	2.24
026	Teacher working alone	3.00	6.00
027	Intrusions	.00	3.14
028	Teacher involved with visitor	.00	2.20
029	Positive interactions	4.00	.52
030	Negative interactions	.00	1.50
031	Teacher touching	5.00	.00
032	Teacher movement	3.00	1.12
033	All activity-related comments or action	16.00	9.77
034	Student organizing comments	1.00	.13
035	Student academic comments	3.00	.13
036	Teacher organizing comments	5.00	1.98
037	Students' academic discussion	7.00	7.66
038	Students' cooperative group academic discussion	5.00	.00
	Total Number of Interactions for Teacher: 905		

SOURCE: Adapted from Figure 2.5 in *Improving Teaching* (1986 ASCD Yearbook), ed. Karen K. Zumwalt (Alexandria, VA: Association for Supervision and Curriculum Development, 1986), p. 25.

Table 8.2 illustrates the type of display that is created from FMI data. Some of the observation variables represent particular behaviors (e.g., "008—Teacher asks clarifying questions"), whereas others are groups of behaviors (e.g., "001—All academic statements").

The display is for the same lesson as that shown in Table 8.1. By comparing the two exhibits, you can see how the FMI complements and expands on the picture of classroom teaching produced by the snapshot. Also, you will note that both displays use the same format.

The Stallings Observation System is complex, but has the virtues of being comprehensive and focused on important aspects of effective teaching. If you wish to learn how to use this instrument, you will need to receive instruction from a certified trainer.[16]

TEACHER EVALUATION RATING SCALES (TECHNIQUE 24)

The purpose of observation in the clinical supervision cycle is to collect objective data about the teacher's classroom behavior. In teacher evaluation, however, the supervisor collects evaluative data for the purpose of judging the teacher's competence. Observation instruments used for the purpose generally consist of evaluative rating scales. The observer makes a check or circles a point on the scale that corresponds to his or her rating of the teacher's performance.

We are describing these scales here, even though they are deliberately evaluative rather than objective. One reason for doing this is that they provide a contrast that can help you better understand the objective, neutral nature of the other observation instruments presented in this section of the book. Another reason is that there may be occasions in clinical supervision when it is appropriate to use evaluative observation instruments. For example, the supervisor may be working with a teacher to help him prepare for an upcoming evaluation. Use of the rating instrument that will be used in the evaluation can help the teacher prepare for it and may also defuse some of the anxiety associated with being evaluated.

A typical teacher evaluation instrument contains 10 to 15 items. Most of the items usually have to do with the teacher's classroom behavior, for example:

1. teaches accurate content
2. makes learning outcomes explicit to students
3. includes both lower-cognitive and higher-cognitive objectives in instruction
4. uses curriculum materials and technology that are appropriate to the lesson objectives
5. motivates students to achieve the lesson objectives
6. uses a variety of teaching strategies
7. demonstrates effective classroom management
8. gives students adequate feedback on their performance, and reteaches if necessary
9. maintains a positive, cooperative classroom climate
10. adjusts instruction appropriately for unexpected events and time constraints
11. assesses student progress and achievement regularly and in a manner consistent with curriculum objectives

These items are only illustrative. A review of the literature on effective teaching (see chapter 2) will suggest other items that can be used instead of, or in addition to, those listed above. The most important consideration is that the evaluator have a rationale for each item included in the instrument. It is also important to make the rationale explicit to the teacher being evaluated. This can be done by showing the teacher the instrument and explaining it prior to the observation visit.

Examples of other items typically found in teacher evaluation instruments include the following:

1. prepares coherent, complete lesson plans
2. demonstrates ethical, professional behavior
3. contributes to colleagues' development and to the school as an organization
4. communicates effectively with parents and other members of the community
5. demonstrates continued professional development

The supervisor obviously would need to make observations outside the classroom context in order to rate these items validly.

Some teacher evaluation instruments include "indicators" that clarify what is meant by each item. It is helpful both to the teacher and the supervisor if these indicators are stated as observable behaviors. For example, consider the item stated above, "Motivates students to achieve the lesson objectives." Indicators of what is meant by this item might include

- exhibits enthusiasm (varied voice inflection, lively facial expressions, energetic body movements)
- praises and acknowledges students when they demonstrate interest or give a correct response
- relates the curriculum content to phenomena within the range of students' experience and interest

These indicators increase the credibility and comprehensibility of the items. They also help teachers identify what they can do to improve their ratings on individual items. An important element of an evaluative rating instrument is the scale itself. A typical scale includes five or seven points, with an appropriate descriptor at key points on the scale, for example:

Low Competence		*Average Competence*			*Exceptional Competence*		*NA*
1	2	3	4	5	6	7	

Unsatisfactory		*Satisfactory*		*Excellent*	*NA*
1	2	3	4	5	

You will note that the scales include an "NA" (not applicable) option. This is because some items on the instrument may not be appropriate for the teacher's lessons or job description.

Each item on the instrument is accompanied by a scale like the ones illustrated above. The supervisor need only circle the appropriate point on the scale for each item.

NOTES

1. Many other checklists are described in Gary D. Borich and Susan K. Madden, *Evaluating Classroom Instruction: A Sourcebook of Instruments* (Reading, MA: Addison-Wesley, 1977).
2. The Pupil Observation Survey was developed at the Research and Development Center for Teacher Education, The University of Texas.
3. Information about the IDEA H Questionnaire is available from Kansas State University, Center for Faculty Evaluation and Development, Manhattan, KA 66502.
4. Their research is reviewed in Ned Flanders, *Analyzing Teaching Behavior* (Reading, MA: Addison-Wesley, 1970).
5. These rating checklists are called Teaching Analysis Guides by Joyce and his colleagues. They are included in a set of three books: Marsha Weil and Bruce Joyce, *Information Processing Models of Teaching* (Englewood Cliffs, NJ: Prentice-Hall, 1978); Bruce Joyce and Marsha Weil, *Social Models of Teaching* (Englewood Cliffs, NJ: Prentice-Hall, 1978); Bruce Joyce, Marsha Weil, and Bridget Kluwin, *Personal Models of Teaching* (Englewood Cliffs, NJ: Prentice-Hall, 1978).
6. Ned Flanders and Edmund J. Amidon, *A Case Study of an Educational Innovation: The History of Flanders Interaction Analysis System* (Oakland, CA: Ned A. Flanders, One Spyglass Hill, 94618), 1981.
7. A brief, excellent package for learning how to use this observation system is *Interaction Analysis: A Mini-Course* by Ned Flanders and his colleagues. It is available from Paul S. Amidon and Associates, Inc., 4329 Nicollet Avenue South, Minneapolis, MN 55409.
8. Some classes may have a guest speaker or a teacher aide. In this situation you may wish to adapt the Flanders Interaction Analysis System to accommodate the additional speaker(s).
9. The use of a timeline to record Interaction Analysis data is a relatively recent development. If you learned the system some years ago, you may be familiar, instead, with the use of matrices to record and interpret Interaction Analysis data. We present the timeline method here because we believe it is generally superior to matrices in ease of coding and interpretation.
10. When a simple interaction category occurs for any length of time, the observer may abbreviate the record-keeping process. For example, if the teacher launches into an extended explanation of a concept, the observer may place a few tallies in the row designated by category 5, and then draw a short arrow with a note indicating approximately how many minutes or seconds this category of verbal behavior was used.
11. Their address is: Innovative Assessment LTD, Suite No. 114, 524 San Anselmo Avenue, San Anselmo, CA 94960. Phone: (415) 454-2447.
12. Kenneth A. Sirotnik, "What You See Is What You Get—Consistency, Persistency, and Mediocrity in Classrooms," *Harvard Educational Review* 53 (1983): 16-31.

13. Jane A. Stallings, "Using Time Effectively: A Self-Analytic Approach," in *Improving Teaching* (1986 ASCD Yearbook), ed. Karen K. Zumwalt (Alexandria, VA: Association for Supervision and Curriculum Development, 1986), pp. 15–27.

14. H. Jerome Freiberg and Hersholt C. Waxman, "Reflection and the Acquisition of Technical Teaching Skills," in *Encouraging Reflective Practice in Education*, ed. Renee T. Clift, W. Robert Houston, and Marleen C. Pugach (New York: Teachers College Press, 1990), pp. 119–38.

15. This research is reviewed in Jane Stallings, "Allocated Learning Time Revisited, or Beyond Time on Task," *Educational Researcher* 9, No. 11 (1980): 11–16.

16. Information about training in the Stallings Observation System can be obtained from Dr. Sandra Simons, 2606 Spring Boulevard, Eugene, Oregon 97403; or Dr. Jane Stallings, Texas A&M University, College of Education, College Station, Texas 77843.

Unit III Exercises

MULTIPLE-CHOICE ITEMS

Answers are on page 255.

1. Teachers' use of redirection and probing can be analyzed by
   a. the verbal flow technique.
   b. the at-task technique.
   c. the movement pattern technique.
   d. a selective verbatim of teacher's questions.
2. Journal writing is intended to promote
   a. effective use of instructional time.
   b. reflective teaching.
   c. teacher sensitivity to the affective domain.
   d. supervisor accountability.
3. The figure shown to the right is most likely from a(n)
   a. selective verbatim record.
   b. verbal flow record.
   c. at-task record.
   d. movement pattern record.

4. The figure shown to the right is most likely from a(n)
   a. selective verbatim record
   b. verbal flow record.
   c. at-task record.
   d. movement pattern record.

5. The specific emitters and targets of verbal behavior in classrooms can be identified most effectively by the

    a. verbal flow technique.
    b. movement pattern technique.
    c. Student Perception of Teacher Style checklist.
    d. Flanders Interaction Analysis system.
  6. The technique most closely related to the ethnographic method in anthropology is the
    a. video recording.
    b. timeline coding technique.
    c. anecdotal record.
    d. selective verbatim.
  7. When first exposed to a videotape of their teaching behavior, teachers tend to focus on
    a. their physical appearance.
    b. their students' physical appearance.
    c. their students' at-task behavior.
    d. verbal flow patterns.
  8. The IDEA H Questionnaire and the Pupil Observation Survey are examples of
    a. supervisor-administered checklists.
    b. teacher-administered checklists.
    c. school-principal-administered checklists.
    d. student self-administered checklists.
  9. In the Flanders Interaction Analysis System the behaviors of accepting feelings, praising, and accepting ideas are examples of
    a. teacher initiation.
    b. teacher response.
    c. student initiation.
    d. student response.
 10. In timeline coding columns are used to indicate _____, and rows are used to indicate _____.
    a. teacher initiation, student response
    b. teacher response, student initiation
    c. behavior categories, time intervals
    d. time intervals, behavior categories

PROBLEMS

The following problems do not have single correct answers. Possible answers are on pages 256–258. Your answers may differ from ours, yet be as good or better.

  1. A teacher under your supervision has a concern about how she "comes across" to students but can't get any more specific than this in stating the concern. What observational techniques might you select? Why?
  2. A teacher tells you he has several problem students in his class. The students create class disturbances and spend little time engaged in learning.

The teacher would like you to collect data on their behavior that would help him better understand why these students are a "problem." What observational techniques would you consider using? Why?

3. Figure IIIa is a verbal flow chart made of an actual sixth-grade class. The teacher had given a presentation on a social studies topic and, at the time of the classroom observation, she was discussing the topic with the class.

FIGURE IIIa   Verbal flow chart for unit III, exercise 3.

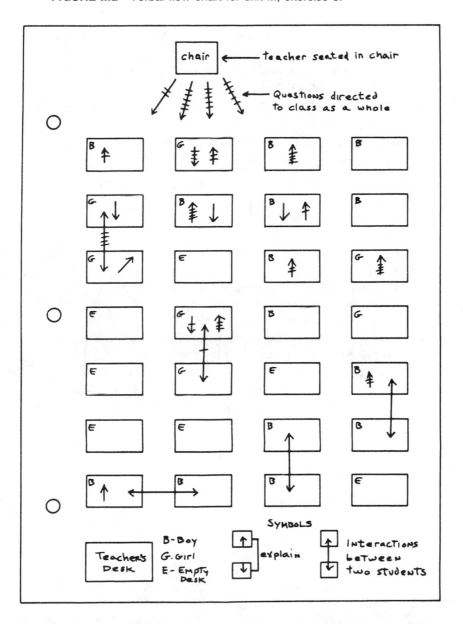

What inferences and recommendations for changes in the teacher's behavior might you make based on the verbal flow data?

4. The following is a transcript of the first few minutes of an actual lesson in a junior high school class. First, make a selective verbatim of the teacher's feedback statements. Second, code the transcript on a timeline using the Flanders Interaction Analysis System. Assume that each line of the transcript represents a 3-second interval.

TEACHER: Who knows what a population explosion means? Who knows what it means?

STUDENT: I think it means like too many people, there's too many people living in like all over the world, there is just too many people. The population has just increased, the amount of people is just going up. It's just expanding, put it that way.

TEACHER: All right. How many people are here in the world right now?

STUDENT: A couple of billion.

TEACHER: A couple of billion. Any other guesses?

STUDENT: I'd say about six million.

TEACHER: Six million.

STUDENT: There is only about a billion.

TEACHER: Only a billion.

STUDENT: I'd say about three billion.

TEACHER: About three billion. All right, Mary is closest because it is over three billion people in the world today. A couple of billion, that is a billion less than three billion, though, unless you meant a couple of billion or three. All right, what do they mean by squeezing to death? What do we mean by squeezing to death, Liza?

STUDENT: Well, there will be so many people in the world that there will be no place for them to go, and they squeeze.

STUDENT: Well, it means that there are a lot of people that are just barely making it in their life. You know, they don't have much money.

TEACHER: All right, there are a lot of people that are just barely making it.

Conferences Based on Objective Data

OVERVIEW

Data recorded by an observer must be shared with the teacher. Good data badly shared may become bad data. In this unit we look at some good ways to provide feedback to teachers, and we consider some of the interpersonal dynamics that are involved in the process. Chapter 11 is addressed to the feedback conference, and chapter 12 looks at direct and indirect styles of supervision.

OBJECTIVES

The purpose of this unit is to help you develop

Explicit techniques for providing useful feedback to teachers to aid them in analyzing, interpreting, and modifying their instructional efforts

An approach to supervision conferences consistent with the goals set forth in unit 1

An appreciation for how the differences in styles and strategies can be accommodated in conferences with teachers

chapter 9

The Feedback Conference

Most of us know how to say nothing; few of us know when.
Anonymous

Several things must take place before a successful feedback conference can occur.

1. Before the conference, teacher and observer have set some goals, identified common concerns, established a rationale for working together, considered the strategies the teacher has been using and intends to use, and translated any abstract concerns into observable behaviors the observer could record.
2. Before observing the data (such as a television recording of the teacher working with a group or with an individual), teacher and observer identified the nature of the instruction, made the objectives explicit, discussed what the teacher would be doing in the recorded session (strategy), predicted what the student(s) should be doing (expectations), considered specific problems or concerns the teacher anticipated before the recorded session, and selected appropriate observation techniques or categories of analysis.
3. The observer is prepared to use one or more devices from a repertoire of data-recording techniques appropriate for the specific situation as related to the goals and concerns, and the observer has recorded data unobtrusively without distressing the teacher.

Now we are ready to begin the feedback conference.

The observer tries to provide objective observational data, analyze the data cooperatively, and reach agreement with the teacher on what is happening. Then teacher and observer interpret the data. The observer elicits the teacher's reactions to the data (inferences, opinions, feelings) and considers possible causes and consequences. Together, teacher and observer reach decisions about future actions. These may be decisions about alternative teacher strategies, different objectives for students, or modification of the teacher's self-improvement goals. At this juncture, teacher and observer may recognize a need for other kinds of information or make plans for the next observation. Often, the feedback conference for one observation becomes the planning conference for the next.

PROVIDE THE TEACHER WITH FEEDBACK USING OBJECTIVE OBSERVATIONAL DATA (TECHNIQUE 25)

If the planning conference has established one or more goals that address genuine concerns and if the observational data are accurate and relevant, then the teacher should find the information useful, and the conference should run relatively smoothly. Many conferences are difficult because the data are "soft" (i.e., subjective, inaccurate, irrelevant). The inherent defensiveness teachers feel toward what they perceive as an evaluative situation is heightened by information that, to them, is suspect and debatable. "Hard" data alleviate this problem. Teachers do not say that what they saw on videotape or heard on audiotape did not happen, even though they may analyze or interpret events in a way that differs from another observer's analysis. Data in paper-and-pencil form (e.g., selected verbatim statements) can be similarly convincing.

We should keep in mind, however, that all data are more or less subjective; even with videotape and film, someone chooses where to aim the camera and whether to take close-ups or wide-angle shots. Sound recordings can be affected by microphone placement and other factors. Checklists and charts are subject to the judgment, skill, and bias of the person tallying frequencies of given behaviors, choosing categories, or making qualitative judgments.

Similarly, in sharing information there is a temptation to add editorial opinion, either through direct comment or through a not-so-subtle use of adjectives. Consider this statement: "Here are some objective, unbiased, nonjudgmental data on your chaotic classroom."

Beginning the Conference

Having important information to discuss is the essential ingredient of a successful feedback conference. This means information that is objective (unbiased), accurate, clear (to both parties), relevant to the agreed-upon concerns, and interpretable in respect to what changes are feasible and reasonable. If the observer has these kinds of information available in an easily displayed and readily understood form, a logical opening for the conference is "Let's look at the data we have observed or collected."

Analyzing comes next, which means simply describing what the recorded information shows is happening without making value judgments. It is best for the teacher to take the lead in doing this.

Interpreting the data includes looking for probable causes of observed effects, or possible consequences, or suggested alternatives. Allowing the teacher to hypothesize several consequences or infer several reasonable causes of observed phenomena is usually a productive strategy. For example, observation of student "at-task" behaviors during a class period may show their interest in the activity waning after 20 minutes. The teacher may interpret this to indicate a weakness in the activity or a normal consequence of limited student attention span. Depending on the interpretation, decisions for change will vary. If the activity is judged inappropriate, it may be modified or changed substantially; if it is interpreted as appropriate but too long, it may merely need to be shortened.

Deciding what changes to make in future instruction can take many forms. Decisions can relate to any elements discussed in the planning conference. For example, the conferees may conclude that one or more of the following should be changed:

* the nature of the lesson, session, or unit
* the objectives of the lesson, session, or unit
* what the teacher does during the instruction
* what the student(s) do(es) during the instruction
* what additional kinds of information are needed to make intelligent decisions through analysis and interpretation

Another way of looking at decisions is to consider their magnitude. At one extreme, the teacher may decide to leave teaching as the result of systematic observational feedback (this has happened). At the other extreme, the teacher may decide not to change a thing (this has not happened, in our experience; teachers who believe they are perfect must be very rare). More often, teachers think of several aspects of the instruction that could be changed. The teacher may decide to experiment with these changes one at a time and analyze the effects. Usually the effects can be observed by the teacher without repeated visits by an observer, but in some cases an observer will be needed. In addition to the observer, others may be available either for direct observation or viewing recordings—colleagues, aides, family members, or even students.

Occasionally a teacher reaches a decision as the result of viewing data without making any comments during the feedback conference. For example, a teacher may resolve to get rid of an annoying mannerism noted in watching a videotape or to spend more time working with a particular student after noting the student's behavior recorded during the observation. One teacher, who was using a low-key style during a videotaped session, displayed a very dynamic style during the next observation (also videotaped). When asked by the observer about the obvious and abrupt change in teaching style, a matter that had not been mentioned in the previous conference, the teacher replied, "It wasn't until after I saw that first tape that I realized how undynamic I was. I swore I'd try something much different the next time!" Such a radical change is unusual, but this teacher found he was capable of a more energetic approach to teaching—at least occasionally.

Science makes use of accurate data to understand, predict, and thereby control. Similarly, when presented with factual information rather than inferential conclusions drawn by the consultant, the teacher is in a position to behave professionally and responsibly in the next step.

Acting on the decisions is a step that should not be overlooked. Teachers may work through the process described above and then not follow through to the point of changing their behavior in the classroom. The infrequency of classroom observation by supervisors, colleagues, coaches, or others can contribute to this possibility.

ELICIT THE TEACHER'S INFERENCES, OPINIONS, AND FEELINGS (TECHNIQUE 26)

Providing objective data can be translated into practice as, "Here's what was recorded from your session; let's have a look at it." The technique we are about to discuss, eliciting reactions, does not call for an opening question like, "How do you feel your session went?"

Cautious teachers hesitate to say, "Great!" for fear the observer will contradict or disagree. On the other hand, if they say, "Lousy," they run the risk of having the observer agree. "Some parts were good; others could be improved" is a safe answer, but this is what the conference is all about anyway. The observer can choose a less threatening opener, after the teacher has had a chance to inspect the information, by asking, "What aspects of the data do you want to talk about first?"

Eliciting the teacher's reactions to the data requires skill and patience. There is always a temptation to jump to conclusions about what has been recorded and observed before the teacher has had an opportunity to reflect on it. A device that works well, especially in connection with tape recordings, is to ask the following questions:

> "What do you see [or hear] in the record [or tape] that you would repeat if you did this teaching again?"
> "What would you change?"
> "If you were a student, what would you want to change?"

We have asked these questions of hundreds of teachers—primary, intermediate, secondary, and college teachers—who have viewed videotapes of themselves. No one has answered all the questions with "I wouldn't change a thing." If "What would you repeat?" gets no response (although it nearly always does—we find things we like in our own teaching), you can proceed immediately to the second question. If the teacher expresses total satisfaction with the lesson in response to "What would you change?" the third question, "What would a student want changed?" should provoke a more thoughtful response. The teacher can be asked to view the instruction from the perspective of different students, say, one who usually has difficulty understanding and one who is usually ahead of the rest.

These questions are phrased in a relatively nonthreatening manner to which most teachers are able to respond openly and with considerable insight. In response to the third question, one teacher said,

"Which student?"

"What do you mean, which student?"

"Well, the slowest, the brightest, the least interested?"

"OK, the slowest."

"All right. What I see that teacher doing is talking too fast, using vocabulary I don't understand, discussing topics that don't affect me. I don't think she likes me; she almost never calls on me even when I know the answer."

This was a healthy insight for the teacher to develop, and the anecdote points out that one function of the observer is to serve as a catalyst, to help the teacher make productive use of the available information.

For most teachers, the steps in the feedback conference are reasonable and appropriate: providing objective data, analyzing and interpreting it, and drawing conclusions with the teacher taking equal part in a collaborative process. Unfortunately, many observers reverse the process. They provide their own conclusions, give some analysis that justifies the conclusions, then search for data to substantiate the analysis. Often, no alternative interpretations are even considered.

For a small percentage of teachers a "conclusions first" conference approach may be needed. For example, it may be more effective to say, "You've been late for work twelve times this month. This has got to stop, or else!" rather than to say, "Here are some data about your punctuality. Do you find anything of interest?" An alternative effective strategy could be "What do you propose to do about this record of tardiness?"

Even stronger examples can be given for medical settings where the teacher needs to point out to the student, intern, resident that the patient being discussed is at risk. In schools and colleges there are also persons (students) "at risk."

There are several assumptions in a procedure that encourages teachers to come to their own conclusions, based on objective information and thoughtful analysis.

- Few teachers set out deliberately to do a bad job. Most have reasonable goals.
- Most teachers have alternative strategies available and can use them if they see a need.
- We don't "see ourselves as others see us." Being able to view our teaching from a new perspective can be an enlightening experience.
- Those insights we discover for ourselves tend to be retained and acted on with more energy and better spirit than those we are told about by others.
- Many teachers prefer a collaborative, collegial approach instead of one in which the observer (supervisor) is regarded as "superior."
- Good data can be more persuasive than mere admonishments.

Persuasive data contain no value judgments. Inferences and generalizations the observer may have formed about the activity are not included in the data presented in a conference with the teacher. Data that might lead the teacher to the same inferences probably should be presented, however. Persuasive data, in addition to being value-free, must be specific and presented in a form that can be understood and used immediately by the teacher. They also must be data the teacher feels are necessary and important at a given time. For example, a teacher concerned about the inability to ask good questions is probably not ready for data and conferences designed to improve lecturing prowess. Or data that might be helpful to a teacher worried about disciplinary problems might be regarded as irrelevant by a teacher who has no problem with discipline. The observer needs a variety of skills to share data in a persuasive manner at a time when the teacher feels that the data are relevant, important, and useful.

A teacher, after studying a seating chart on which an observer has recorded which students were responded to by the teacher (and in what ways), may begin to understand why some students feel "turned off" and plan activities that create opportunities to respond in positive ways to those students. Many teachers who have analyzed charts of their direct and indirect behaviors (using Flanders's categories) have modified the indirect-direct ratio. Teachers who have had access to verbal flow patterns on seating charts (who talks to whom) often have been stimulated to experiment with different seating arrangements.

A high school science teacher studied observational charts that showed what percent of his students were at task for various time periods. The percentages were strikingly high, which might have been expected to please this instructor. Yet the teacher concluded that they were too high. Every year a number of students dropped this course; after the instructor saw the data, he realized he was "keeping their noses to the grindstone" so much that the course was unduly punishing. He decided to restructure the course.

When an observer feels that a teacher is drawing acceptable inferences and suggesting reasonable alternative plans for the future, a simple reinforcement is all the technique needs. "That sounds like a good idea, Pat. Why don't you try it?"

Another teacher had been having some real problems with lesson preparation and control of students. She was observed on two successive days, the observer taking verbatim notes of her questions and control statements. At the feedback conference, the observer began the conference as follows:

"How do you feel about the two lessons?"
"Well, I feel that it went better today than yesterday. But how did I look?"
"You know I'm not going to answer that."
"I know."

It would have been better for the observer to start the dialogue with

"Here are the questions and control statements you wanted to analyze. Let's have a look at them."

If the teacher asks "How did I do?" an appropriate answer is "Let's see." Then teacher and observer turn to the data.

ENCOURAGE THE TEACHER TO CONSIDER ALTERNATIVE LESSON OBJECTIVES, METHODS, REASONS (TECHNIQUE 27)

Once an observer has analyzed the data, the tendency is to say to a teacher, "Here's what I would do if I were you." This short-circuits the system. If teaching were a straightforward physical skill, then viewing the performance and giving advice like "Keep your eye on the ball" would be effective. Translated to advice about teaching, this tends to become "Be firm, fair, and consistent." This is undoubtedly good advice, but it does not tell what to be firm about (discipline? standards? questionable rules? teacher opinions?) or what is fair and consistent for all (activities for the physically handicapped? individualized academic assignments?). Moreover, there are always feasible alternatives for teaching anything. When change is desired, one purpose of the feedback conference is to get the teacher to consider several alternatives and choose the most promising. Teachers should be able to give alternative explanations of why things might be happening the way they are and also to suggest several ways to change the situation, or the strategy, or the activities.

Beginning teachers have a more limited repertoire of possible approaches than do more experienced teachers. One benefit accruing from systematic observation and teacher-centered conferences should be teachers who, on their own volition, do self-analyses using objective data and thus develop a wider range of alternative approaches.

For example, a group of beginning teachers in an intern teacher program read about social-class discrimination by teachers in schools. They recorded their own interactions with students in their classes, played them back, and were surprised to learn that they, too, were favoring middle-class children.

Another group of inexperienced teachers asked for help in learning how to control student participation in recitations and discussions. They were asked to note several students who were often active participants in a lesson and several others who seldom participated. In the next lesson they were asked to see if they could limit those who talked the most to no more than three contributions and get those who rarely participated to make at least three contributions. Every teacher reported being able to accomplish this assignment without any special instructions; simply being aware of the two groups of students was all that was necessary.

Many aspects of teaching can be observed, recorded, and analyzed as easily as counting student contributions to a recitation or discussion. You may wonder why teachers are not more aware of such obvious patterns as paying more attention to one side of the room or calling only on students in front seats. The answer is that these things are not obvious to teachers while they are preoccupied with the details of teaching. These things are not obvious to observers either, unless they are watching for them.

Observers often feel that if they record specific information, such as the nature of the teacher's responses to individual students, they will miss other important elements of the teaching-learning situation. Our experience suggests that we see more as observers when we have something specific on which to focus our attention. Making an audiotape recording, in addition to whatever charts or codes the observer is keeping on paper, ensures backup information about the lesson if it is needed.

A common worry among beginning elementary and secondary teachers is the problem of discipline. Students can get out of hand whether they are first graders or high school seniors. Feedback on this aspect of teaching can bring startling results. One of our beginning teachers asked that we videotape her troublesome fifth-period class instead of the well-behaved first-period class we had taped twice before. She volunteered the tape for analysis in a seminar on a day when classroom discipline was to be discussed and a film was to be shown that illustrated both ineffective and effective techniques. When her classroom tape was played later in the session, the teacher was able to see herself using many of the ineffective techniques portrayed in the film.

PROVIDE THE TEACHER WITH OPPORTUNITIES FOR PRACTICE AND COMPARISON (TECHNIQUE 28)

As a source of alternative teaching methods, a supervisor may be asked to play a more direct role as a model for a teacher by demonstrating a particular method or technique in the classroom. Curriculum specialists in particular are often asked to do such demonstrations. When this is done, the teacher becomes the observer and records data to be analyzed and interpreted in a postdemonstration conference. For example, an elementary teacher was experiencing difficulty explaining "pi" and the formulas for circumference and area. She asked a mathematics specialist to take over a lesson while she observed the explanation and recorded student questions. During the feedback conference, information about the observer's lesson was incorporated into information taken from the teacher's experience and plans.

Another frequent strategy is to suggest that one teacher observe another in order to compare styles or strategies or to pick up some different techniques. If the observing teacher has some knowledge of systematic observation and recording, the feedback conference can result in a mutual sharing of ideas and perspectives. In a small group that takes turns sharing videotaped examples the observers can learn about their own teaching vicariously while watching others.

Time for collecting information and providing feedback is always limited. One way to increase the amount of feedback is for the teacher to collect some of it. This can be done with teacher-made tape recordings (audio or video), by getting systematic feedback from students, or by using teacher aides or colleagues as observers.

Strategy	*Self-Observational Device*
Lecture: explanations, directions	Audiotape recording, selective verbatim
Discussion, seminar	Verbal flow chart made by student or teacher using tape recording
Demonstration	Videotape recording
Individualized instruction: seatwork, resource centers, laboratory, shop	Classroom traffic (movement) chart drawn by aide
Simulations, games, self-instructional materials	At-task chart prepared by teacher as students participate
Heuristic approaches: problem solving, inquiry lessons, guided discovery	Selective verbatim of teacher or student taken from tape recording

If the teacher has collected and analyzed some of the data, much time can be saved in a subsequent conference with the observer. Some tasks the teacher can perform also will make the teacher better informed at the time of the conference. For example, transcribing selected verbatim from a tape, charting student participation, or plotting frequencies from a student questionnaire will make the teacher aware of elements that need improvement or emphasis.

SUMMARY

In this chapter we have described the following techniques essential to a productive feedback conference:

- Provide the teacher with feedback using objective observational data. If the data are inadequate, inaccurate, biased, or irrelevant to the teacher's concerns, the process cannot get started. The teacher must feel that the information being analyzed is a valid representation of what is really happening in the classroom. Information that relies on memory is less persuasive than information that is objectively recorded.

- Elicit the teacher's inferences, opinions, and feelings about the observational data. If the data are accurate and objective, but the observer immediately draws opinionated inferences from the data, the teacher may feel compelled to respond defensively rather than interpret the data in a self-directed and productive way. It takes self-control and practice to provide another person with data in a nonevaluative, nonthreatening manner. The use of adjectives or nonverbal cues may communicate opinions or conclusions to the teacher before he or she has had a chance to work through the steps.

- Encourage the teacher to consider alternative lesson objectives, methods, reasons. If the teacher expresses dissatisfaction with something observed in the lesson, several reasonable hypotheses may help explain why an event is occurring; it is a mistake to zero in on only one possibility. Similarly, several feasible alternatives are usually available for dealing with a problem; more than one should be considered before settling on the best alternative. Here the supervisor can help the teacher avoid two traps: (1) "functional fixedness," proceeding to judge all information on the basis of a single hypothesis (which may be wrong); and (2) "a working definition of insanity," considering only one solution to a problem and when that doesn't work, doubling and redoubling our efforts with the same unsuccessful approach. The collaborative setting of the conference should provide teacher and observer with a wider range of hypotheses and proposed solutions than either conferee could generate alone.
- Provide the teacher with opportunities for practice and comparison. Just because the teacher has settled on a plan of action, we should not expect to see the problem solved immediately. Teachers need time to try out new approaches, develop new skills, or compare several strategies. An observer can follow up at a later time to observe, record, and reinforce teacher progress.

Ideally, the feedback conference takes the following form:

1. The observer displays the data recorded during the observation. This is done without evaluative comments.
2. The teacher analyzes what was happening during the lesson as evidenced by the data. The observer simply helps to clarify what behaviors the recorded data represent.
3. The teacher, with the help of the observer, interprets the behaviors of teacher and students as represented by the observational data. At this stage the teacher becomes more evaluative since causes and consequences must be discussed as desirable or undesirable.
4. The teacher, with assistance from the observer, decides on alternative approaches for the future to attend to dissatisfactions with the observed teaching or emphasize those aspects that were satisfying.
5. The observer reinforces the teacher's announced intentions for change when the observer agrees with them or helps the teacher modify the intentions if there is some disagreement.

Observers are often surprised at how easily these steps can be accomplished. When supplied with adequate information and allowed to act on it, most teachers can analyze, interpret, and decide in a self-directed and constructive manner. When things do not go well in a feedback conference, the difficulties can usually be traced to failure on the part of the observer to use effective techniques, such as those we have been considering.

chapter 10

Direct and Indirect Styles of Supervision

Take my advice: don't give advice.
Anonymous

The techniques in the previous chapter on feedback conferences can be used by a supervisor or peer observer who has systematically collected observational data to analyze with a teacher or colleague. How the data are interpreted and what decisions are reached will depend to a considerable extent on the supervisor's or consultant's style. Styles of consultation can be described in many ways; we shall use a common distinction: direct versus indirect styles.

Ned Flanders differentiates direct teaching styles (i.e., lecturing, directing, criticizing) from indirect styles (i.e., accepting feelings, encouraging, acknowledging, using student ideas). Arthur Blumberg uses similar categories for supervisor behavior and has gathered some evidence that teachers prefer an indirect style of supervision.[1]

The direct and indirect behaviors an observer may employ can be placed on a continuum, though no scale is intended.

Accept and use feelings	Give encouragement, praise	Use teacher's ideas	Ask questions		Lecture	Give directions	Criticize
	Indirect		▲		*Direct*		

CONSULTANT BEHAVIORS

Another range of possible conference behaviors on the teacher's part can be constructed using the work of Robert Spaulding.[2]

Escape	Withdraw	Respond to internal stimuli	Respond to external stimuli	Seek help	Transact	Share	Self-direct	Attend	Control	Annoy	Hurt

| *Flight* | *Passive* | ▲ | *Aggressive* | *Fight* |

TEACHER BEHAVIORS

Think of these as "coping" behaviors that one may use to survive a one-on-one conference.

The behavior of either conferee can be described with labels used by Everett Shostrom.[3]

Warm	Sensitive	Dependent	Supportive	Controlling	Critical	Strong	Aggressive

CHARACTERISTICS OF CONFEREES

These characteristics can be translated into verbs that describe a range of verbal behavior the supervisor or teacher can employ.

Care	Guide	Appreciate	Empathize	Respect	Express	Lead	Assert

One can also view the observer's actions as aversive (dominative, punishing) or supportive (approving, receptive). Setting limits and setting goals are actions that usually lie between these extremes but can be pushed toward one end or the other.

Approving	Receptive	Setting Goals	Setting Limits	Dominating	Punishing

Supportive   *Aversive*

Although teachers indicate a preference for observers who emphasize the supportive, caring style, these are not the only appropriate behaviors for an observer. A caring style at times may be indicated by doing something aversive (e.g., when a parent prevents a child from playing on the highway).

This chapter recommends several techniques usually regarded as indirect, but they also can be used by direct observers. Indeed they should be so used when persuasive data are shared. The techniques are concerned with listening, acknowledging, clarifying, encouraging, guiding (rather than directing), supporting, and dealing with feelings. The techniques that follow are especially useful for consultants who want conferences to be "teacher-centered." Whether an observer's essential style is direct or indirect, self-centered or teacher-centered, these techniques can be used to improve the quality of interaction between the conferees.

LISTEN MORE, TALK LESS (TECHNIQUE 29)

Many observers dominate the conversation. The teacher has little chance to identify goals and objectives, analyze and interpret information, or reach decisions about future actions. Teachers talk to students about two-thirds of the time they teach, and observers talk in about the same proportion to teachers. The exact ratio varies, but too many observers do most of the talking. It is difficult to attend to a teacher's concerns in a conference or encourage a teacher's plans for improvement when the observer monopolizes the conference. Avoid this tendency when applying the techniques in the remainder of this chapter.

ACKNOWLEDGE, PARAPHRASE, AND USE WHAT THE TEACHER IS SAYING (TECHNIQUE 30)

Observers who insert an "I understand" or "I know what you mean" in the course of a teacher's conversation indicate that they are listening. Accurate paraphrases also show that they understand the teacher. Using the teacher's ideas can be even more convincing than merely acknowledging (hearing) or paraphrasing (comprehending) them. Applying an idea to a different situation is but one example; pointing to a logical consequence is another. Paraphrasing can be overdone if too many responses are similar, or if they are inappropriately placed. For example, if a teacher says, "The car was going 60 miles an hour," it doesn't contribute much to respond, "What you are saying is that the automobile was traveling a mile a minute." An effective paraphrase must be a genuine effort to communicate that we understand what the other person is getting at. Using an idea of the teacher's shows that the observer heard, understood, and is pursuing the thought. Of course, it can be pursued so far that it ceases to be the teacher's idea and becomes the observer's. Generally, however, having a person you respect use your idea is rewarding.

ASK CLARIFYING QUESTIONS (TECHNIQUE 31)

The teacher's statements often need to be probed to clarify the observer's understanding and to get the teacher to think carefully about inferences and decisions. "Tell me what you mean by that" or "Can you say a little more about that?" are examples. So is "What would you accept as evidence that. . . ."

In many instances, if we do not clarify, miscommunication is the result. Occasionally someone will say, "You're absolutely right! Moreover, . . ." And then the person proceeds to say the exact opposite of what you thought you said. Of course, that could be a conscious strategy or a case of not listening at all, but a clarifying question avoids unintentional misunderstandings.

An example of paraphrasing and asking clarifying questions took place in a high school where the principal gave the faculty an administrator appraisal form to fill out anonymously. After analyzing the compiled responses, the principal said in a faculty meeting, "What you seem to be telling me in this survey is that I'm not as accessible as you would like." Several teachers said, almost in unison, "Could you tell us what 'being accessible' would look like?" To which the principal replied: "Well, I'd keep my door open more and welcome 'drop-in' chats. And if you stopped me in the hall and asked a question, I'd try to answer it briefly instead of pointing out that I was on my way to a meeting."

Having announced and clarified his intentions in public, he was destined to become "Mr. Accessible" in the next few months. Of course he had some help from wags on the faculty who could not resist asking, "Are you feeling accessible?"

Several points can be made with this example: (1) the paraphrase translated a statistic into flesh-and-blood behavior, (2) the clarifying question checked the perceptions of the subject and his observers, and (3) the public announcement of a resolution to change virtually ensured success. The same process takes place in the feedback conference. Note that the principal had objective data, analyzed and interpreted the data, made a decision, made use of paraphrasing and clarifying questions, and received verbal support in his resolve to change. These are exactly the steps we should follow in helping teachers improve their teaching.

GIVE SPECIFIC PRAISE FOR TEACHER PERFORMANCE AND GROWTH (TECHNIQUE 32)

To say "That was a nice lesson" is not specific praise. Saying "That was an excellent answer you gave to Billy" or "Removing Fred from the group was an effective way to handle the problem" makes the approval explicit. It is especially important to note positive instances where the teacher has shown growth toward an avowed goal.

There is some possibility that an observer will reinforce more than was bargained for. A workshop leader received this comment from a participant on the post-workshop evaluation: "Stopping the tape recording to explain what was happening was really helpful." So the leader stopped the tape about 20 times during their next workshop, until someone sent this note: "Why don't you let the tape play long enough for us to hear what's going on?"

Again, an elderly lady who had never eaten apple pie remarked that when she was a girl, she turned down her first opportunity to do so and gained considerable attention: "Imagine that! Carrie doesn't eat apple pie." The attention was such that in subsequent situations, she felt compelled to continue her refusal, although she confessed, "I always thought I might have liked it."

Yet in our experience, the possibility of too little reinforcement for teachers is much more likely than too much. Teaching often seems a thankless task to those who toil in the schools of our nation. They seldom lack critics, however.

AVOID GIVING DIRECT ADVICE (TECHNIQUE 33)

This does not say never give direct advice, just wait a while. Let teachers analyze and interpret. Often the decisions they reach will be very similar to yours. For most teachers, having their ideas for change reinforced by someone they respect is more likely to produce results than having to carry out someone else's idea. On the other hand, there are times when it is better to say what we think rather than let indirectness become manipulative.

Some people are naturally compliant, submissive, obedient; perhaps they enjoy being told what to do. Nevertheless, our experience with teachers indicates that most of them prefer to feel responsible for their own actions. People who choose teaching as a career expect to be in charge of their classes; they expect to make professional decisions about goals, subject matter, materials, methodology, evaluation, and other aspects of the educational process.

The line between "guided discovery" and "manipulation" is a fine one. The observer must decide when "Here's the way it looks to me" is preferable to making the teacher feel that guessing games are being played.

PROVIDE VERBAL SUPPORT (TECHNIQUE 34)

The emphasis of the observer is on helping the teacher identify professional goals relating to classroom performance, then obtaining valid feedback to assist in reaching those goals. It is often difficult for teachers to separate personal goals from professional goals, and it is especially difficult to separate emotional problems from professional ones. Many of the problems administrators identify as deterrents to instructional improvement by their teachers have their basis in personal aspects of the teacher's life—for example, apathy, lack of organization, or emotional instability in the classroom.

It would be convenient if we could exclude personal problems from a discussion of techniques to use in conducting conferences, but they often enter the discussion despite all efforts to stay on a professional level. Most observers have had the experience of a teacher crying at some point in a conference. Analyzing behavior is an intensely personal process that often defies a scientific or cold-blooded approach.

Hence, we need ways of dealing with these situations as they arise. It does not seem reasonable for an observer to be in tears along with the teacher, yet some expression of sympathy or empathy is in order. If the problems seem to be medical or psychiatric, the course of action is clear: seek help by referring the teacher to an appropriate specialist. Ordinary teacher observers and school administrators are not competent to make medical diagnoses ("He's an alcoholic" or "She's mentally ill"), and it is definitely not advisable for them to attempt psychiatric therapy or psychological counseling without the necessary special training and experience. Even medical school teachers and their observers (about teaching) shy away from diagnosing outside their specialty.

On the other hand, if the problem does not seem to require specialized, professional, medical, or psychiatric treatment, a sympathetic listener can often help a person work through a problem. In a previous edition, we quoted a university student: "You're the first one around here who has helped me!" This student had sought aid from several advisers in solving a personal problem. One faculty member took the time to listen to the particulars, then said, "It seems to me you've identified several possible alternatives. You could drop out of school and work full-time for a while, or you could take a reduced load and work part-time; and you also need to decide whether to get married now or wait." With his own alternatives outlined, the student said, "I see now what I need to do. Thank you." (He did not share his decision with the professor.)

Client-centered counseling doesn't always work out as quickly or as well, but for a number of reasons it may be an appropriate strategy for consultation with a teacher. The observer does not necessarily know more about teaching biology, kindergarten, French, or physics than the teacher; is probably not aware of as many factors in this particular classroom situation as the teacher; does not expect to spend the rest of the term, year, or career in this teacher's classroom; and will probably rely on the teacher to do most of the follow-up decisions. It is within the domain of the observer to consider what the teacher says about personal problems in the light of how they pertain to performance in the classroom.

The level of trust the two people have established is a major variable in how helpful an observer can be to a teacher with a personal problem that may be interfering with classroom effectiveness. Several factors influence trust building. We tend to trust those who trust us. We tend to trust those whose competence we respect. One way to build a teacher's confidence in our competence as observers is to demonstrate our ability to provide useful feedback and to conduct productive conferences.

In some cases, an observer needs to take full charge of the dealings with certain teachers: selecting what kinds of data will be collected and then analyzing and interpreting that information, drawing conclusions about which goals are being met and which are not, and deciding what needs to be done in the future. At the other extreme, an observer may encourage some teachers to set their own goals, select appropriate information to use in assessing the achievement of those goals, and make decisions about future efforts. As pedagogical strategies, these approaches are either didactic or heuristic. How much structure observers provide for a conference will depend on their estimate of what kind of atmosphere will provide maximum potential for the growth of a particular teacher. We have found that when teachers are given a choice of observers some choose one they know to be quite direct whereas others prefer one who tends to be indirect. Teachers who prefer the direct approach may say, "I know where she stands" or "He tells it like it is" or "I'm tired of people 'bouncing everything off the wall.' " Those who like an indirect style may say, "I feel more comfortable with Mary; she doesn't act like she has all the answers" or "Fred helps me do my own thinking and treats me like a colleague" or "I've had enough of the 'hardsell' approach."

The classroom observer is often cast in a double role: as a colleague helping to improve instruction and as an evaluator. It is sometimes awkward to deal with these two functions simultaneously. For example, to say "I'll devote the first few visits to helping you improve and save the evaluating until later" does not reassure the teacher, nor can the observer forget what has been seen. With teachers who are doing reasonably well, this need not be a problem: "I'm expecting to write a favorable evaluation anyway, so let's concentrate on some areas you'd like to work on" is one approach. Teachers on the borderline deserve to be informed of this fact, but the conference can still be positive and productive. Fair dismissal procedures also require that teachers be given early notice of deficiencies and assistance in attempting to overcome them.

In a few cases, the teacher may be in an "intensive evaluation" situation. (Some school districts encourage such a teacher to have an attorney or teacher's organization representative in attendance at any conferences with an evaluator.) Obviously, the tone of the conference will be different in the intensive case. Yet observers do not have to turn from Jekyll into Hyde. A skillful parent serves as both counselor and disciplinarian and can do so in a consistent style. Observers, too, should be able to fulfill both aspects of their role skillfully.

Dissonance theory provides a rationale for changing teachers' classroom behavior through observational feedback and teacher-centered conferences. The writings of Leon Festinger, Fritz Heider, and others supply powerful insights into the dynamics of what Robert Burns expressed in poetic form as the gift of seeing ourselves as others see us.[4] We each have an externally perceived self and an internally perceived self. We develop discomfort when we become aware of a discrepancy between what we believe to be "the real me" and what "the perceived me" seems to be doing in the eyes of others or in the information collected through systematic observation. For example, a teacher who believes that teachers should smile a lot feels that he smiles a lot; if he views videotapes of himself that show no smiles, he has dissonance. This dissonance can be reduced in several ways, such as

1. "The videotape is wrong."
2. "It was a bad day, I was nervous."
3. "It isn't really that important to smile so often."

In other words, he can (1) deny the information, (2) reduce the importance of the information, or (3) reduce the importance of the behavior. Another possibility is that he can resolve to make the perceived self more like the "real" or ideal self. That requires changing his behavior.

The goal of supervision for instructional improvement is to get teachers to change their behavior in ways that both they and their supervisors regard as desirable. In some cases only the observer (and not the teacher) sees a suggested change as desirable. Now the observer experiences dissonance. Among the options for reducing this dissonance are the following:

1. "You'll do it my way, or I'll send you to Siberia."
2. "Let's look at some more data about what is happening."
3. "Let's work on something you are concerned about."

In other words, the observer may (1) reduce dissonance by forcing compliance from the teacher, or (2) and (3) attempt to achieve consonance through increased understanding of what is on the teacher's mind.

There are times when it is necessary to force teacher compliance to the observer's demand—for example, when laws or official school policies are at stake. Most problems that observers and teachers work on are not that clear-cut. They concern ways of dealing with students; choosing strategies for teaching certain concepts, skills, or facts; finding alternative ways of managing the many variables in teaching; selecting elements of teaching style that can be modified by the teacher through the use of feedback, practice, and experimentation. It is unlikely that a teacher can eliminate a fundamental personality characteristic, such as dominance, emotional stability, or empathy. Nevertheless, a teacher can learn to use strategies that reduce the tendency to dominate or can develop classroom management techniques that reduce emotional stress. Some outward and visible signs of empathy can be observed, practiced, and incorporated into a teacher's repertoire without resorting to psychiatric therapy or profound religious conversion. Most people who choose teaching as a career have basic qualities that are compatible with the requirements of the job; systematic feedback can inform and convince those who do not.

ACKNOWLEDGE AND USE WHAT THE PERSON IS FEELING (TECHNIQUE 35)

Carl Rogers reminds us that when a child attempts to do something difficult and says, "I can't," a typical parental response is, "Of course you can!"[5] The response is intended to be positive, but it denies feelings. It might not hurt to say, "It is difficult, isn't it, but you'll get it."

Researchers have found that feelings are seldom acknowledged verbally in the classroom.[6] The occurrence in conferences is less well documented, but we suspect that it is unduly limited. When the goal is to change behavior, affective aspects cannot be ignored. The emotions that can be expressed in a conference range from rage to despair, from exhilaration to depression. Clinical observers should not ignore the significant emotional content of what teachers are saying any more than they would ignore important cognitive statements.

One way to respond is to describe what you are observing: "You appear to be quite angry about that" or "This seems to make you anxious." Don't be surprised if the teacher's response is "Oh, no, I'm not really angry" or "Who's anxious? I'm not anxious." We tend to deny feelings, as if it were bad to have them, especially in a teaching situation. A psychologist once remarked, "I always knew when my mother was angry at me because she showed it immediately, and I could take that; but my father would wait to 'have a talk with me later,' and that was an agonizing experience." Expressing feelings can be healthy and helpful. After an especially satisfying performance before a large class of graduate students, the instructor was told by one student, "I enjoyed seeing that you were relishing the experience." That is a good observation to share. Telling a teacher "You appeared to be enjoying the responses you were getting" or "I shared your apprehension when Dickie volunteered" can have a desirable effect on the tone of the discussion.

COUNSELING

For many years we advised observers to avoid taking on a counseling role with teachers. We thought it best for observers to spend what time they had helping teachers improve their instructional efforts rather than attempting to work on marital, financial, or psychological problems. We felt that the "amateur psychiatrist" would do more harm than good. In the case of serious problems, we still feel this way, but we have modified our position somewhat.

The more we work with observers, the more we recognize that it is impossible for them to separate teachers' instructional problems from their personal problems. What is needed is an approach that avoids the pitfalls of inept amateur therapy yet deals honestly with problems expressed by the teacher that have significant impact on classroom performance.

For example, if a teacher says, "I'm spending so much time fighting with my spouse that I just can't get my lessons prepared," the observer might do one of several things:

- threaten to fire the teacher if work does not improve
- offer advice on how to improve a marriage
- concentrate on ways of handling schoolwork at school
- recommend a counselor
- provide nondirective counseling

Any of the above might work, depending on the situation and the nature of the individuals involved. An objective approach consistent with other techniques in this chapter might be the following:

OBSERVER: Here are some of the things you've mentioned that would be desirable. Let's indicate them briefly in one column. Here are some things you have identified about your current situation. Let's put them in another column. Now you can add or subtract from either list, but the essential problem is to ask what it takes to get from here to there.

It is conceivable that a conscientious supervisor might perform all the tasks of planning, observing, and giving feedback (as recorded and coded by reliable means) and still not be regarded as helpful by the teacher. We suspect that when this happens, other personality factors or interpersonal dynamics account for the discrepancy. The data we have on what teachers want from an observer suggest a fairly open and democratic approach for most teachers. Yet we can use open and democratic procedures to communicate content that is quite structured. Self-guided discovery, teacher-guided discovery, and didactic teaching are examples of procedures that lie along this continuum.

Carl Rogers, who pioneered client-centered counseling in the 1940s, argues for "person-centered" approaches in a wide range of human activities.[7] He contrasts our usual notions of power and control with another view of influence and impact.

Some Notes on Leadership: Two Extremes

Influence and Impact	*Power and Control*
Giving autonomy to persons and groups	Making decisions
Freeing people to "do their thing"	Giving orders
Expressing own ideas and feelings as one aspect of the group data	Directing subordinates' behavior
Facilitating learning	Keeping own ideas and feelings "close to the vest"
Stimulating independence in thought and action	Exercising authority over people and organizations
Delegating, giving full responsibility	Coercing when necessary
Offering feedback and receiving it	Teaching, instructing, advising
Encouraging and relying on self-evaluation	Evaluating others
Finding rewards in the achievements of others	Being rewarded by own achievements

For most teachers, influence and impact are needed from observers, not power and control.

MANAGEMENT

Douglas McGregor's Human Side of Enterprise suggests two approaches to management, theory X and theory Y.[8] They are not opposite poles on a continuum but two different views about work—including teaching and observing. Theory X applies to traditional management and the assumptions underlying it. Theory Y is based on assumptions derived from research in the social sciences.

Three basic assumptions of theory X are:

1. The average human being has an inherent dislike of work and will avoid it if possible.
2. Because of this human dislike of work, most people must be coerced, directed, and threatened with punishment to get them to put forth adequate effort toward the achievement of organizational objectives.
3. The average human being prefers to be directed, wishes to avoid responsibility, has relatively little ambition and wants security above all.

McGregor indicates that the "carrot and the stick" theory of motivation fits reasonably well with theory X. External rewards and punishments are the motivators of workers. The consequent direction and control does not recognize intrinsic human motivation.

Theory Y is more humanistic and is based on six assumptions:

1. The expenditure of physical and mental effort in work is as natural as play or rest.
2. External controls and the threat of punishment are not the only means for bringing about effort toward organizational objectives. Human beings will exercise self-direction and self-control in the service of objectives to which they are committed.
3. Commitment to objectives is a function of the rewards associated with their achievement.
4. The average human being learns, under proper conditions, not only to accept but also to seek responsibility.
5. The capacity to exercise a relatively high degree of imagination, ingenuity, and creativity in the solution of organizational problems is widely, not narrowly, distributed in the population.
6. Under the conditions of modern industrial life, the intellectual potentialities of the average human being are only partially utilized.

McGregor saw these assumptions leading to superior-subordinate relationships in which the subordinate would have greater influence over the activities in his or her own work and also have influence on the superior's actions. Through participatory management, greater creativity and productivity are expected, and also a greater sense of personal accomplishment and satisfaction by the workers. Chris Argyris, Warren Bennis, and Rensis Likert cite evidence that a participatory system of management can be more effective than traditional management.[9]

Likert's studies showed that high production can be achieved by people- rather than production-oriented managers. Moreover, these high-production managers were willing to delegate; to allow subordinates to participate in decisions; to be relatively nonpunitive; and to use open, two-way communication patterns. High morale and effective planning were also characteristic of these "person-centered" managers. The results may be applied to the supervisory relationship in education as well as to industry.

NOTES

1. Edmund Amidon and Ned Flanders, "Interaction Analysis as a Feedback System," in *Interaction Analysis: Theory, Research, and Application*, ed. Edmund Amidon and John Hough (Reading, MA: Addison-Wesley, 1967), pp. 122–24; Arthur Blumberg, *Supervisors and Teachers: A Private Cold War* (Berkeley, CA: McCutchan, 1974).
2. Robert I. Spaulding, "A Coping Analysis Schedule for Educational Settings (CASES)," in *Mirrors for Behavior*, ed. Anita Simon and E. Gil Boyer (Philadelphia: Research for Better Schools, 1967).
3. Everett L. Shostrom, *Man, the Manipulator* (Nashville, TN: Abingdon, 1967).
4. Leon Festinger, *A Theory of Cognitive Dissonance* (Stanford, CA: Stanford University Press, 1968); Fritz Heider, *The Psychology of Interpersonal Relations* (New York: Wiley, 1958).
5. Carl R. Rogers, personal communication, September 1964.
6. Amidon and Hough, *Interaction Analysis*, p. 137.
7. Carl R. Rogers, *Carl Rogers on Personal Power* (New York: Delacorte, 1977), pp. 91–92.
8. Douglas McGregor, *The Human Side of Enterprise* (New York: McGraw-Hill, 1960).
9. Chris Argyris, *Management and Organizational Development* (New York: McGraw-Hill, 1971), and *On Organizations of the Future* (Beverly Hills: Sage, 1973); Warren G. Bennis, *Organizational Development: Its Nature, Origin and Prospects* (Reading, MA: Addison-Wesley, 1967); R. Likert, *New Patterns of Management* (New York: McGraw-Hill, 1961), and *The Human Organization* (New York: McGraw-Hill, 1967).

Unit IV Exercises

MULTIPLE-CHOICE ITEMS

Answers are on page 255.

1. If one attributes the data-collection techniques of unit III to behavioral psychologists such as B. F. Skinner, the feedback techniques of unit IV should be attributed to
   a. J. B. Watson.
   b. Sigmund Freud.
   c. Carl Rogers.
   d. Leon Festinger.
   e. David Ausubel.
2. From the following, choose the *best* remark for getting the conference down to business:
   a. How do you feel?
   b. How's your family?
   c. You had a good lesson.
   d. Let's take a look at the data I recorded.
   e. You need to be stricter.
3. If a supervisor suspects that a teacher is an alcoholic or is mentally ill, it would be best to
   a. confront.
   b. refer.
   c. prescribe.
   d. counsel.
   e. ignore.

4. Major steps in the feedback process are
   a. provide data.
   b. analyze data.
   c. interpret what is happening.
   d. make decisions on future actions.
   e. All the above are correct.
5. When a teacher asks a supervisor, "What would *you* do?" the supervisor should
   a. refuse to answer.
   b. describe exactly what to do.
   c. give several alternatives.
   d. encourage the teacher to think of several alternatives.
   e. say, "What would *you* do?"
6. Which of the following fit Carl Rogers's notions of influence and impact (as opposed to power and control)?
   a. Having teachers make their own tape recordings of lessons.
   b. Having teachers turn in lesson plans.
   c. Filing evaluations that are not seen by the teacher.
   d. Giving merit pay.
   e. Asking teachers for feedback about supervisory conferences.
7. A behavior that is either direct or indirect is
   a. lecturing.
   b. giving directions.
   c. giving praise.
   d. asking questions.
   e. criticizing.
8. Two behaviors from Spaulding's list that would describe the authors' ideal conference are
   a. respond to internal stimuli.
   b. control.
   c. transact.
   d. seek help.
   e. share.

PROBLEMS

The following problems do not have single correct answers. Answers are on pages 256–257. Your answers may differ from these, yet be as good or better.

1. Think of a teacher you have known who had a definite problem with classroom management (student discipline). Then (a) list several alternatives this teacher might try. Next (b) write a sentence that you would use in suggesting these alternatives to the teacher.
2. Identify a teaching strategy that is not in the list on page 157—for exam-

ple, a field trip or committee meetings—and devise a "self-observation" plan a teacher could use to collect data about the lesson.

3. Consider the categories suggested by Spaulding (p. 160). Put them in the first column of a three-column list. In the second column, suggest (with a brief phrase) a common student behavior in the classroom that fits each category. In the third column, identify teacher behaviors in conferences with supervisors that would fit each category. For example:

Spaulding's list	Student Behavior (classroom)	Teacher behavior (conference)
•		
•	•	•
•	•	•
•		
Respond to external stimuli	Distracted by another student sharpening pencil	Interrupting conference to deal with a student in the hall
•		
•	•	
•	•	•
		•

Other Applications of Clinical Supervision Techniques

OVERVIEW

The other units have concentrated on *what* are the techniques of classroom observation and conferences with teachers, *who* uses them and *how* they are used. This unit will expand *why* they are used, not just for teacher personal growth, administrator evaluation, but also in larger contexts, such as implementing a new curriculum or introducing a new approach to teaching.

OBJECTIVES

The purpose of this unit is to help you develop understanding of

The relationship between processes of instructional supervision and teacher evaluation

Some aspects of analyzing teaching that can be applied aside from supervision

Several examples of instructional programs that have used supervision techniques

Some different roles that are evolving for teachers and administrators

The nature of the process we call "peer consultation"

chapter **11**

Clinical Supervision
and Teacher Evaluation

The easiest way to identify specific behaviors is by observing them. Final scores, whether in sports or tests, indicate whether you have a winner or loser, but only observation can yield the information necessary to change a loser to a winner. To be useful, observation must be valid, objective, and recorded. A recorded observation enables observer and performer to "play back" the performance so that salient cause-effect relationships can be identified.

Madeline Hunter

In chapter 1 there is a reference to the "sting" of evaluation. A decade and a half after that sentence was first published (in 1980), the evaluation of teachers still stings. During the intervening years, a few developments have affected the relationship between our techniques of clinical supervision (which concentrate on teacher growth and development) and the legal accountability requirements for evaluating teachers.

A study in Canada by Keith Acheson[1] described programs in each of the four western provinces that incorporate collegial observers as well as evaluative personnel in staff development. Some of these programs separate summative evaluation from formative or developmental activities. We endorse this separation; however, in most situations, those who are charged with responsibilities that call for clinical supervision techniques are also required to make summative evaluations of some kind. Therefore, we shall address both concerns simultaneously in this chapter.

Another historical tendency with respect to the preservice preparation, inservice development, and periodic evaluation of teachers was brought home to us by a colleague from Germany, who has followed the development of microteaching at Stanford University in the early 1960s, the experimentation with minicourses at the Far West Laboratory in the late 1960s, emphasis on competency-based education for teachers as well as for students in the 1970s, the shift from quantitative to qualitative research in the 1980s, and the move toward collaborative school organizations in the 1990s. In all these endeavors, an objective observer can provide perceptions that are informative and useful for instructors and leaders who are caught up in their own subjective interpretations of day-to-day activities, just as an objective observer from another country can see the forest more clearly than those who are busy with the trees. What we see (with the help of our friend) is an encouraging trend toward liberating teachers from the isolation and powerlessness they have often felt. Enlightened professional development techniques and activities have given teachers the opportunity to analyze and improve what they do.

If these kinds of insights can be provided by observers who also evaluate (that is, retain, promote, renew, dismiss, reprimand, grant tenure, reward, punish), then let us proceed. If they are better supplied by peers, colleagues, and collaborators, then let us continue to experiment, test, and improve those kinds of arrangements. In the meantime we shall continue to include the cycle of planning, observing, and giving feedback from clinical supervision within the cycle of summative evaluation. We shall also extend our view of that cycle to include the larger concerns of setting, situation, structure, and style. Chapter 12 will consider some variations on the evaluator-supervisor mode of analyzing teaching and will also look at some alternative roles that observer/analysts may play.

THE TENSION BETWEEN ACCOUNTABILITY AND PROFESSIONAL GROWTH

In everyday language, evaluation, supervision, and other functions that use analysis of teaching sound pretty much the same. There are important differences, however, when we consider who will do it and why. An evaluator can either value or devalue something. A supervisor can either oversee, inspect, and look for what is wrong, or have "super vision" to perceive what will make things better or even better. Analysis of what teachers do is essential to supervision. It is also essential to teacher evaluation, peer coaching, collegial observation, and peer consultation.

There are several roles developing in education that fit the general title, instructional leaders. Those who traditionally have been called supervisors, especially clinical supervisors as we have defined them, certainly qualify. Those who evaluate teachers also deserve the title; although as we have already pointed out, evaluation introduces a sting to supervision. Stated more strongly, it is the fly in the ointment. Nonetheless, the need for accountability coexists with the need for professional growth in teaching.

In this chapter and the next, we shall look at how clinical supervision relates to these other roles, and we shall advocate using the techniques that are described in units II, III, and IV in performing the roles. Goal setting, planning for observation, observation, and feedback are functions of all the roles.

Our solution has been to place the planning, observation, and feedback in an expanded schema that includes district standards (or criteria of effective teaching), job descriptions (consideration of the unique situation), goal setting, formal evaluation (report writing), programs of assistance for teachers with serious deficiencies, and dismissal—which requires consideration of contracts, grievances, arbitration, hearings, litigation. Before describing this schema, we need to address two issues that arise from combining the accountability requirements of teacher evaluation with the professional growth goals of clinical supervision.

The Threat of Evaluation

We have mentioned the "sting" of evaluation. There are a number of ways of dealing with it. One is to emphasize it. Those of us old enough to remember the use of iodine as first aid for cuts also recall parents who believed medicines that didn't sting, taste bitter, or cause gagging couldn't be effective. One can take the iodine approach to evaluating teaching. Many evaluators believe that fear is an effective motivator for teachers.

Another way to deal with the sting is to remove it. We have worked with groups of teachers who observe in one another's classrooms and give only positive feedback. Unconditional positive regard is something we have all been seeking since our mothers pushed us out of the nest. Knowing that someone has such regard for us can also be a powerful motivator.

An alternative is to use both of the above sources of motivation in an intermittent reinforcement menu. This must be what appeals to gamblers in casinos as well as to teachers in classrooms.

There is abundant evidence from our research and that of our colleagues, students, and others that the threat of evaluation can destroy the potential of clinical supervision techniques to foster teacher self-analysis, reflection, and growth. Nevertheless, we shall no doubt have to cope with both aspects of the plan-observe-feedback cycle simultaneously in the foreseeable future.

Our best solution, for the present, is to have the observations of the evaluator-supervisor of preservice or in-service teachers augmented by those of peers (other teachers whose data will not be used for judgmental, threatening purposes). The techniques both kinds of observers can use are those described in the following chapters. The difference lies in their intended outcomes and the degree of trust the observed teacher is willing to bestow.

Consistency of Evaluation with Components of Clinical Supervision

As we have noted in chapter 1, clinical supervision has three major components that are repeated several times during a year. A trained observer (1) meets with the teacher and plans for the next observation; (2) observes a lesson systematically (and non-judgmentally) and records information related to the objectives set during the planning conference; and (3) meets with the teacher to (a) analyze (together) the data recorded by the observer, (b) interpret the meaning of this information from the teacher's perspective, and (c) reach decisions about the next steps.

Laws concerned with teacher evaluation often require a goal-setting conference, "multiple" observations (which means "two" to many evaluators), and a postevaluation interview or conference.

Some authorities, believing it is sufficient for observers merely to observe and then confer with teachers, advocate elimination of the planning conference. Our view of what can be accomplished by expert observation of teaching implies a need for planning the observation with the teacher. The logic goes like this: The goal of observation is feedback-information that is useful, relevant, objective, accurate, understandable. The goal of feedback is analysis, interpretation, and decision making by the teacher, with the assistance of the observer. If these goals are to be reached, the teacher and the observer need to plan the observation together.

The planning (when it is in conjunction with formal evaluation) needs to be consistent with official standards or criteria, and for in-service teachers it should be compatible with the job description. The observation, recording of data, and feedback need to be in concert with the planning. If this is the case, and there are several observations, the evaluator should be able to write a reasonable and just summative report at the conclusion of several clinical supervision cycles.

CLINICAL SUPERVISION AND TEACHER EVALUATION

Although the primary purpose of clinical supervision is to help teachers develop and improve through cooperative planning, observation, and feedback, it is often a part of a larger system that has as its purpose decisions about tenure, promotion, retention, and dismissal. In this section we describe the additional components we feel are needed to build a system of teacher evaluation that is consistent with the tenets of clinical supervision. These components are district standards, job descriptions, performance goals, formal evaluations, plans of assistance, postevaluation conferences, and postdismissal activities. Figure 11.1 is a graphic representation of how these are all related.

District Standards

The teacher needs to be aware of the criteria that will be used to evaluate performance. These include specific criteria for a given teacher in a particular situation and also general criteria or standards that are applied to all teachers in a district. These general criteria are best developed by a committee of teachers, administrators, and others before being adopted by the school board as official policy and before copies are placed in the hands of all teachers.

The total number of standards needs to be kept under control. One way to accomplish this is to identify 15 to 20 general standards, each with three to five "indicators" stated in more explicit, behavioral terms.

An Example.   One example of district standards that was developed by this process (over a period of several years) is included on the following pages.[2] Note that the committee organized their standards around a model of what a competent teacher

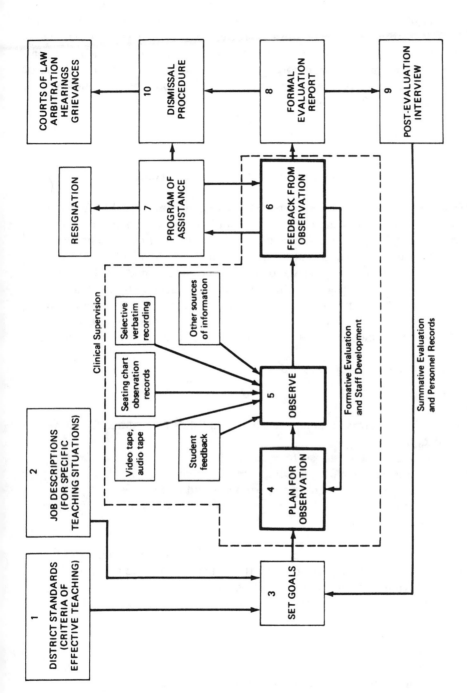

FIGURE 11.1 The teacher evaluation process. (Note that boxes 4, 5, and 6 refer to Figure 1.5.)

SOURCE: Adapted from Keith A. Acheson, *Techniques in the Evaluation of Teachers* (Salem, OR: Confederation of Oregon School Administrators, 1982).

should do before teaching, during teaching, and after teaching. The logic of the sequence is appealing: knowing about students, setting objectives relative to that knowledge, planning instruction based on those objectives, and conducting instruction that reflects the plans. Knowledge of subject matter and classroom management are components of teaching that will be important to any group of educators. Evaluation of students and communication with peers and parents are some of the competencies that are demonstrated after teaching or outside the classroom setting.

District Standards of Competent Performance

A standard is composed of three parts: (1) a statement which establishes a general behavior, (2) a list of indicators which specify how that behavior will be identified, and (3) a principal's judgment as to the level of competent performance. The statement and indicators are listed for each standard. The level of expected performance of these standards will be determined by the professional judgment of the principal. The judgment is influenced by the teacher's assignment, class size, experience, and available resources. To determine if the requirements of the standard have been met, the statement of general teacher behavior, all of the indicators, and the performance level must be considered.

Section I—Instructional Development

Area: Diagnosing

Standard 1   The competent teacher establishes procedures for gathering data by
a. completing the diagnosis for each student
b. using the diagnostic tools which are pertinent to the teacher's goals
c. using a variety of diagnostic instruments and techniques
d. requesting assistance from others, when needed, for more comprehensive diagnosis

Standard 2   The competent teacher interprets diagnostic data to identify the needs and concerns of both the individual and the group by
a. identifying the achievement level of each student
b. explaining the significance of the achievement level diagnosed

Area: Prescribing

Standard 3   The competent teacher utilizes diagnostic data to establish instructional objectives and relates these to individual needs by
a. writing instructional objectives

b. preparing objectives that show the data gathered in diagnosis are utilized

c. preparing objectives in terms of student performance

d. preparing objectives that are measurable

e. preparing both short- and long-term objectives for any assigned class

Standard 4   The competent teacher plans lessons to meet individual and group needs by

a. planning lessons that are consistent with the objectives

b. planning lessons that include appropriate activities which meet individual and group needs

c. planning to use appropriate resource materials related to instructional objectives

d. planning alternatives to meet the needs of individual students

e. accepting and using student feedback in planning instruction

Area: Facilitating

Standard 5   The competent teacher utilizes knowledge of subject matter by

a. using words and content appropriate to the subject area and students' abilities

b. using available media effectively and efficiently

c. requesting and using materials and facilities based on instructional objectives

d. knowing and utilizing community agencies, groups, and individuals to further the educational program

Standard 6   The competent teacher uses effective classroom management techniques by

a. showing respect for students

b. providing an atmosphere in which students remain at task

c. exhibiting consistency when dealing with behavior problems

d. exhibiting positive verbal and nonverbal influence on students

Standard 7   The competent teacher applies learning theory by

a. utilizing and building upon students' interests and prior knowledge

b. providing feedback as students progress toward goals

c. allowing for a balance between intake of information and the expression of student ideas

d. providing the individual with activities to develop attitudes, appreciations, and values

District Standards of Competent Performance (*continued*)

Standard 8   The competent teacher uses a variety of instructional techniques appropriate to the students' needs by
a. giving directions in a clear, concise manner
b. phrasing questions so students may respond appropriately
c. using strategies which involve students in higher levels of thinking
d. pacing the activities within a lesson according to the needs of students

Area: Student Performance Evaluation

Standard 9   The competent teacher establishes procedures for assessing student performance by
a. selecting means of evaluation which are appropriate to the objectives
b. planning measurement procedures for specific purposes
c. utilizing procedures whereby students receive feedback on their individual performance
d. presenting information that indicates evaluation has taken place for each student

Standard 10   The competent teacher interprets the results of student performance assessment by
a. identifying the reasons why students have or have not met the performance objectives

Standard 11   The competent teacher utilizes the results of student performance assessment by
a. using objective data to arrive at a grade or indicator of student progress to be reported to parents
b. providing feedback that facilitates the student accomplishment of goals
c. planning changes in teaching strategies based on the results of the evaluation

Section II—Professional Development

Area: Communication

Standard 12   The competent teacher communicates effectively with students by
a. listening to and considering student comments and suggestions
b. being open to suggestions about ways in which to present material
c. conveying an attitude that promotes participation in activities

Standard 13   The competent teacher communicates effectively with colleagues and staff by
a. participating in the group decision-making process
b. listening to and considering suggestions from the staff
c. sharing ideas and resources with others

Standard 14   The competent teacher communicates responsibly to the public the significance of the school program by
a. answering parents' inquiries promptly, honestly, and with discretion
b. initiating when necessary communication with parents
c. having available or locating information to relate District philosophy to the community at large

Area: School Relationships

Standard 15   The competent teacher has a consistent and professional attitude toward accomplishment of own school goals by
a. contributing to the decision-making process and abiding by group decisions
b. accepting shared responsibilities in and out of the classroom during the school day
c. maintaining consistency in record keeping as defined by building or District administrative regulations and procedures
d. using adopted courses of study or adjusting teaching objectives to include such adoptions
e. carrying out reasonable requests given by proper authority

Standard 16   The competent teacher has a consistent and professional attitude toward the accomplishment of District and State goals by
a. adhering to and enforcing school law, state board regulations, school board policy, and established administrative procedures
b. adhering to the Employee Conduct and Responsibility requirements as stated in the Board Policy Handbook

District standards serve several purposes. They serve as the reference for contract renewal, promotion, and tenure decisions. They also figure prominently in fair dismissal hearings, arbitration, and litigation about teacher evaluation.

Over the years, our notions have changed about what the criteria of good teaching should be. In the 1950s we looked at the characteristics of a good teacher—personality variables, qualities of character, and the like. In the 1960s attention shifted to what teachers do, or should do, as part of the teaching process. These behaviors were often called "competencies." Since the 1970s we have tended to talk about "teacher effectiveness" in terms of what students are able to do before and after working with a particular teacher.

Teacher evaluation in the past has sometimes made use of several sources of information. Observation by supervisors is one. Another is student ratings of teachers. Systematic observation instruments used by others besides supervisors form another possibility. So does self-evaluation. Gains shown by students, as measured by test scores or other criteria, are another possible source. Scores on standardized teaching tests might be used.

Unfortunately, the most common source of information has been the evaluator's subjective feelings, which are influenced by the teacher's personality, style, philosophy (in relation to the evaluator's), staff relations, social patterns, and other factors, all of which may be important but are not central to teaching effectiveness.

Job Descriptions

Related to district standards are job descriptions. They should contain some of the same language and be consistent with the standards. In addition, they explicate the duties and responsibilities of the teacher. The district standards would be the basis for judging incompetent performance, whereas the job description would be the basis for judging neglect of duty.

Once a district has a set of standards (like the ones we have looked at), there are several possibilities for how they can be used in the process of evaluating teachers. The characteristics can be emphasized: "is neat, orderly, cooperative" or "is creative, enthusiastic, energetic." Using personal traits as the basis for summative evaluations has a long tradition but has not been very effective in either encouraging teachers to change or dismissing those who don't.

Another possibility is to use the processes as absolute standards: "reinforces positive behavior immediately and explicitly" or "does not plan lessons to meet individual needs." Beginning teachers and teachers who are insecure may welcome the reassurance of an explicit set of expectations. It is also possible that the most spectacular teachers any of us have ever known don't give a hoot about such expectations.

A third possible use of official standards is to emphasize student outcomes: "made, on the average, a gain of one year in reading comprehension." Most teachers are apprehensive about too much emphasis being placed on what their pupils accomplish: "But you gave me a bunch of turkeys this year." As the coach of a professional football team said in turning down an attractive college job, "I don't want my career to depend on what a bunch of adolescents do on a Saturday afternoon."

A fourth possibility is to borrow an idea from business and industry and have "job targets" as an aspect of "management by objectives." To do this well, one needs explicit and irrefutable descriptions of the essential elements of a particular job.

A fifth possibility—the one we advocate—is to have a set of standards, which apply to all teachers, and job descriptions that describe unique duties and responsibilities that apply to teachers with specific assignments in specialized areas of the school program. Some examples of teachers with specialized assignments are counselors, special education teachers, and resource center coordinators.

The following job description illustrates an assignment in which performance would be assessed on the basis of the primary accountabilities in addition to the general standards for all teachers.[3]

Position Description

Position: Teacher

Reports to: Principal (or His/Her Designee)

Position Purpose:

Implements, supervises, and maintains a high quality learning environment for students within the specific curriculum and standards of the District.

Nature and Scope:

The teacher is a professional with the responsibility for implementing a curriculum. Inherent in this responsibility is the requirement of related academic knowledge, technical skills, and professional attitudes and judgments.

The teacher must have the ability to diagnose the needs of learners and to evaluate their performance. The teacher must also be able to prescribe learning activities appropriate to student needs and to constructively evaluate these activities. The teacher effects an optimum learning climate through appropriate and maximum use of all resources available and through the use of effective instructional and classroom management techniques.

In addition to the requirement of technical competence, the teacher maintains an attitude and conduct which is consistent with the District policy of professional conduct. The teacher follows building and District procedural guidelines and policy.

Primary Accountabilities:

1. Identifies the needs of students through diagnostic procedures and relates instructional objectives to these needs. Plans, prepares, and executes appropriate lessons, utilizing appropriate resource materials and activities.
2. Maintains student records as required by the school.
3. Communicates with parents, students, and other professional staff regarding student progress (behavioral and academic).
4. Follows a curriculum that is prescribed by state, district, or building.
5. Assures students of learning opportunities within a classroom environment that facilitates learning.
6. Meets the District's Standards of Competent Performance at all times.
7. Follows district and school policies, procedures, rules, regulations, and guidelines and the provisions of the contract.

The standards and job descriptions provide guidelines for teachers to refer to in setting annual goals for self-improvement, staff development, and professional advancement. The concerns teachers can translate into goals or targets can come from a variety of sources. In the past, leaders who evaluated teaching have used various criteria of teaching performance—traits, competencies, and effectiveness: that is, what kinds of people teachers are, what they can do, and what they accomplish. Here we will look also at the situation within which they teach, in particular the organizational nature of the school. Other factors that need to be recognized are the social system within and around the school; the legal, governmental, and political conditions; the economy within which the school exists; and the influential culture(s) of the community referred to as parts of the "setting."

Goals can serve two kinds of needs—growth needs and deficiency needs. Teachers with deficiency needs (as identified by evaluations with respect to district standards or job descriptions) must attend to these before concentrating on goals that are strictly for personal growth. Although building on strengths is a desirable activity, it should not prevent a teacher from eliminating undesirable practices or cultivating desirable ones that have hitherto been missing.

Performance Goals

To evaluate a teacher on the basis of the complete list of district standards would be a large undertaking if it were to be done objectively. An alternative is to concentrate on a few items that are of concern to the teacher (or the observer) and agree on these as goals for a given year. The formal evaluation then is based on the progress that was made toward accomplishing the goals. If a teacher develops a serious problem in mid-year, the goals should be modified to address the problem.

Teachers have a tendency to look for "safe" goals when they know they will be evaluated on the basis of them. The observer needs some skill at negotiating (or insisting on) goals that are important. Skill is also required in stating goals clearly. Here are some questions that can be asked about a goal statement:

- Is the called-for behavior (a) observable, (b) measurable, (c) describable?
- Is it clear what the criterion level will be? (How much is enough?)
- Under what conditions will the behavior take place?
- Is it related to the district standards or job description?
- Is it important?
- What resources will be required?
- How will the teacher proceed to reach the goal?

Figure 11.2 shows a form used in a school district to record the goals of educators (teachers, administrators, and others) for a given year.

Eugene Public Schools
School District No. 4J, Lane County
Eugene, Oregon

EDUCATOR GOAL PLAN

Educator's Name_____

Assignment _____ Year _____ Building _____

I. **GOAL STATEMENT**

List the activities/behaviors you have planned to accomplish this goal.

II. **MONITORING**
List the planned activities and/or procedures for measuring goal accomplishment.

Approved by _____(Supervisor's Signature) Date _____

III. **ANALYZING AND ASSESSING**
Educator: Comment on the degree to which this goal was accomplished and list
the data used to support your judgment.

Educator's Signature _____Date _____

Supervisor: Comment on the degree to which this goal was accomplished.

Supervisor's Signature _____ Date _____

1984 - Form EG-3 (One sheet should be used for each goal developed by/for
the educator.)

FIGURE 11.2 Educator goal plan.

SOURCE: Eugene Public Schools, School District 4J, Lane County, Eugene,
OR, 1984.

Formal Evaluations

Sometimes teachers are not very good at writing clear goal statements, and some administrators are not very good at writing formal evaluations. The written evaluations tend to be euphemistic and not explicit. When a dismissal occurs and the teacher has had 10 years of these vague kinds of evaluation, it is difficult to make the case.

If one purpose for the formal evaluation is to assist the teacher's growth in instructional effectiveness, then vague generalities in the report are not very helpful. Crisply stated goals and explicit yearly evaluations could be computer-stored and accessed as a data base for making decisions about in-service staff development.

Plans of Assistance

"Due process" requires that before a tenured teacher is summarily dismissed for lack of competence, there be an effort to help remedy the deficiencies. One way to do this is through an official plan of assistance. In some states this is explicitly required by law. A point of contention in dismissal hearings is often whether a plan of assistance was properly designed and carried out.

When a plan of assistance is called for, often the principal who put the teacher on notice is then expected to design and conduct the remedial program. If there is tension between the principal and the teacher (and there often is), then it is difficult to conduct a truly helpful program. We recommend the formation of a small committee to assume this responsibility. One member should be a neutral (objective) administrator; another can be a person chosen by the teacher to serve as advocate for the teacher. The third person can be someone with special knowledge, expertise, or skill in the area(s) of the teacher's deficiency. In Oregon, the Fair Dismissal Appeals Law requires that tenured teachers who are deficient in complying with district standards are entitled to a program of assistance.

The committee should reach agreement on what the plan of assistance will consist of, how long it will last, and what will be accepted as satisfactory evidence that the deficiency has been remedied. The committee can call on other people and resources to carry out the planned activities.

Postevaluation Conferences

The teacher and observer should meet to discuss the formal evaluation before it is placed in the permanent personnel file. The teacher should have the opportunity to write a rebuttal that will be filed along with the evaluation if there is irreconcilable disagreement. The postevaluation conference is also a good place to begin outlining the next year's goals for most teachers. For a few teachers, this conference will be held to discuss a dismissal notice.

Postdismissal Activities

When the evaluation process results in a dismissal, there are almost always additional activities. These may take many forms: grievances, arbitration, hearings, or even lawsuits. There are several implications for clinical supervision techniques in connection with these occurrences. Consider an observer on the witness stand being cross-examined by the teacher's attorney.

"On what basis were these judgments made?" (systematic observational data recorded in the classroom, chapters 5 through 8)

"Did the teacher receive any feedback from these observations?" (feedback conferences, chapters 9 and 10)

"Was any help provided to the teacher?" (see chapters 9 and 10)

Several problems develop from these relationships. The use of systematic classroom observational data as evidence in a dismissal may tarnish the image of objective data as helpful to a teacher's growth. The remedial, corrective, or negative nature of a plan of assistance may diminish the luster of those same techniques that were used to promote strengths. When observation is regarded as inspection, when data become evidence, and when feedback equals criticism, the trust relationship so vital to good supervision is difficult to establish or restore. One way of dealing with this dilemma is to separate formative (growth) activities from summative (judgmental) evaluation by using colleagues for the former and evaluators for the latter.

We have studied approximately 25 dismissal cases in some depth in connection with preparing expert testimony. Several things become obvious in reading the personnel files and listening to the testimony at these hearings. If the school district administrators do a conscientious job of carrying out all the elements previously described, and if they have documented all the events carefully, they will prevail. If, on the other hand, they have been careless, arbitrary, or capricious, the teacher will win.

CONCLUSION

Clinical supervision is the heart of a good teacher evaluation system. The planning, observation, and feedback cycle should occur several times so that the teacher has an opportunity to grow and improve as well as to be evaluated. Where plans of assistance are required, the clinical cycle is again the key tool, but is used more frequently and with greater intensity.

School administrators tell us that when intensive assistance has been called for, approximately half of the teachers recover, a quarter resign voluntarily, and a quarter are dismissed (and usually appeal the decision). In cases where dismissed teachers have been reinstated by an arbitrator or hearing panel, it is usually because the district has failed to provide due process, such as a satisfactory program of assistance. Some of the records for an unsatisfactory program have been:

- setting an unreasonable number of goals for the teacher
- not providing feedback after observations
- displaying evidence of prejudice or vindictiveness
- not providing sufficient time for the program to have an effect

NOTES

1. Keith A. Acheson, "Teacher Evaluation Policies and Practices in Four Western Provinces and Four Northwest States," report of a study supported by the Canadian Embassy, 1986.
2. Adapted from Beaverton, Oregon, Schools Personnel Handbook.
3. School District 48J, Beaverton, OR.

chapter 12

Analyzing Teaching within Various Roles

Watch the doughnut, not the hole.
From a song

Why would anyone want to analyze teaching? An administrator might do it as part of the evaluation process (chapter 11), to make decisions about job retention, promotion, or salary increases. A teacher might do it for purposes of personal development, remediation, or as a part of intensive assistance if there are serious deficiencies. Colleagues might do it collaboratively as a staff development activity.

An obvious reason for analyzing teaching is to understand it by having knowledge about it. This understanding helps the teacher to gain control over teaching through self-analysis which, in turn, guides the teacher toward improvement. This is a scientific or technical rationale. We study things to know more about them so that we can understand them better. When we understand them well enough to make reasonably accurate predictions about what will happen under various conditions, then we feel we have some control over them. The progress that has been made in understanding and controlling various kinds of technology—for example, airplanes and other flying machines or electronics—has been phenomenal. Our efforts at understanding and predicting weather have been encouraging; controlling it has been less successful. Our progress in understanding, predicting, and controlling teaching and learning has been less spectacular.

Who analyzes teaching? Teachers themselves often engage in self-analysis, though not often in a systematic manner. Mentors, such as those who work with beginning teachers, must analyze the efforts of their proteges. Colleagues can work together doing peer consultation. Coaches, who may range in style from Vince Lombardi to Carl Rogers, are analysts. Supervisors have traditionally been charged with analyzing the teaching of others for "formative" (developmental) purposes. Evaluators (usually administrators) engage in analyzing teaching for "summative" (report writing) purposes.

Where does this analysis take place? Traditionally, we have assumed that it occurs in a postobservation conference between a teacher and an observer. Realistically it's more likely to happen in the car, in the shower, out in the woods, wherever the teacher is reflecting on what has gone on in teaching.

When does it happen? It may go on during the teaching, before a conference, after a conference, despite the conference. It may occur in a group setting, some time later, when several teachers get together to play excerpts from tapes (audio or video) and give one another supportive feedback.

How does it proceed? When it is self-analysis, the process may be relatively random. In a structured conference it may be decidedly sequential. In a peer consultation setting it may be orchestrated and choreographed by the participants themselves.

If the analysis involves another person (as opposed to self-analysis), there is a logical sequence to the process. The "other person," whether supervisor, colleague, or evaluator, will make some observation of the teacher teaching, share with the teacher what was observed, then (with the participation of the teacher) develop an interpretation of what the analysis implies, either for improvement or to satisfy the accountability requirements for supervision and evaluation.

This kind of analysis can help teachers by providing them with objective feedback on the current state of their instruction. It can help them diagnose and solve instructional problems. It can help teachers develop skills in using instructional strategies.

ANALYSIS OF TEACHING DEFINED

Analysis of teaching, therefore, is the systematic and interactive study of instructional processes and factors by obtaining persuasive data to compare with established goals in order to provide relevant information for appropriate decision making by the teacher about different ways of improving teaching. Systematic analysis of teaching may also be defined as the process of helping the teacher reduce the discrepancy between actual teaching behavior and the teacher's vision of ideal teaching behavior.

Our definition (for this chapter) will be that analysis of teaching is an activity in which teachers deliberately plan (often with the assistance of another) to collect and assemble data about their teaching behavior for the purpose of

- describing accurately what is happening,
- explaining why it is happening,
- predicting what might happen if alternatives were tried,

- choosing among several alternatives,
- acting on the choice,

and then repeating the cycle a number of times.

After considering several frameworks to organize the subject, this chapter describes the analysis of teaching in the context of the clinical supervision cycle. Subsequent sections look at the analysis of teaching from the perspective of the leaders' (or analysts') styles and roles, the effect of organizational structure, and the need to account for diverse teaching styles and strategies. Finally, several metaphors and some lighthearted examples shed light on the essential characteristics of analysts, followed by some serious discussion of the implications for new roles that we see emerging.

FRAMEWORKS FOR ANALYZING TEACHING

Most will agree that teaching is a complex activity; hence, it can be analyzed in many ways. In order to analyze our own or someone else's teaching for the purpose of enhancing, enriching, and improving it, however, we need a relatively simple framework for organizing our thoughts and for arranging the information (data) we have available. One practical framework is as follows:

1. *The setting.* What are the cultural, economic, political, governmental, legal, and social contexts in which the teaching is taking place?
2. *The situation.* Where is the teacher coming from in relation to the demands of the job? Is the teacher a beginner, experienced but new to the setting, old and burned-out, solid, working with a new boss . . . ?
3. *The structure.* Within what kind of an organization is the teacher working? Is it dictatorial, autocratic, feudal, supportive, collaborative, autonomous, or abdicative?
4. *The style.* What style of learning, behaving, and leading fits this teacher, and if the teacher is analyzing in collaboration (or conflict) with a colleague (or critic), then how does that person's style affect the interaction?
5. *The strategies.* What are the models or ways of teaching the teacher uses to reach the goals that have been chosen, and if a colleague is involved, what are the strategies that person is using to work with the teacher?
6. *The skills.* Which explicit techniques (observable behaviors) does the teacher use to deal with students, and what techniques does the colleague use to deal with the teacher?

Another framework that journalists use may help us set the scene—the interrogatives who, what, where, when, why, and how. In our scenario the "who" is the teacher, but there is often another "who" involved as evaluator, supervisor, coach, mentor, colleague, or friend. How these people typically behave and how they interact can be analyzed and modified just as teaching can.

An evaluator may only be concerned with whether the teacher is meeting the minimum standards or criteria. A supervisor may be looking for evidence of growth toward an avowed goal. A teacher may be looking for reassurance that an annoying mannerism is occurring less often. A colleague playing the role of friendly critic or peer consultant might be looking for interactions with students that could be classified as warm and sympathetic, organized and businesslike, or stimulating and imaginative. A researcher might treat teaching strictly as a string of observable behaviors that can be coded to answer such questions as: How many questions were asked?, What percent of the questions were of higher order?, What kinds of reinforcement were used?, What percent of reinforcement was positive? Negative?

The "what" is the teaching, that which happens between teacher and student in relation to learning and the content of instruction. We noted elements of effective teaching in chapter 2.

The "where" relates to "setting," "situation," and "structure," but it also pertains to where the analysis takes place. Our emphasis has been on the feedback session between an observer and a teacher (postobservation conference), but if the analysis of teaching is a reflective activity, the "where" is inside the teacher's head and the "when" may be during the teaching, before the conference, in the conference, after the conference, despite the conference, at the supermarket, during sleep, in a meeting. These "wheres" can also be thought of as "whens."

Another "when" needs to be emphasized; that "when" is "often." We probably hear and see more systematic analysis of football, hockey, basketball, baseball, movies, ballet, opera, or books than we do of teaching, particularly our own. We undertake unsystematic analyses of the "Gee Whiz!" or "Good Grief!" type ("Gee, it was wonderful" or "Gosh, it was awful"), but analysis of the type advocated here occurs too seldom in most schools and for most teachers.

Of course the primary "why" of analysis is growth. This may consist of fine-tuning existing skills, developing and practicing new ones, experimenting with an expanding repertoire of strategies, or overcoming a troublesome deficiency. Why analysis is being done can include personal awareness, professional growth, accountability, research. The analysis may be used only for feedback to the teacher or it may be used in making decisions about curriculum implementation, program development, or other concerns about an innovation.

The "how" of analysis has a number of stages, each of which calls for various strategies and skills. These stages include goal setting, planning for observations and other forms of data collection, observing and recording, providing feedback, interpreting what is happening, making decisions about modifications, and then acting on the decisions. The process should recycle several times per year. The kinds of data that might be used include observation data of several kinds, inspection of artifacts, such as student work, teacher-made tests, lesson plans, or syllabi. The kinds of data available affect what can be accomplished in the analysis. For example, a verbatim list of questions allows the teacher to analyze the wording and the cognitive level. An audiotape allows analysis of the pacing, vocal inflections, pronunciation, volume. A videotape permits analysis of gestures, facial expression, and other non-verbal behaviors. A number of other possibilities have been considered in earlier chapters.

Also contained in the "how" are the explicit (observable) behaviors that the teacher and a colleague use while analyzing teaching. We call these "skills" or "techniques," implying that they can be learned, practiced, improved upon, fine-tuned. Many of these techniques can be classified as "interpersonal skills," but there are many more: knowledge of content and context, understanding of human growth and development, familiarity with a range of teaching strategies and models, capacity for introspection, and willingness to take risks, to experiment, and to tolerate another's style and idiosyncrasies.

ANALYSIS OF TEACHING AND
THE CLINICAL SUPERVISION CYCLE

As noted in chapter 1, clinical supervision has three major components that are repeated several times during a year. A trained observer (1) meets with the teacher and plans for the next observation; (2) observes a lesson systematically (and non-judgmentally) and records information related to the objectives set during the planning conference; and (3) meets with the teacher to (a) analyze (together) the data recorded by the observer, (b) interpret the meaning of this information from the teacher's perspective, and (c) reach decisions about the next steps.

Some authorities, believing it is sufficient for supervisors merely to observe and then confer with teachers, advocate eliminating the planning conference. Our view of what can be accomplished by expert observation of teaching implies a need for planning the observation with the teacher. The logic goes like this: The goal of observation is feedback—information that is useful, relevant, objective, accurate, understandable. The goal of feedback is analysis, interpretation, and decision making by the teacher, with the assistance of the observer. If these goals are to be reached, the teacher and the observer need to plan together.

The Planning Conference

If the decision making is ultimately the concern of the teacher—and we believe that it must be if teaching is going to change and improve or be reflective, and if the teacher is aware of and interested in more than one approach to teaching—then it follows that an observer needs to know:

- what kind of lesson will be observed
- what specific strategies, tactics, and behaviors the teacher will be attempting to use

- what sorts of behaviors the teacher expects from students
- what explicit concerns the teacher wants to address by means of observational data
- what sort of observational data will be most useful

Is it possible to analyze teaching without observing it? We could use information that is not observational but is instead "collected" from lesson plans, student test scores, examples of student work, hearsay from other teachers, impressions from conversations with the teacher in the lunchroom or corridor, feelings about how the teacher looks or talks, opinions expressed by parents, and the teacher's membership in community organizations. Although these sources may yield useful information, they are at best indirect measures of the quality of teaching.

Analyzing teaching requires something to start with, something to talk about, and someplace to head for. We suggest beginning with data—factual, accurate, relevant, and understandable. Inferences and opinions developed by the observer (or collector) may be accurate or perceptive; on the other hand, they may be biased, distorted, and inappropriate.

The Observation

Let us consider just six of the observation recording techniques: selective verbatim, verbal flow, at task, class traffic, interaction analysis, and wide lens (including audio and video recordings). These have been described in other chapters and can be viewed in the ASCD program, "Another Set of Eyes."

The Feedback Conference

Something to Start With.   Of the six methods for recording we have chosen, the least likely to be biased or distorted by the observer is "Selective Verbatim" transcribed from a tape recording. The one most prone to subjectivity is the wide-lens technique, Anecdotal Record. The observer chooses which incidents to note, how to record them (perhaps using judgmental adjectives), and what to ignore. Class Traffic and Verbal Flow simply require accuracy and concentration on who is moving or talking and where. At Task and Interaction Analysis require judgment calls in choosing the coding to record at a given moment, but they are usually accepted by teachers as reasonably accurate unless there is lack of trust for the observer.

Something to Talk About.   Given the hard data, we have something to start with. "Here's what I saw happening" is a reasonable statement for an observer to make. Note that it does not state why it is happening, or what should be happening. Interpreting what is happening involves the teacher's analysis, conjectures, hypotheses, and predictions—leading to decisions for the future.

It is easy to find observers (supervisors, principals, or evaluators) who conduct the process backward. Instead of starting with data (facts), then analyzing and interpreting the data before reaching decisions, they start with a conclusion or pre-conception, interpret any evidence in the light of that prejudgment (prejudice), and pursue the self-fulfilling hypothesis by selecting only data that fit. For example: "Two students were not paying attention" rather than "Twenty-eight were at task." Jerome Bruner has called this "functional fixedness"—proceeding on the basis of a single hypothesis that happens to be wrong.[1]

For many teachers, self-concept or confidence level is fragile enough that having their teaching analyzed in the backward fashion just described can have devastating effects. An extreme literary analogy is the film *Gaslight* in which a husband (played by Charles Boyer) deranges his wife (played by Ingrid Bergmann) by telling her she only thinks the lights are dimming when they actually are (through the efforts of the husband's confederate, played by a young Angela Lansbury). This analogy was used in a teacher dismissal arbitration to describe the overwhelmingly negative feedback provided by a principal and vice-principal in a "program of assistance" for a teacher. The teacher previously had 18 years of positive reinforcement for his efforts.

Someplace to Head For. Let us assume we have some hard data from a systematic observation of a lesson by an observer who is unbiased, objective, and interested in aiding the teacher's worth through collaborative analysis. How shall the analysis proceed?

The obvious first step is to share the data. Ideally, this should be done soon after the observation by giving a copy of the "raw" data to the teacher. Carbonless copies or photocopies are possibilities. If a videotape or an audiotape has been made, it can be given to the teacher for viewing or listening before the analysis conference with the observer.

The next step is to elicit and attend to the teacher's perceptions of what he or she learned from the data. "What do you see that you would repeat if you taught this lesson again?" is a good question to ask. Teachers invariably find something they like in such a record as a videotape or audiotape. The other types of records (seating chart coding, verbatim transcriptions, traffic patterns, interaction timelines or charts, anecdotal notes) can also provide positive reinforcement that some of the teacher's intentions are being realized.

"What do you see that you would like to change?" never fails to produce a response. Asking this question countless times has not identified a teacher who has taught (or thought he or she taught) a perfect lesson. Truman Capote, in an interview, claimed to have written a perfect story. Even if true, this feat would be different from completely achieving your objectives with 30 wriggling reactors. In teaching, the equivalent of a 300 game in bowling or 18 under par in golf is to reach "some of the people some of the time" (as opposed to "all of the people some of the time" or "some of the people all of the time.") This has to do with "fooling the people," not teaching them.

A third step that can help a teacher analyze from "inside" the teacher's head (as opposed to "outside" analysis) is "If you were a student in that class, what might you want the teacher to change?" Picking a specific student for whom to answer the question can be useful and revealing. Many teachers will comment on students' individual needs regarding the level and pace at which information is presented. Another thing that teachers identify is the amount of structure that different students desire or require. No matter how explicit, linear, sequential, or ordered the structure, some students want more. No matter how flexible, varied, random, and tolerant the limits, some students want more.

Some Ways to Help Get There.   Thus far we have looked only at ways to help the teacher analyze the available data (with the exception of the "gaslight" approach, which was portrayed as not helpful). What are some ways the observer can help the teacher besides question-asking (heuristic) approaches?

One technique is to assemble the data in such a way that patterns or phenomena become more obvious. For example, the pattern of student engagement and disengagement becomes more apparent when "at-task" and "not-at-task" (technique 11) behaviors are transferred from a seating chart record to a table that summarizes over time. As the result of this revelation, a teacher may decide that half as much time would have been enough for an assigned activity. This may not seem to be a significant outcome, but if this teacher has spent twice as much time as necessary 6 hours a day, 180 days a year, for 25 years, it is. Likewise, interaction patterns (technique 22) emerge from a timeline but are less apparent on a seating chart.

Another technique that goes beyond displaying the data in a revealing way is to comment on facts in a nonevaluative manner. For example, in relation to Verbal Flow (technique 12) recorded on a seating chart, the observer might say, "I noticed that if we draw a diagonal from the northwest to the southeast corner, nearly all the interaction is on one side of it." This is quite different from saying, "You ignored half the class." In Class Traffic charts (technique 13) most teachers would notice that one corner is not visited by the teacher or that one student spent 5 minutes looking nonproductive at the water faucet in that corner. If the teacher does not notice or comment on these facts, the observer can do so—without accusatory tone or judgmental language. The teacher may have a convincing rationale for what was done or not done.

The skeptical reader may question the wisdom of allowing the teacher to choose what to analyze or to interpret what the observer points out. Remember, however, evaluating teaching need not consist of finding what is wrong with it, berating it, or devaluing it. We are so accustomed to assuming that the only reason for observing a teacher is to look for what is wrong that the notion of helpful feedback seems alien, even though school districts usually list "improvement of instruction" as the primary reason for teacher evaluation and supervision; accountability-related reasons are listed second. Nonetheless, the threat of evaluation generally makes teachers so defensive about being observed by anyone other than their students that the potential for growth-producing analysis is severely compromised.

Where Are We Headed?   We have been considering what to talk about, how to talk about it, some ways to help get somewhere. Where? The goal is making decisions. These decisions are about alternatives, changes, resolutions for future efforts by the teacher. Hence, the decisions (if they are reasonable and feasible) are best made by the teacher. Only the teacher can change the teacher's behavior. Moreover, we are more likely to act on decisions we have made ourselves than ones others have made for us.

Teachers can make a wide range of possible decisions as the result of systematic observation and nonjudgmental feedback. The following general categories of decisions occur fairly often.

Things to change: strategies, tactics, arrangements, goals, objectives, occupations (that is, leaving teaching for greener pastures)

Things to strengthen: skills, resolve, techniques, knowledge

Things to eliminate: mannerisms, habits, affectations, redundancies, irrelevancies

Things to experiment with: new approaches, different materials, varied groupings

Things to modify: techniques, attitudes, objectives

Things to learn: new subject matter, different methodology, understanding of the implications of research

Ways of going at it: There are as many ways of going at the evaluation (or supervision or analysis) of teaching as there are kinds of teachers, kinds of observers, and kinds of teaching.

The four approaches described below involve a teacher working with a student teacher. You decide how helpful each approach will be for the student teacher.

The first one we'll call the "I'm right; you're wrong" approach. This teacher-observer's "data" consist of inferences and conclusions rather than recorded behavior that can be analyzed by the observing teacher and the student teacher, interpreted, and then used to decide upon options for change. The shortcut has eliminated planning together, systematic and objective data collection, analysis of what the data show, and interpretation of causes and consequences; instead, it has jumped to conclusions.

The natural progression for this "concluder" is to deal with the student teacher in a concrete and sequential manner within an autocratic command system using direct, didactic teaching strategies (and insisting on the student teacher using these same approaches). The transactions will be parent to child and the followership pattern expected will be for the student teacher to behave as an immature, inexperienced, grateful neophyte while the teacher plays an omniscient, omnipotent role.

A second possible approach is one in which the transactions are adult to adult; the organizational context is collaborative and collegial; the strategy for learning is heuristic; the leadership style is participative and delegative; the learner is independent, mature, willing, and able. The goals are mutual, realistic, and important.

A third possibility is to *sell* the student teacher on particular ways of doing things. This may involve modeling the behaviors, providing guided practice in using them, leading cheers when they are used properly, using a theory or rationale that justifies the approach, and treating the neophyte as willing and potentially able to emulate the wizardry of the mentor.

If you would like an all-purpose sentence that captures the ideas (or biases) expressed so far, here is a skeleton:

	supervisor	*tells*		*follower*
	leader	*sells*		*learner*
The	*teacher*	*participates with*	the	*neophyte*
	evaluator	*delegates to*		*colleague*
	observer			

within an organizational structure that is

autocratic
feudal
motivational
supportive
collegial
autonomous

using a model or strategy of teaching that is

didactic (telling)
experiential (experiencing)
maieutic (helping, midwifing)
heuristic (discovering)
transcendent (seeing the "big picture")

and a personal style that is

concrete-sequential
abstract-sequential
concrete-random
abstract-random

to meet needs for

housekeeping
controlling
clarity
variety
surgence (enthusiasm for students and for subject matter)

and evaluates on the basis of

traits
standards
goals
concerns

A fourth option is to abdicate all responsibility, turn the class over to the student teacher, and head for the boiler room for a semester of smokes and jokes. This can be labeled the "sink or swim" method. Professor Harold Hill, in *The Music Man*, called it the "think" method—just think how you'd like to be able to play this horn you've bought.

LEADERSHIP STYLES AND ROLES

In an earlier section, we noted that one element of a framework for understanding the analysis of teaching is the style of the analyst. This element also relates to the "who" in the second framework; analysts look at teaching and interact with teachers in different ways depending on whether the analysts are task- or relationship-oriented, dictatorial or collaborative, intuitive or logical-sequential, and so forth. Hence it is useful to examine how the style of the analyst or instructional leader affects his or her analysis.

Our first look at style will be concerned with leadership. Paul Hersey and Kenneth Blanchard have developed a schema that relates human interactions with task accomplishment and structure.[2] Leaders who are high on task but low on relationships will tend to tell their followers what to do. Leaders high on task but also high on relationships will try to sell their followers on what they ought to do. Those who are lower on task and structure but high on relationships will tend to participate or collaborate with their troops. Persons who do not have a high commitment either to task or relationships can feel comfortable if they delegate the task to someone else.

In order to expand the scope of leadership styles to cover the range of structures (school organizations) that will be described later, let us consider what might lie beyond sell and tell on the continuum of structure (control) and getting the task done. Obviously, yell and hell are candidates if only for the sake of rhyme. Another way of expressing the shift from "sell" (persuasion) to "tell" (giving orders) and "yell" (issuing commands) to "hell" (dictatorship) is to think of the words "indirect" to "direct." Other words we commonly use to express this distinction are "controlling" or "dominating" as contrasted with their opposites. Such organizations as schools, colleges, political parties, churches, and clubs can be ranged along this continuum.

At the other end of the continuum a leader may go beyond participating with teachers in planning and conducting staff development, even beyond delegating the responsibility. If teachers are mature, independent, autonomous, and competent, then liberating them from some of the rituals of bureaucratic behavior may be in order. We shall not advocate abdicating the responsibilities of leadership altogether, though most of us have seen it happen in schools and governments.

There are a variety of names for the roles that leaders might play within the framework:

evaluator	supervisor	peer
judge	coach	colleague
critic	tutor	collaborator
inspector	mentor	consultant
referee	teacher	connoisseur

Let us take a more detailed look at a few of these leadership roles.

Role of the Analyst as Evaluator

In Olympic skating the judges (analysts) are quite clear on whether they are watching speed skating, figure skating (both required and interpretive), or hockey. In analyzing teaching we have not been so clear. There is as much difference among direct instruction, inquiry, and T Groups as there is among figure skating, speed skating, and hockey.

The kinds of events in which one skis for a while, shoots a rifle, jumps on a bike, swims, runs, jumps, and then does somersaults come closer to what we're after in analyzing teaching. We have a set of criteria for the decathlon. Let's consider a pentathlon of teaching. Using Abraham Maslow's hierarchy of human needs (physiological, safety, belongingness and love, esteem, and self-actualizing) as a model,[3] let us arbitrarily select housekeeping, control, clarity, variety, and "surgence" as our hierarchy of teaching needs (see Figure 12.1). A similar hierarchy exists in baseball: throwing, catching, hitting, running, and sliding. Sliding is the self-actualizing, surgent, quintessence of the game. If you can slide into second, kick the ball out of the second baseman's hands, steal third (the same way), and then steal home, you can make up for the fact that your teammates don't throw, catch, hit, or run well. Making judgments about the merits of Ty Cobb or Willie Mays, then, is relatively straightforward. You analyze the statistics on throwing, catching, hitting, running, and sliding.

The hierarchy of teacher needs starts at the housekeeping level. If you can't find the chalk, the chalkboard, the paper, the books, the door, you can't teach (unless you're a university professor). If you can't control the class, at least to some minimum level, then instruction cannot take place. Now, the depressing fact is that many teachers and administrators are apparently content with merely achieving acceptable housekeeping and control.

FIGURE 12.1   Three sets of needs in ascending order of importance.

SOURCE: Model adapted from Abraham Maslow, *Motivation and Personality* (New York: Harper & Row, 1970), pp. 35–47.

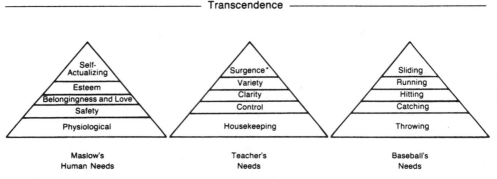

*Enthusiasm for students and subject matter

The next level, where clarity (of explanations, directions, assignments, control statements, and other communication) is the criterion, can result in learning (by students); hence teachers may facilitate achievement (a part of the fourth level for Maslow) by developing and employing clarity (the third level of our hierarchy). Another means of achieving success as a teacher, getting students to learn, is to develop and use a variety of strategies, activities, and techniques (skills).

We know of several hundred teachers who have entered into peer consultation, which uses the goal setting, planning, observation, and feedback techniques from this book. Most of them have used the process to expand their repertoire of strategies and skills. A few have gone beyond that stage to contemplating and reflecting on the deeper meanings of teaching—a self-actualizing activity that leads to surgence. Some teachers have used peer consultation to tinker with existing skills and strategies, and a few have managed to avoid and evade it even after taking as many as 5 days of training and being provided with substitute time for observations and conferences.

Above each of the hierarchies, there is room for transcendent needs (or metaneeds). Maslow discusses these in *The Farther Reaches of Human Nature.*[4] Aspiring to reach this level as an instructional leader may be overly ambitious for most of us (who are even having difficulty with self-actualization, surgence, and sliding). However, high levels of expectation are generally more useful than low ones.

The role that emerges from the foregoing discussion is that of judge or evaluator. The essential task is to apply standardized criteria to a product or performance and then proclaim its relative goodness. Analysts of teaching have fewer standardized criteria and their measures are less clear than those of, say, analysts of baseball. One can, however, make gross judgments on our pentathlon for teaching. For example:

Housekeeping could range from deplorable to commendable.

Control could range from chaotic to consummate.

Clarity could range from totally lacking to crystalline.

Variety could range from missing altogether to bountiful.

Surgence could range from apathetic to exuberant.

Putting each of these on a scale from 1 to 5 would create a list that might solve the problem of summative evaluation, but it would not be very useful for a teacher who is interested in fine-tuning skills, enlarging a repertoire of strategies, or adapting styles to individual needs.

Role of the Analyst as Critic

An observer and an observee each take on a role in the drama of planning, observing or being observed, and giving or receiving feedback from the observation. The roles an observer might assume are described from a leadership perspective (because of the traditional view of supervisors as observers), though it is possible (indeed preferable) that the observer be a peer, colleague, collaborator, coach, consultant, or even protege/student. To begin, we might note what kinds of observers record, critique, or otherwise take part in the analysis of other professionals. Actors have coaches, directors, critics, and commentators; so do athletes. Doctors have clinical professors, colleagues, peer review teams. Lawyers have judges, juries, arbitrators, panels, and other spectators who watch their performance. They also have colleagues who provide feedback. Engineers get feedback on whether their bridges fall down, whether anyone buys their designs, and who bids for their services. Researchers have their reports "refereed" before they are published in scholarly journals. Authors have their work reviewed by editors before publication. Our experience is that editors of educational tomes send the work to be reviewed by other authors (sometimes even competitive, envious, invidious, treacherous ones).

This brings us back to peer review. When the vicious aspects are removed, genuine peer review is the best form of feedback. If you are a wizard by vocation you don't especially want feedback from bumpkins; you want it from other wizards. Authors have their work examined critically after publication through book reviews. The list could go on; ballet, opera, sculpture, painting, and the other visual and performing arts all have their critics, commentators, and connoisseurs. These analysts often separate a performance into its technical and artistic aspects—figure skating provides a very clear example.

Teaching also has its technical aspects, many of which can be measured or quantified. It also has qualitative or artistic aspects; these dimensions are much more difficult to scale. The image of judges at the Olympic Games of Teaching holding up numbers for technical and artistic achievement comes to mind. Until teachers have such panels, they must be satisfied with the critical analysis given by their supervisor or evaluator. We have seen cases where the critic's competence to assess what is taking place in the classroom was in question.

Role of the Analyst as Coach

What might an outstanding coach do instead of merely marking a five-point checklist? Let's begin with an analogy. Here is Digby Duffer who wants a lesson from the golf club pro. Digby slices, takes his eye off the ball during the downswing, bends his elbow, dips his shoulder, doesn't rotate his hips, et cetera. Peter Par, the pro, has to focus on what Digby needs to address first; he knows you can't work on everything at once. Discussions of what are the best shoes, tees, or clubs won't help Digby much, nor will the merits of the pitch and roll versus the chip and spin. This Duffer needs to begin with hitting the ball (not the turf) with the club (not the caddy) on the downswing (not the backswing). Now, compared to teaching, golf is a piece of cake! For instance, consider the following section.

Role of the Analyst as Educator

The object of the golfer's intentions sits there (on the tee, grass, or sand), immobile, inarticulate, neither cooperative nor defiant. But, suppose your golf ball could hop off the tee at the last instant, mutter disparaging remarks about your best effort, go home and tell its dad that you abused it. Assume it could carry a genetic weakness of intellect (about following its direction toward the green) that its politically powerful parents refuse to recognize or admit. Well sir, Mr. Peter Par, thank your lucky stars. Imagine having these creatures 30 at a time to address!

Most educators have to deal with groups of individuals who vary a great deal in personality, temperament, needs, talents, and interests. Instructional leaders must deal with individual differences among teachers just as teachers must cope with individual differences among students. We can range these individual differences along a continuum as we did with leadership styles. First, however, we need to recognize that the organizations within which people function have their own diverse characteristics.

ANALYZING WITHIN ORGANIZATIONAL STRUCTURES

The way an organization is structured influences how its members will behave. In Table 12.1 we see a number of factors that are affected by the nature of the organization.

Starting with the autocratic command column and moving to the left, one can see historical progression from despotic to democratic forms of governance. Communication patterns move from "down only" to "up and down" and then "across." How we deal with differences can vary from not recognizing them to treating them as data.

Analyzing teaching in a school, college, or university that is run by autocratic command will differ from analysis of teaching in a collaborative, collegial setting. The norms for behavior that exist for the institution will be reflected in the classroom. The range of teaching behaviors will be limited by what is sanctioned by the administration.

In the organization labeled "Think Tank," the members are all "transcendent" in the sense that they are at or above the self-actualizing level. The organization depends on the individual contributions they are making to society. Let's assume they are all Nobel Laureates, the leaders in their respective fields. Would it make sense to have them punch a time clock, or be closely supervised to make certain they are "working"?

Rather than to "boss," the management role is to provide support and resources to further the endeavors the members choose. The role of the member is to be a unique specialist "doing your own thing," using the creative zeal and insight that led to being selected for this role. The communication patterns are bound to be "across." The notion of talking down to a colleague or taking a problem "up" to the boss seems alien. It is interesting to speculate on how differences are handled in such organizations. We suspect that unresolved issues and contradictory opinions would result in books by each of the contestants arguing their case in a broader forum.

The motivational organization is well illustrated by many of the service clubs that do good things for communities and develop leadership for worthwhile projects. This supportive form of organization emphasizes cooperation, congeniality,

TABLE 12.1 Characteristics of seven kinds of organizations

	Liberate *Transcendent (Think Tank)*	Delegate *Specialist Division of Labor*	Participate *Collegial Collaboration*	Sell *Supportive (Motivational)*	Tell *Custodial (Maintenance)*	Yell *Autocratic Command System*	Hell *Competitive Cold War*
Depends On	Individual contribution to society	Specialized competence	Cooperation	Leadership	Economic resources	Power	Winning
Management Based On	Providing resources and support	Integration	Togetherness	Support	Material rewards	Authority	Glory
Employee Status	Autonomous	Expert	Responsibility	Performance	Security	Obedience	Contestant
Employee Psychological Result	Self-actualizing and altruistic	Doing your thing	Self-discipline	Participation	Organizational dependency	Personal dependency	Free-floating hostility
Employee Needs Met	Seeing the effects	Achievement	Self-realization	Higher-order	Maintenance	Subsistence	Victories
Moral Measure	Continuing to work doing own thing	Production	Commitment to task and team	Motivation	Satisfaction	Compliance	Ethnocentrism
Basic Roles	Unique specialist	Nominal peers Specialty-related	Colleagues Task-related	Partners	Benevolent owner Grateful subject	Boss and Subordinate	Competitors
Basic Skills	Creativity, surgence, insight	Specialty and complementary	Specialty plus interdisciplinary and collaboration	Serving as a model or good example for others	Majestic wisdom and judgment Obedience and compliance	Boss: managing, directing, evaluating Sub: listening, doing, reporting	One-upmanship, debating, blaming and compromising

(continued)

	Liberate	Delegate	Participate	Sell	Tell	Yell	Hell
	Transcendent (Think Tank)	Specialist Division of Labor	Collegial Collaboration	Supportive (Motivational)	Custodial (Maintenance)	Autocratic Command System	Competitive Cold War
Nature of Relationship	Mutual respect	Polite and respectful	Open, trusting Developing informal, personal	A Covenant	Noblesse oblige Paternalistic allegiance	Status-determined Formal impersonal	Impersonal Distant Mistrustful
Power Distribution	Shared	Nominal half-and-half All power is in own area	Nominal half-and-half Flexible according to task need	Shared Delegated	Controlled Bestowed	Fixed: boss has it all	Nominal half-and-half Used to counter and cancel each other
Communication	Across	Task focused Restrained	Mutual	Across Friendly	Up and Down	One Way	Across Hostile Distorted
How Differences Are Handled	Writing an article or book	Avoidance Compartmentalized into discipline areas	In the open Used as information for problem solving	Negotiated	Mediated by the liege	Not recognized	To spar and wage war indirectly through task

SOURCE: This table is derived from a variety of sources. The framework is from Abraham Maslow, *The Farther Reaches of Human Nature* (New York: Viking Press, 1971), pp. 284–286, which in turn draws on Keith Davis, *Human Relations at Work*, 3d ed. (New York: McGraw-Hill, 1967), p. 480. The notion of a competitive cold war within an organization was suggested in a speech by Sherman Grinnell in Atlanta, c. 1976. The term "free-floating hostility" is from Meyer Friedman and Ray H. Rosenman, *Type A Behavior and Your Heart* (New York: Knopf, 1974). An earlier version of this table appeared in Keith A. Acheson, *Techniques in the Evaluation of Teachers* (Salem: Confederation of Oregon School Administrators, 1982); the above version s from Keith A. Acheson, "Instructional Leaders for the 1990s: Improving the Analysis of Teaching," *Oregon School Study Council Bulletin* 33, No. 6 (February 1990).

and shared (revolving) leadership. Differences are negotiated through democratic procedures—debating and voting.

The collegial-collaborative organizations, at least in education, exist on paper more often than they do in school buildings. One is more likely to see mere congeniality than genuine collegiality or collaboration. There is clearly a trend toward this kind of organization in education, but one is much more apt to find feudal institutions out there than the kind outlined in the table.

The autonomous form of organization is much more suitable for a think tank than the more directive forms of organization that one finds in schools, colleges, universities, and other educational institutions with which we are familiar.

Some Examples of Organizational Forms

The kinds of organizations represented in the table exist in many forms. For an example of an autocratic command system one could study the Ford Motor Company when Henry, Sr., was at the helm or analyze the Family Saud in present-day Arabia.

The custodial or maintenance system that functioned throughout the Middle Ages was based on land ownership. In present-day China the word for "feudal" is used to describe the more conservative citizens. The supportive, motivational organization can be examined on given days of the week at the luncheon meetings of service clubs. Many student organizations operate along similar lines.

Two examples leap to mind to illustrate the specialist division of labor: a medical clinic and a university. A number of modern-day electronic firms combine the compartmentalization of specialists with the autocratic tendencies of the two owners who invented their blidget in a garage a few years ago.

The competitive cold war takes over in specialist organizations when there is a budget crunch followed by a scramble for scarce resources. Some universities have had an uncommon amount of experience with this state of affairs.

Collegial collaboration is the form of organization preferred by most educational writers who have been studying school organizations in recent years. It also represents what a number of writers see as the evolving nature of the relationships teachers are seeking with their peers and colleagues (as opposed to traditional supervision and evaluation arrangements). In a number of our graduate courses and workshops, practicing teachers and administrators have been asked if they know of schools that are operated as either autocratic, custodial, supportive, specialist, competitive, or collegial institutions. The answer, in general, appears to be "all of the above."

Effect of Organizational Structure on Role of Leader

What is the effect of the organizational structure on the role of the supervisor or evaluator of teachers? It is a profound one. In programs based on collegial, collaborative precepts, school principals must modify their role as "boss" to become the team leader. The communication patterns also change from "top down" to "across." The ways differences are handled also tend to follow the table, that is, in a collaborative setting they are treated as data to be discussed, whereas in the autocratic setting there are no differences (the boss has all the answers).

The autonomous organization appears to be the kind of arrangement many teachers would like. The function of the administration is not to manage what people will do but to provide assistance to the laureates who are doing the work of the organization, that is, teaching. Going a step beyond autonomy, of course, one can find anarchy. These different points of view enter into another variable as well—strategies of teaching.

The effect of the structural variable on the context in which teaching will be analyzed is important and unavoidable. Instructing in Summerhill is not the same as instructing at Annapolis.

Discussion of differences implies disagreement. Being able to disagree is not the same as being disagreeable. In the collegial, collaborative organization, disagreeable people may be as disruptive as they are in any other organization. One trait of being disagreeable is always to look for what is wrong without recognizing what is good, what is working well, what is commendable.

The instructional leader of the 1990s will have to handle disagreements among teachers, between teacher(s) and leader(s), and within a single individual (who will likely become disagreeable as the result of internal conflict). Thus we realize the need for leaders who can be conciliators, negotiators, and therapists. The effects of personal style on these situations are examined next.

TEACHING STYLES

When we begin to work with someone else analyzing, we must remember that "the teacher is the teaching."[5] That is, we are not merely talking about what the teacher does; we're talking about the person—personality, character, body, and soul. As we work with learners (students), we pay some attention to individual differences in learning style. It becomes evident that some learn best by seeing (diagrams, charts, pictures, movies, demonstrations). Others learn best from hearing (lectures, interaction, jingles, slogans, radio). Others need physical, kinesthetic experience (hands-on, field trips, projects, on-the-job, hard knocks).

Some appear to respond well to rules and regulations and to orderly, structured, sequential learning activities. Others march better to a drummer that allows options, variations, independent investigation, intuitive leaps, random thoughts. As a consequence, teachers are more effective if they use a variety of strategies and techniques. Similarly, teachers vary in their styles of learning and behaving. Supervisors and other analysts are more effective if they recognize these variations and use a variety of strategies in working with teachers.

Style is an overarching variable in teaching. Individuals who are comfortable being low-key in their private lives are unlikely to do well being bombastic in their professional roles. Autocratic, domineering, linear individuals have a difficult time allowing students to discover through heuristic teaching strategies. However, in education as well as in writing, the elements of style can be modified. The delightful book *Elements of Style* can help a writer turn long, contorted sentences (and thoughts) into shorter, straightforward ones.[6] Similarly, teachers who communicate little enthusiasm can learn to do so through training, practice, and feedback. Other modifications of inherent style seem possible.

There are many ways of classifying different styles. We shall allude to the categories used by Anthony Gregorc and by Isabel Briggs Myers and Katharine C. Briggs,[7] and there are many others.

Classifications of Styles

Style enters into the analysis of teaching at three levels. If there is an observer (supervisor, colleague, mentor, evaluator), then the inherent style of that individual will be involved. The variations of style among teachers (and within an individual) must be recognized. Finally, the styles of the learners in the teaching situation must be considered.

There are numerous schemes for categorizing personal styles, learning styles, and leadership styles. We shall consider only a few in relation to the analysis of teaching. Hersey and Blanchard's categories have already been mentioned, expanded, and related to different kinds of organizations that are part of the context of teaching.[8]

Gregorc has suggested and elaborated "concrete sequential," "abstract sequential," "concrete random," and "abstract random."[9] These can be depicted as a two-by-two matrix (see Figure 12.2), if we accept the premise that people tend to process information primarily as concrete or abstract and that they do so mainly in a sequential or random fashion.

The Myers-Briggs Type Indicator looks at extroversion-introversion, sensing-intuiting, thinking-feeling, and judging-perceiving.[10] These categories (which are based on the work of Carl Jung) generate a four-by-four matrix or 16 categories. Many of the characteristics of style can be ranged along the continuums displayed in Figure 12.3. We have arbitrarily chosen to mark one dimension "right" and "left"— as in politics and religion—with order, orthodoxy, and authority to the right and liberal, experimental, autonomous values on the left.

A second dimension, which can be marked as "up" or "down" (high or low), runs from "surgence" to "apathy." The third dimension, for our purposes, runs from "out" to "in" and represents the degree of involvement that an individual has in a given activity.

Thus, in the case of an educational innovation, such as team teaching, peer coaching, or cooperative learning, a teacher or a principal may have conservative enthusiasm and modest involvement. Another may have super and liberal enthusiasm but minimal involvement.

FIGURE 12.2 Diagram of Gregorc's categories.

	sequential	random
concrete	CS	CR
abstract	AS	AR

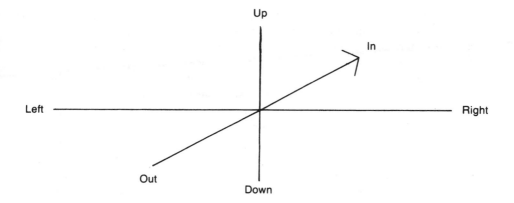

FIGURE 12.3 Continuums of style.

SOURCE: Keith A. Acheson, "Instructional Leaders for the 1990s: Improving the Analysis of Teaching," *Oregon School Study Council Bulletin* 33, No. 6 (February 1990): 16.

Let's label these dimensions as follows:

HIGH-LOW: enthusiasm for the idea

RIGHT-LEFT: attitude toward change

IN-OUT: direct involvement

It appears, then, that the HIGH-LEFT-IN people will lead the way. LOW-RIGHT-OUT folks will not be helpful. HIGH-LEFT-OUT individuals may lead cheers but won't participate in substantial ways.

We shall not attempt to describe in detail how these styles differ in actual practice, but will rely on the experience of the reader to flesh out what the variations are on the skeleton we provide. At the skill level we won't attempt to show correspondence between a particular skill (or technique) and a strategy or style, because the techniques advocated in this book can be used within any strategy or style. Some matches are more likely than others. For example, participators are more apt to use listening than are tellers. Sellers are less likely to encourage colleagues to try their own alternatives than are delegators.

STRATEGIES OF TEACHING

We have looked at differences in style as they affect leadership behavior, organizational structure, and individual preferences. Another key variable that affects the behavior of teachers working with students (and also leaders working with teachers) is the strategy (or "game plan") they have in mind. These strategies have many names: for example, demonstration, discovery, didactic, heuristic. We shall continue to use a right and left alignment of these variations with direct strategies to the right and indirect ones to the left.

For those who prefer a structured approach to learning, didactic, direct strategies have great appeal. They also resonate with teachers who prefer telling to delegating. There are times and situations when direct instruction is the strategy of choice. Advocates of direct instruction see these times as almost always, and these situations as rampant. On the other hand, proponents of heuristic, discovery approaches to teaching see their favorite strategies as nearly always useful. Our position is that there are times when a didactic tactic (telling) is best; in other situations, providing an appropriate experience to learn something "on your own" (delegating) is preferable. In other milieus, helping "maieutic" or midwifing procedures (participating) would be best. In some instances (especially when everyone in the group is at least self-actualizing), heuristic, transcendent or "big picture" considerations should come to the fore. Sometimes persuasion (selling) is appropriate.

The number of permutations and combinations of the variables we've listed thus far is staggering. However, they tend to coalesce along the structural dimension of our model. So, Ghengis prefers yelling; Carl favors discovering; Siegfried uses telling; Hilda likes inquiry; Madeline does well at selling. As analysts, instructional leaders should be more open to appreciate wider variations among these models and among the people who use them than they typically have been.

For one author, a 65-year career as an analyst, starting as participant observer (student) in a Montessori kindergarten and including 46 years as a teacher in schools, colleges, and universities has revealed despots, bosses, snoopervisors, consummate consultants, trusted peers, crafty consultants, greedy gourmets, caustic critics, conceited connoisseurs, compleat coaches, and obdurate observers. It has disclosed shouters, pouters, cajolers, pejorators, implorers, imploders, molders, moulders, jumpers and bumpers, pleaders and plodders. Based on this experience, it seems unlikely that we shall develop a standardized model of the ideal analyst, nor shall we standardize the ideal teacher.

What was simple and focused when this book was first written—planning for observation, observing and recording, then giving feedback from the observation—has become more complex because of the persistent requirement that supervisors provide summative evaluation of teaching (for accountability) as well as formative information (for development, growth, analysis).

Our resolution of this dilemma, as discussed in chapter 11, has been to put planning, observation, and feedback in an expanded schema that also includes the following concepts and activities: standards (or criteria of effective teaching), job descriptions (consideration of the unique situation), goal setting, formal evaluation (report writing), programs of assistance for teachers with serious deficiencies, and consideration of contracts, grievances, arbitration, hearings, and litigation. The key element within all these activities is the process of analyzing teaching.

SKILLS

The skills (techniques) that one needs to analyze teaching effectively are the same as those of clinical supervision. They have been described and illustrated in the units that precede this one.

CONCLUSION

Most teachers who voluntarily undertake a program of instructional improvement that includes peer observation by colleagues who have been trained in systematic observation techniques find it useful and beneficial. Some principals are able to function as colleagues in a peer observation program; others find it difficult to establish the level of trust necessary to be accepted by teachers as truly helpful. There are several reasons for this difficulty according to the teachers we've interviewed, and the reasons vary among individuals. A few principals deliberately emphasize evaluation through judgmental statements, ignoring the data that both observer and teacher had agreed would be recorded. Moreover, they dominate the postobservation conference. A few principals appear to gain complete acceptance as colleagues or collaborators. Two of the factors of acceptance that teachers identify are these:

- A willingness to be observed teaching as well as to observe another's teaching
- A personal style that is approachable, empathic, supportive, enthusiastic, flexible

Teachers have also described principals who were supportive and enthusiastic about the program but not personally involved in it. The personal involvement of the leader appears to be very important to teachers who want more than pro forma "evaluation." In one view, "analysis of teaching" is a subtopic of "feedback" within the cycle of clinical supervision: plan, observe, feedback. This perspective assumes the availability of an observer, which is often not the case. Many teachers are rarely observed by another educator, and when they are it is for the purpose of a "ritualistic" formal evaluation rather than for personal and professional growth.

Teaching deserves to be analyzed, especially by the teacher. Doing so with the help of a trusted, respected, competent colleague is to be preferred, but much useful self-analysis can be accomplished using adaptations of the same techniques that work in a collaborative mode.

We admire the role a colleague can play, but we also regard self-analysis as a desirable activity. With or without the enriched perception a peer can provide, the teacher needs something to look at, listen to, or analyze; someplace to head for, that is, a goal; and some way to get there, a strategy.

Other variables that affect the analysis of teaching are as follows:

- the setting, situation, and organization (structure) within which the teaching takes place
- the inherent information-processing style of the teacher, especially as it affects interactions with students and colleagues
- the range of strategies, methods, and techniques (skills) of teaching that can be employed, both by teachers and leaders
- the variations in leadership styles among leaders and followers as they affect teachers interacting with students, teachers interacting with colleagues, and teachers interacting with administrators

These variables need to be addressed with more vigor and competence than has been evident in the past. In the following sections we shall consider again the kinds of roles that may be involved in using the techniques of goal setting, planning, observing, and giving feedback that are described in subsequent units.

NOTES

1. Jerome S. Bruner, "Some Theorems on Instruction," in *Theories of Learning and Instruction*, ed. E. R. Hilgard (Chicago: National Society for the Study of Education, 1964).
2. Paul Hersey and Kenneth Blanchard, *Management of Organizational Behavior: Utilizing Human Resources* (Englewood Cliffs, NJ: Prentice-Hall, 1969).
3. Abraham Maslow, *Motivation and Personality* (New York: Harper & Row, 1970).
4. Abraham Maslow, *The Farther Reaches of Human Nature* (New York: Viking Press, 1971).
5. Ted Aoki, personal communication.
6. William Strunk and E. B. White, *The Elements of Style* (New York: Macmillan, 1979).
7. A. F. Gregorc, *The Style Delineator* (Cambridge, MA: Gabriel Systems, 1982); I. B. Myers and M. H. McCaulley, *Manual: A Guide to the Development and Use of the Myers-Briggs Type Indicator* (Palo Alto, CA: Consulting Psychologists Press, 1985).
8. Hersey and Blanchard, *Management of Organizational Behavior*.
9. Gregorc, *Style Delineator*.
10. Myers and McCaulley, *Manual*.

chapter 13

Peer Consultation*

Nothing new that is really interesting comes without collaboration.
James Watson, Nobel laureate, co-discoverer of the double helix

A process that uses the planning, observation, and feedback techniques of clinical supervision as described in units II, III, and IV is peer consultation.

We shall concentrate on three questions: (1) What is peer consultation? (2) Why do teachers get involved in peer consultation? and (3) Where does peer consultation appear to work best? We will investigate the first question through a look at the literature, some comparisons, and a review of research conducted within the Program for Quality Teaching (PQT) of the British Columbia Teachers' Federation over the past decade. We will try to answer the second question by analyzing individual experiences through interviews. For the third question, we will consider the levels of participant involvement and describe what conditions and factors influenced the chances for success of various programs.

About two hundred interviews have been conducted with teachers, principals, and other educators who have been associated with peer consultation. The interviews were analyzed according to the three key questions. Questionnaires surveyed PQT participants at the end of the first year and fifth year. Notes from observations

* We acknowledge the work of Neil Stephenson Smith[1]; Mohammed Shamsher[2]; Smith and Acheson[3]; Acheson, Shamsher, and Smith[4]; and all who have participated in the British Columbia Teachers' Federation *Program for Quality Teaching* since 1982.

of teachers doing peer consulting, written feedback from participants at instructional sessions, and follow-up interviews with selected teachers, facilitators, and developers at the end of the fifth year of operation (for PQT) and after one to four years of operation for other projects added to the data base. Another unavoidable source of information was participation as developers, presenters, or active members in the project(s).

Our research was not designed to evaluate the effectiveness of peer consultation (e.g., in relation to student achievement), but to describe how teachers and administrators, with different goals and organizational needs, have interpreted it. Contacts with actively involved educators include elementary schools in inner-city Winnipeg, Manitoba and suburban Portland, Oregon; several school districts in Saskatchewan and Alberta; two high schools and a medical school in Oregon; a community college in Alberta, in addition to those in British Columbia. These contacts have been followed up by personal visits at varying intervals (months or years).

WHAT IS PEER CONSULTATION?

Peer consultation is a school-based process in which teachers work in consort with colleagues in a reciprocal process to provide one another with descriptive feedback and discussion about observed teaching to enhance professional growth and organizational development. This definition was also used to analyze other models of collegial observation in relation to their implementation. The underlying theoretical and philosophical principles differed. They were divided into two broad categories: (1) peer coaching for technical proficiency and (2) peer consultation for critical reflection.

Peer Coaching toward Technical Proficiency

Here coaching practice seemed to be aimed at safeguarding adoptions of new models of instruction. Most of the models of instruction linked with peer *coaching*, for example, Instructional Theory Into Practice (ITIP) and Teacher Effectiveness Training (TET), are grounded in behaviorist learning theory. The coaching practices connected with these models appeared to work from the same theoretical system. Teachers' behaviors with colleagues in the coaching relationships corresponded to those they employed with the students in their classrooms; demonstration-practice-feedback-reinforcement-refinement. A key word was *training*—"to bring a person to a desired state or standard of efficiency by instruction and practice." The responsibility of the peer coach was to ensure that his or her partner deviated as little as possible from the prescribed model of instruction. Written and verbal feedback given the teacher by the peer coach reinforced "correct" behaviors and identified errors. Teacher performance was judged according to the criteria defined by the model of instruction studied. The observed teacher's responsibility was to apply the feedback to the refinement of practice in using the model.

There seem to be three advantages in this type of peer coaching: First, from the teachers' perspective, there was an opportunity to work with colleagues toward the mastery of a model of instruction that was common to all. Most of these programs asserted that the models of instruction led to increased student learning in areas of basic skills as measured by standardized tests. Students were expected to benefit by experiencing a more consistent education in terms of discipline and teaching strategies.

Second, in many schools where peer coaching was used, teacher evaluation became more standardized as evaluators adopted the approved behaviors from the instructional skills programs as criteria for judging effective teaching.

Third, from the district perspective, a tightly linked, standardized instructional system could be projected. Teaching behaviors and related student learning were controlled through centralized administration of training and peer coaching, reinforced by a standardized system of pupil testing and teacher evaluation. In simple terms, peer coaching appeared to be a vehicle for controlling organizational uniformity.

We see six disadvantages in the peer coaching models: (1) Implementation is typically "top-down," that is, designed for the classroom but initiated outside the classroom. This gives teachers little sense of ownership of the process. (2) Teachers are apt to feel constricted by the expectation that they must *adopt* the proposed methods, rather than *adapt* them to their classroom programs. (3) Teachers indicate that they feel constrained by the implicit expectation that they use only the prescribed model of teaching. There is also some doubt as to the validity of the research linking the instructional skills to student outcomes on standardized tests. (4) At the outset of most implementations, teachers believed that learning new instructional methodologies through coaching was exclusively for their professional growth. They were dismayed when the new models of instruction became the exclusive standard by which administrators evaluated their teaching. In extreme cases, if teachers did not adhere to the standards of the new model, unsatisfactory reports would be written, even in cases where students were meeting learning objectives defined in the curriculum. (5) Teachers felt there was not enough flexibility in the methods connected with most programs of peer coaching. They were discouraged from using inquiry or critical thinking, whose divergent outcomes were difficult to fit with behavioral objectives that they were expected to pursue. (6) Finally, one of the greatest problems for teachers was to be asked to judge each other's performance. To what extent teachers were disaffected by the judgment of colleagues remains unclear, but our findings clearly identify the sensitivity that most teachers have about the evaluation of their teaching. Also worth noting is that most programs of peer coaching did not emphasize the development of interpersonal communication skills needed to maintain healthy relationships between teachers and coaches. It is possible that the lack of such training added to the problems in the implementation of peer coaching.

The disadvantages of peer-coaching models can be summarized by saying that teachers appeared to be intolerant of having their powers of self-evaluation and decision-making significantly reduced. The research on these models indicates that most teachers, once the external accountability measures were removed, rejected the prescribed models and the peer coaching that supported them.

Peer Consultation toward Critical Reflection

The second general group of peer-consultation types include Instructional Finetuning and Reflection, Reflective Practice and Innovation, and Organization Development. They differ from peer coaching in an important way. They are aimed at the development of practices selected and evaluated on standards defined by the teachers, not by external experts. Underlying these types are the humanistic and cognitivist theories of learning that place the evaluation and control of instruction in the teacher. Accordingly, the principal role of the consultant is to (1) provide his or her partner with specific feedback as requested on aspects of teaching *chosen by the teacher* and (2) provide support for the partner's critical reflection in planning and feedback conferences.

The general advantages of this "peer consulting toward critical reflection" group are (1) opportunity for change and development of new knowledge about teaching is granted to the teachers at the classroom level; (2) teachers learn a variety of tools for providing colleagues with objective feedback related to different learning methodologies; and (3) teachers are given the professional freedom to experiment and test their own theories of teaching and learning without fear of reprisal from a judgmental peer or administrator/evaluator.

These kinds of peer consultation have four disadvantages: (1) A high degree of self-initiative is required of teachers. It is voluntary, and the numbers of teachers currently interested in this kind of professional endeavor may be a minority. This leaves those teachers with low self-initiative unaffected. (2) The organization of such a professional-development system is loosely coupled, which translates into less administrative control over the teaching methods, teacher evaluation, and student-learning outcomes. The de-emphasis on matching teacher-evaluation strategies with standardized student testing adds to the problem of accountability. (3) There is little evidence to support the notion that peer consultation for critical reflection positively affects student learning. (4) Critical reflection is not a high priority in the present culture of schools in which practicality is celebrated. Altered perspectives, financial and symbolic, are required before a new kind of leadership can emerge. Many administrators currently in service may be unable to accommodate these changes.

Discussion about the Comparative Analysis

Summarizing the two groups of peer-assistance types (*coaching* and *consulting*) has highlighted some important differences in what people tend to think are all the same practices. The most striking is that the first group of peer-coaching types aim to change the behaviors of teachers by using a system of high structure and centralized support. Formal bureaucratic structures, including teacher-evaluation procedures and standardized pupil testing, are set in place to enforce this behavioral change. Such systems as these reflect low estimates of teachers' skills and a belief that teachers are lazy and unimaginative. They appear to be designed as a catch-net for marginal teachers, reluctant teachers, and those who simply need a high degree of structure before they can enter into anything new. Our review reveals that, in spite of all the formal accountability measures, these centralized, top-down programs have not caused long-lasting change. Our involvement with workers in the field over an appreciable length of time substantiates this claim.

The second group appears to be designed for teachers who operate from the opposite end of the spectrum, although this is not stated by any of the program architects. The support systems in this group tend to be less formal, and they become highly dysfunctional if attempts are made to bureaucratize them. In our experience, any attempts from central administration to control the peer-consultative process failed abruptly. The success of peer consulting seems to be dependent on the health of the immediate culture and the shared meaning within the group. Administrators were most functional when they were able to help teachers come to some common understanding of what was going on and to support teachers in their pursuit of the goals that *they* (the teachers) defined.

Administrators were most successful when they helped teachers work toward these goals, rather than impose externally defined criteria, such as standardized pupil assessment and teacher evaluation to guide teacher activity. The literature on peer-consultation types in the second group, however, did not provide substantial evidence that long-term change has occurred, nor does our personal experience. However, the concept is relatively new, and what we predict, based on what we have observed in PQT and other programs during a decade, is that the peer-consultation notion, for teachers, will persist and grow.

Continuum Relating Peer Consultation Types to Other Educational Factors

To help understand how peer consultation fits into the larger educational scene, a continuum (Figure 13.1, p. 222) may clarify the relationship of the peer-consultation types to other educational factors and influences. This figure is intended to help establish the fit between different styles of communication, teaching, peer consulting, and leadership. One idea emerging from our work is that there seems to be very little thought given to the relationship among these levels of operation in our North American system of education. This omission leads to circumstances, for example, where very self-directed and mature teachers might suddenly find themselves in an educational innovation that is very prescriptive and is led by a principal who is infinitely directive and judgmental. Or, conversely, laissez-faire administrators might end up in situations where they are asked to lead a very tightly prescribed instructional program. It must, however, be stated at the outset that there is no *fixed* relationship among any of the elements identified on this spectrum. It merely represents a rough assembling of understandings that may clarify the families of educational functions most closely associated with peer consultation.

At the top of the continuum we have placed Ways of Communicating. These approximate the range of communication styles that peer consultants might use with one another. On the left side, the style is didactic, even prescriptive, and is often associated with peer-coaching techniques that inform colleagues about where they have deviated from the expected practice. Here the colleague observer often is ex-

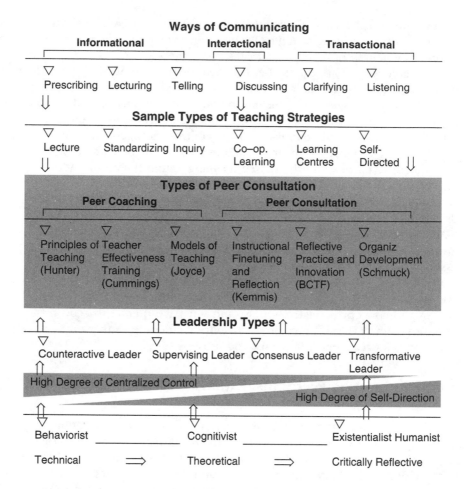

FIGURE 13.1 Continuum relating peer consultation types to other educational factors.

SOURCE: Smith, Neil Stephenson, "Peer Consultation as a Means of Professional Growth" (Ph.D. Dissertation, University of Oregon, 1989).

pected to control the assessment and flow of information. Standards are fixed and externally developed from principles created outside the teacher's classroom. On the right side are modes of communication that are nondirective and transactional in nature. Some examples of communication on this side are questioning, clarifying, and listening. The orientation in this family is communication that fosters self-evaluation and self-direction. The aim is to work toward human development with less emphasis on technical proficiency than would be found on the left side. These types of communication are more often associated with practices of peer consultation and organization development than with peer coaching as we have seen it.

On the second level of the spectrum are Samples of Teaching Strategies. We recognize and admit that we have over-simplified and stereotyped, but nonetheless believe that cooperative learning, self-directed learning, and learning centers are located on the right side. If implemented in heuristic fashion, these correspond to the focus on self-direction and self-evaluation, and correspond closely with peer consultation for reflective practice. On the other side, the more didactic styles of teaching (for example, lecture and standardized learning) relate more to the practice of peer coaching. Although it is inaccurate to place all the peer coaching models on the didactic side of the scale, it is accurate to suggest that most peer coaching deals with directive coaching processes that attempt to lead a teacher toward a specific model, usually some form of direct instruction. Although the architects insist that the elements of effective teaching are transferable to all types of teaching strategies, this style of coaching would not work if the peer coach could not quickly compare the observed practice to prescriptive guidelines.

On the third level, three learning theories are identified, ranging from behavorism with emphasis on technical functions, through cognitivism, to humanism with a tendency toward critical reflection. Underlying all these is centralized control. This control is usually opposed to the amount of self-direction afforded to the learner (who may be a student or a teacher).

Leadership Types relate to peer consultation types. For example, the supervising leader would be better suited to coaching toward direct teaching models than would the transformative leader. Different leaders fit certain peer-consultation programs. Educators should consider how peer consultation and peer coaching relate to the broad spectrum of education. It could prevent "forced fits" when caught in innovations for which they are philosophically and practically ill-suited.

There are drawbacks to this notion. For example, consider Teaching Strategies. The Lecture, if shaped in heuristic manner, can be a powerful catalyst for self-directed learning and discovery. Similarly, the types of peer consultation called Reflective Practice and Innovation could easily be used by a person who wants to learn more about direct instruction. We urge you to view the continuum only as a general representation of the issues raised.

THE NATURE OF PEER CONSULTATION IN PRACTICE

Why Did Teachers Choose to Become Involved?

Teachers who entered PQT typically had 10–15 years of teaching experience. This was also true in other K–12 projects, although an occasional hardy first- or second-year teacher volunteered (having experienced "mentoring" in some cases). Teachers in community colleges, vocational colleges, and medical school programs usually had fewer years of direct teaching experience, though all had some experience as teachers.

Interviews and interactions showed that many lacked confidence in their teaching abilities and were reluctant to be observed by colleagues for fear of being judged.

Like weathered consumers, most entered these programs with a healthy cynicism about the underlying motivations and stability of such projects. Many felt abandoned, manipulated, insulted, or bored by previous projects to which, regretfully, they had dedicated themselves. In PQT, most were confident the 3-year partnership between the teachers' federation and the local school board was a potentially solid program. Most were committed to finding out about the philosophical and practical possibilities of peer consultation *prior* to volunteering.

Teachers felt much could be learned about their own teaching and from the teaching of their colleagues. Most preconceptions of peer consulting lacked a realistic notion of the time commitment required to make it meet their needs, and the difficulty of finding some space in busy schedules.

Teachers joined PQT and its counterparts with different goals:

1. To learn ways to collect data and confer with colleagues. Many had been involved in peer observations in the past and wanted to learn different ways to collect information that could be used with a variety of models of teaching.
2. To learn how to work with colleagues in conferences that were interesting and challenging, but not alienating. Many teachers had worked with peer observation before and had found it to be either too benign or too critical in its impact.
3. To work with colleagues in the study of teaching. They looked upon the classroom, clinic, shop, or laboratory as a rich source of ideas to regenerate teaching commitment, and saw colleagues as an untapped source of professional knowledge. Most of the inservice they had experienced was apart from the realities of their situations. They saw in peer consultation a way to make the study of their own work (as teachers) a legitimate activity.
4. To reduce feelings of professional isolation. Working with a colleague or colleagues on a common project was perceived as a way to develop important professional relationships that transcend staffroom chatter and, at the same time, preserve personal autonomy.

Inservice Preparation for Peer Consulting

Interviews and questionnaires reveal that only after some months of application and practice did most teachers begin to recognize two aspects that were essential for their preparation as peer consultants. One was learning to communicate with a colleague nonjudgmentally. The second was learning to select aspects of one's own teaching that are relevant and important to the practice of self-evaluation and to be able to look at them in a critical yet constructive manner.

Different sources of data reveal that a few teachers find a 5-day instructional session overly complex or unnerving (particularly undergoing the stress of microteaching) to the point that they do not trust the process enough to commit themselves to it. Medical instructors who have traditionally believed that they can "see one, do one, teach one," saw an evening and a morning in a pleasant retreat as perhaps "not enough." Subsequent monthly meetings of 2 hours at a variety of hospitals, restaurants (for breakfast), or homes proved to be instructive and satisfying.

Different generations of instructional groups operated as different subcultures within their milieus, separated not by dissimilar knowledge, but by separate training experiences. In some places, people who were influenced by one training session had difficulty integrating with groups who had attended other sessions. In others, this was not a problem. This phenomenon may present a challenge for educators. Those who are planning systems of long-term change and educational renewal should examine carefully the natural development of subcultures that can emerge from separate training sessions. The split-cultures that developed in our studies tended to detract from the possibility of organizational collaboration. Yet we also found that attempts to involve everyone in processes like peer consultation all at once, even in a small family-like school, or subgroup, is not always a viable answer to this problem.

Peer Consulting: What Is It, Really?

From the outside, the popular image of peer consulting is something like this: Teachers are given time off from their classes, they observe one another, they learn from the observations and possibly learn new things from one another, and isolation is reduced. In reality, we found that peer consultation is difficult and complex. In one sense, the process does have a simple elegance. Its mechanics are logical and comprehensible. It appears to enable teachers to engage at levels of complexity suited to their needs. It seems adaptable to investigating and learning about most functions of teaching. Our research revealed that most teachers were able to complete planning conferences (or describe what they were interested in observing), observe and collect data pertinent to their colleagues, and subsequently provide requested information and supportive analysis in the feedback conferences.

However, peer consultation is also enigmatic and mysterious. Reaching a stage of harmonious operation and providing a colleague or colleagues with interactions that promote critical reflection is often a formidable challenge. Generally, the peer-consultative process is seen as a plausible means of professional development, but it requires certain conditions to function well. Three areas are especially worthy of mention: (1) levels of engagement, (2) teacher commitment, and (3) coping with time shortage.

1. Levels of Engagement. Teachers operated in peer consultation at different levels. In most cases they were working toward higher levels of engagement. Some maintained their activity at one level, satisfied with what it provided. First was the level of avoidance in which teachers maintained their belonging status, but in reality never became involved in practicing peer consultation. Perhaps 10 percent engaged in this dance at the edge of the pool, never getting wet, but, interestingly, never throwing in the towel. Reasons for avoidance might include low self-esteem, low trust of colleagues' abilities to observe nonjudgmentally, fear of being observed, and the perception that teaching is a "performance" rather than a dynamic process of professional decisions.

The majority of PQT teachers engaged in peer consultation at the second level. They used it for everything from making simple adjustments in their current techniques to experimenting with new theories and models of teaching. Teachers typically started with safe observations involving students' work, then moved to observations they considered higher risk, such as teacher-student interactions. Teachers at this level most commonly found (1) increased collegiality in their work, (2) increased understanding of their teaching, (3) improved abilities to analyze their own teaching, and (4) increased knowledge of the teacher-evaluation system. They were usually successful in developing skills of self-evaluation. Some were successful in their pursuit of effective dialogue with colleagues about theoretical and philosophical considerations, a luxury seldom afforded in the culture of the staff room.

At the third level, critical reflection, 10–15 percent of PQT teachers found peer consultation useful as a means to examine their teaching critically and to guide fundamental changes in how they conceived their teaching practices. With the support of colleagues, they ventured into serious examinations of their beliefs about teaching and learning. A few struggled with the transition from one paradigm of teaching to another that was entirely different.

Eight PQT teachers volunteered in the third year of the program to become part of a research group whose goal was to develop narrative descriptions of their work and to share this knowledge about their teaching with others by publishing it in provincial teachers' journals. By the spring of 1989, both of these goals had been accomplished. In the first medical teacher group, a similar goal was accomplished following their year of meetings.

There is no shortage of difficulties in learning the art and practice of critical reflection. Time limitations, conservative norms of the culture for teachers, emphasis on practicality in schools, lack of familiarity with the concept of reflection, and low self-esteem of teachers are some of the factors that work against critically reflective practice. When motivation is high and situational factors are favorable, teachers succeed in learning the skills of promoting one another's critical inquiry and self-evaluation.

The work necessary for some teachers in PQT and similar programs to succeed at the top level was not cheap. If, however, self-review and school-based development are things that we would like to nurture in preparation for the schools, colleges, and universities of tomorrow, perhaps teachers and administrators who are succeeding at breaking the norms of today represent an important foothold on new ways of functioning in teaching institutions. Moreover, if the levels of engagement represent a sequential development, then the more teachers practice peer consulting, even at the levels of fine-tuning, the more likely teachers will be prepared to work toward higher levels of reflective practice. Ideally, projects such as these, carefully studied, will help identify how higher levels of understanding teaching in classrooms, clinics, and elsewhere can be reached.

2. Teacher Commitment.   Teachers who became engaged in the process had varying degrees of commitment. This commitment was affected by a number of important conditions and influences.

Clarity of Personal Goals.   This was a major influence on how deeply teachers became involved in peer consultation. Those who were unsure of their goals, or how well they were meeting them, had serious problems analyzing their experiences. It not only diminished their commitment but negatively affected their peers.

Clarity of Group Goals.   Almost as important as individual goals was the clarity of the goals that shaped a common purpose among teams of teachers. The whole function of organizational development procedures, where attended to, helped the group function as a healthy entity, support the structure, and ease decision making. Ill-defined goals and an unstructured group of aimless individuals led to a quick breakdown.

Understanding Self-Evaluation and Self-Direction.   Many teachers, even the most confident and competent, lacked clear concepts of their own abilities and ways of assessing them, perhaps a natural consequence of the organized isolation that finds teachers in a vacuum devoid of useful feedback from colleagues.

Teachers have few reliable sources of data from professional colleagues for constructing reliable self-concepts. Related to this is a tendency by many to be caught in tension between self-determination and traditional dependence and comfort provided by deferring to authority.

This tension surfaces in teachers' comments that reflect a strong desire for personal autonomy in decisions that affect their teaching and a reluctance to take the steps necessary to realize the desire. Self-evaluation is a skill, as well as an attitude, needed to examine critically one's own strengths and weaknesses. It is not easy, nor is it commonplace, in our system of education.

Many teachers had difficulty with this in attempting to progress beyond the neophyte stages of consulting. Our educational system functions almost exclusively on evaluation by others and seems to have given teachers little preparation for self-evaluation. And in most classrooms, clinics, or offices the students are still implicitly given to believe the myth that the teacher is one whose knowledge is complete, and for whom weaknesses are never considered. The teachers' reinterpretation of their roles as experts to include being life-long learners, or models of self-reflection in the eyes of students, represents a radical departure from the traditional norms.

What has become clear is that teacher commitment to pursuing peer consultation and adopting a course of critical reflection regarding their own work must be conceived as a developmental process. For teachers to move from one extreme to the other involves major adjustments affecting the way they think of themselves as teachers and as human beings. The challenge becomes existential as well as technical and theoretical.

For many, to become genuinely reflective (and critical) of their work through peer consultation demands the support and nurture of empathic colleagues to help them sort through the more difficult questions regarding their teaching. In our study of peer consultation, the role of the trustworthy and supportive colleague was of paramount importance among all the conditions for successful consultation.

3. Time Shortage. For years we have heard principals and other administrator/evaluators say, "We like your observation techniques and would use them . . . if we just had time." Now, when peer consultation is discussed with teachers, we hear the same lament. There is precious little time available for all the functions we expect schools to perform these days. However, if our priorities include staff development near the top, then we can make time for this activity.

Other Factors. There are several other factors that affect the peer-consultative process.

Relationships with Colleagues. The list of prerequisites for successful peer consultation extracted from patterns of behavior in the case studies are strikingly similar to those for a successful marriage. Teachers who shared experiences in the instructional sessions, who had similar goals, who practiced open communication in their conferences, and who were similarly committed to peer consulting, were those who seemed to thrive in the process. Conflicts in relationships were most commonly reported in areas of differing values or interpersonal communications and problems of a colleague judging a partner's work.

Most teachers perceived a marked improvement in collegial relations as a result of peer consultation. They experienced improved relations with people in their groups, and noted special differences in the depth and quality of relations with their immediate consulting partners. Many talked about the importance of having at least one other person in the school who really seemed to understand their classroom, who was willing to share in sorting out their concerns and problems, and who would also share in the successes and failures of new attempts. In questionnaires and interviews, teachers indicated no discernible impact on relations with colleagues who were not involved in their projects.

Trust Levels. Teachers felt that trust with colleagues increased as a result of the instructional session and subsequent peer-consultation practice. Coming to understand and know others' commitment to teaching, sharing risks together, and exchanging roles in observations engendered mutual confidence and comfort among colleagues.

Teachers spoke about the competitiveness that prevails in school culture. This competitiveness often precluded sharing, responding to, and supporting colleagues' successes or changes. These teachers reported that peer consultation shifted teachers away from a spirit of competitiveness toward true collaboration.

In the interviews and questionnaires, other factors that increase inter-colleague trust were mentioned, including mutual respect. As teachers began to appreciate each other's talents and personal qualities, their confidence to adventure into new territory increased. Reciprocal responsibility was another factor mentioned. Teachers emphasized that a regular exchange of roles was essential. In situations where a person wanted to be the observer, but not the teacher, tension and conflict arose. Shared risk taking was a third factor. Taking risks together, both in the in-service and in the teaching situation, seemed to increase the levels of trust. With failures came support from colleagues and a renewed sense that the process was not going to destroy confidences. Separation from evaluation systems was also an important factor; when observed by administrators, teachers avoided mistakes at all costs. No risks meant very little learning. In evaluation, flawless and simple performance became the teachers' priority.

Leadership, at School Level and Beyond. Along with teachers' capacities for self-leadership, various types of institutional leadership interacted positively or negatively with peer consultation. In roughly half the schools, administrators demonstrated a combination of high commitment to peer consultation and an ability to facilitate teacher self-direction through collaborative leadership. This type of leadership appeared to produce a safe and productive climate for peer consulting. Teachers felt honored and supported by this approach, and felt that the decisions that they made in the classroom were trusted.

These administrators (1) were able to listen to and understand teacher's perspectives; (2) did not mix peer consultation with teacher evaluation; (3) did not act as the judge of teachers' peer consultation efforts; (4) did not try to control the content of peer consultation; (5) placed a high value on the time that teachers spent in peer consultation; (6) actively supported peer consultation in discussion with other teachers, but were careful not to proselytize about it; (7) modeled the kinds of attitudes and skills that were consonant with peer consulting, for example, risk taking, trusting others, good listening skills; (8) were able to judge their appropriate degree of direct involvement in the process, and to respect teachers' autonomy and decision-making capacities; and (9) were adept at resolving conflicts among group members.

The combination of low commitment to peer consultation and a high degree of directiveness seemed to influence the process most negatively. Three leadership types were identified in the case studies that did not fit well with the peer consultative process: (1) the cheerleader, who was interested more in the form of peer consultation than the function; (2) the supervising leader, who had a sincere interest in seeing the process succeed, but was intent on judging the teachers' work and controlling the outcomes according to the leader's personal standards; and (3) the counteractive leader, who used a low level of commitment and a high level of directiveness to actively sabotage teachers' progress.

Leadership at upper levels was also important. Teachers relied on the administration for (1) budget support and (2) symbolic support that made teachers feel that their work in the project was valued, and that peer consultation was part of the institution's long range plans.

Teachers also played important leadership roles in implementation. Although most did not choose to become involved in administrative tasks, they played vital roles in sustaining group vision and motivating their peers, often simply through example. In situations where groups lacked strong administration and teachers had to assume the leadership responsibilities, the demands were too great. The implementation in these cases appeared to be less successful, and groups were typically more fragmented.

Peer consultation is only a part of the restructuring and reforming that needs to take place in the educational system. It is, we believe, a very important element in that process. We have observed it in public, private, and separate schools in western Canada and the northwestern states. We have seen it take place in community colleges, graduate schools, vocational colleges, a medical school. It is surprising that in all these settings it is unusual for teachers—be they primary, elementary, secondary, college, university, professional, or otherwise—to share their hopes, concerns, aspirations, and achievements with their closest colleagues, their peers. To do so, in a nonthreatening, nonjudgmental situation that provides some feedback from the real, not theoretical or hypothetical, world is a highly desirable and useful activity for many teachers.

NOTES

1. Neil Stephenson Smith, Peer Consultation As a Means of Professional Growth: A Study in British Columbia Schools (Ph.D. diss., University of Oregon, 1989).
2. Mohammed Shamsher, "Peer Consultation As a Means to Reflective Practice and Classroom Research: A Case Study of the Program for Quality Teaching in British Columbia Schools" (Ph.D. diss., University of Oregon, 1992).
3. Neil Stephenson Smith and Keith A. Acheson, "Peer Consultation: An Analysis of Several Types of Programs" (Eugene, OR: Oregon School Study Council, February 1991).
4. Keith A. Acheson, Mohammed Shamsher, and Neil Stephenson Smith, "Peer Consultation for Professional Growth and Reflective Practice," unpublished manuscript, 1996.

chapter 14

New Roles for Teachers, Supervisors, and Administrators

. . . instead of looking on discussion as a stumbling-block in the way of action, we think it an indispensable preliminary to any wise action at all.

Pericles

Public concern for the quality of education puts pressure on school administrators to evaluate and improve the competency of their teaching staff. There is no simple formula for measuring teacher competency, however, nor are any new methods guaranteed to improve the quality of instruction. Nevertheless, through a combination of clinical supervision, teacher evaluation, and in-service education on one hand and incentive programs coupled with innovative instructional leadership on the other, administrators can increase the likelihood of attracting and retaining competent and devoted professionals in their classrooms.[1]

We have looked at what clinical supervision is and how it can be conducted. Teacher evaluation was considered in chapter 11. In chapter 12 we looked at some ways of analyzing teaching for various purposes and considered analogous roles from other professions and vocations. Peer consultation has been discussed. We shall next look at some new roles that are emerging in the domain of instructional leadership. In-service education and incentive programs will be a part of developing and implementing these new roles in preservice and in-service programs. We believe that the techniques of clinical supervision should be made available (through in-service education) to many teachers as well as to principals and other administrators. Career ladders for teachers should recognize these skills as prerequisite for various new roles within instructional leadership.[2]

SOURCES OF TENSION

Supervisors of in-service teachers may have a number of other responsibilities: teaching, administration, management, public relations, curriculum, budget, student discipline, health, safety, nutrition, and many more. As one of our administrator colleagues pointed out, when confronted with the fact that school administrators seem more concerned with budgets than supervision, "If you want to get fired, making a mistake in the budget is much quicker than making an omission in supervision." This is still true. However, there is a clear call from those who pay for education asking for an emphasis on improving instruction and an insistence on accountability for those who provide it. The organizations that represent teachers are also recognizing this need. They are saying, "Let's evaluate teachers regularly. If they need help, let's provide it. If they are still unable (or unwilling) to improve, let's dismiss them and replace them."

To carry out the ultimate purpose of clinical supervision (the improvement of instruction), we need some new roles. One might be for someone other than the principal to do public relations, nutrition, inoculation, budgets, and discipline so the principal has more time for instructional leadership activities such as clinical supervision. For the principal of a small school, who also teaches, coaches, and does almost everything else to provide excellence to the patrons of a rural, or isolated, school, sharing the role of classroom observer with teachers may create a new role for the teachers and modify one for the principal. On the other hand, a department head in a large school might simply expand an existing role by taking a more active part in observing and providing feedback to teachers.

What are the appropriate titles for these roles and who can fill them? It seems to depend on the situation. In some provinces of Canada, principals belong to the same professional association as the teachers they supervise. In some parts of the world the person may be called "inspector." In others it may be "mentor" or "peer consultant" or "instructional leader."

We have concluded, after discussions with and surveys of many school people in several states, provinces, and countries, that for the typical school principal (and other building administrators if it is a big school) two observations per teacher per year would represent a substantial increase over what is currently happening. There are, of course, notable exceptions. Studies of exemplary programs have identified districts where a high priority is placed on regular and frequent observation of instruction by consultants whose training and experience qualify them to be instructional leaders.[3]

If these instructional leaders are principals or other administrators, they must have the time, and use it, to be in classrooms making objective and relevant observations. If the consultants are teachers, then they need the time and the skills to carry out the planning, recording, and feedback phases of the clinical supervision cycle. Two cycles per year are not enough to generate and sustain substantial changes in teaching behavior. Six or eight cycles would be more realistic.

If the building administrator is making two of these for formal (summative) evaluation purposes, then four or more could be made by colleagues for developmental (formative) purposes.

The immediate reaction to such a plan is concern for its cost. If every teacher were willing to devote 1 hour per month either to observing or conferring with others (if qualified) or to replacing one who is qualified, most schools could accommodate this within their schedules. In return for this "donated" time, each teacher would receive the benefits of several observations and conferences with a qualified colleague who would be serving as a constructively critical friend. Additional time, in the form of paid substitutes, can be provided by the school board.

We shall pursue these new roles simultaneously—a new role for principals, which includes more supervision and consequently less of something else, and a new role for teachers as collegial observers and as givers and receivers of feedback with colleagues.

A PERSISTENT PROBLEM

One of the most persistent problems in supervision is the dilemma between (1) evaluating a teacher in order to make decisions about retention, promotion, and tenure and (2) working with the teacher as a friendly critic or colleague to help develop skills the teacher wants to use and to expand the repertoire of strategies that can be employed. We have struggled for many years with the tension that results from these different purposes for observation, feedback, goal setting, planning, and other activities of clinical supervision. In some respects the two outcomes, evaluation and help, are compatible. Many jobs combine the two functions. For example, the vice principal of a school may be in charge of student counseling and discipline. Of course, students who are called to the office may be apprehensive about whether they will receive therapy or be expelled. Parents are both evaluators and disciplinarians, and at the same time they are supervisors and counselors. Some parents, and some administrators, handle this double-agent role gracefully and convincingly (though we never did believe "This is going to hurt me more than you").

Supervising and evaluating teachers demands an especially delicate balance. Effective supervision requires a high level of trust. Teachers often regard any evaluation that is less than laudatory as an attack on their character. To evaluate them as teachers is to evaluate them as persons. It is difficult to trust someone who is (in your mind) slandering and defaming your heart and soul.

Another way to reconcile the tension between supervision and evaluation is to agree that both are for the same ultimate purpose: the improvement of instruction. All instructors can improve; some have only growth needs; some also have deficiency needs; some have intensive needs; a few have desperate needs.

OUR POSITION

Despite the foregoing rationales for a single role, our position is that it would be best to separate the role of clinical supervisor or helpful colleague from the role of evaluator. We may label the functions of the former as "formative" and the latter as "summative."

An implication of this separation is that others besides the evaluator will plan with and observe teachers and provide feedback strictly for the purpose of improvement. The consultant's observations will be for the purpose of writing a formal, summative assessment of the teacher. Data or other documentation from the formative phase will ordinarily not be used in summative evaluations.

Another implication of separating the two functions is that we shall have to adapt to some new roles in many schools. These schools are accustomed to having administrators as supervisors and evaluators. Our formative friends would be colleagues (other teachers), department heads, team leaders, "mentors," not line administrators. A third implication is that these collegial consultants need certain skills and understandings in order to fulfill their new roles effectively. Many of the skills (or techniques) that an effective collegial consultant needs are the same as those of a clinical supervisor, which have been described in other chapters. Depending on the role that is developed in various situations, the instructional leader who is not an administrator may need additional skills and training. We shall explore some of these possibilities in this chapter.

A fourth implication of creating new roles for teachers is that the role of the administrator will need to change with, adapt to, and complement the new roles that teachers will play. We shall consider some new roles that teachers will play. We shall also consider some new roles that principals or other administrators might play.

NEW ROLES FOR TEACHERS

We have mentioned two out of three topics that have received increased attention in recent years: teacher evaluation and teacher supervision. The third topic of concern is teacher effectiveness. Are these all part of the same thing? Are they related in some systematic way? Are they separate and immiscible?

One way to relate them is to think in terms of outputs, that is, ends and means. The product of teacher evaluation is decisions about retention, promotion, or dismissal. The product of teacher supervision should be improved teaching. The result of teacher effectiveness is student learning. These observations might lead us to conclude that our three topics are quite different and distinct.

Another approach would be to ask who works with these concepts. The school principal is usually expected to evaluate teachers, supervise them, and help them to be more effective. Viewed from this perspective, the three concepts all fit into a single role. Could they be separated into different roles? Could colleagues take responsibility for "supervising" (that is, observing and giving feedback to) each other? Could teacher organizations take the lead in "quality control" by organizing support groups or other staff development activities? Can teachers be evaluated by others besides school administrators?

With these questions in mind, let us step back and view the topics from a historical perspective. Education as a profession has tended to move from an "inspector" model of employee monitoring to a more democratic, collaborative one. The participation of the teacher in setting goals for self-improvement, choosing sources of feedback, and making decisions about desirable changes has received increased attention over the years. The responses to surveys of teachers and supervisors in several countries have indicated that this is the kind of supervision teachers (and many supervisors) are seeking.

The most available source of expertise is teachers themselves; they have the ability to analyze their own teaching on the basis of objective data, to observe in others' classrooms and record data teachers cannot record themselves, to help one another analyze these data and make decisions about alternative strategies. Some new roles for teachers can allow them to do these things without becoming evaluators. In our scenario, the principal (or other responsible administrator) will still do the formal evaluation. Evaluators need the skills and techniques of clinical supervision as well, but first we are considering what parts teachers can, and should, play.

Several forces are pushing us to create new roles in the schools for instructional leaders. One is the increased role conflict felt by building principals who are expected to be hard-nosed evaluators of teachers and also kindly, sympathetic, helpful supervisors of instruction. Another pressure comes from task forces and special commissions that recommend career ladders for teachers along with other incentives and rewards to stimulate and improve the performance of the schools.

Some momentum is developing within the profession through teachers' organizations that are promoting more careful screening at entry levels, more support and better staff development opportunities for in-service teachers, and better on-the-job supervision. Tougher teacher evaluation laws emphasize the need for better programs of assistance for teachers with serious deficiencies and, when necessary, fair dismissal procedures.[4]

Perhaps the most important reason to look for alternative sources of instructional leadership is that traditional arrangements are, in many cases, not getting the job done adequately. The functions of supervision are not being carried out well in many schools. Teachers are not being observed regularly or systematically, nor are they being provided with useful feedback that they can use to improve instruction or increase effectiveness. Some reasons why the functions of instructional leadership are not being performed well are:

- lack of time
- insufficient knowledge of a range of observational techniques by supervisors and other observers
- inadequate understanding of a variety of instructional strategies by teachers and supervisors
- need for interpersonal skills used by observers to provide feedback for teachers

If others besides the principal are to take part in supervision and improvement of instruction, then we first need to consider what roles they will play. We shall refer to these roles by a single label, instructional leader.

Supervision and evaluation are the two activities that are most important to the instructional leader in dealing with teachers. Related topics are recruitment, selection, staff development, in-service training, assignment, dismissal, and due process. Because supervision of teachers is moving away from the role of an inspector toward the role of a friendly critic or collegial observer, we shall emphasize, as appropriate for teacher colleagues, what a friendly critic (or critical friend) should do. Suitable activities would include the observation and feedback activities of supervision that have been described in other units and the setting of teacher goals by the teacher and an instructional leader or colleague (chapter 3). They would not include formal report writing or other procedures that are associated with summative evaluation.

Behaviors of the Instructional Leader

What might we expect to see an instructional leader doing?

Interacting with Teachers.   This might be before or after an individual observation, in informal conversation, or in a group meeting. Leadership cannot take place in isolation from the teachers.

Planning, Assessing, and Modifying the Curriculum.   Much of this activity will take place in conjunction with others. Surveying materials will require individual activity.

Being in the Classroom.   Observing students, teachers, and activities is often neglected by principals, and the reason is usually lack of time.

Placing High Priority on Instructional Leadership Responsibilities.   To translate this statement into observable behavior, consider the following. Given the choice among several options, which will most school people choose—chasing a dog from the playground, taking a phone call from a parent, or keeping an appointment with a teacher for a postobservation conference? Those who analyze time management point to two forces governing such decisions—which activities have the highest "payoff" and which do we like to do. If educators believe that instructional leadership activities, such as meeting with a teacher to discuss an observation, are both potent and enjoyable, then there is a chance that priorities can be rearranged from what they now appear to be.

Keeping Informed about Forces Affecting Instruction.   School leaders should know about research on how the brain functions and how computers can be applied to school programs. Besides knowing about pertinent research and new technology, instructional leaders have a companion responsibility to share this information with other teachers. Many teachers are unaware of the existence of different models of teaching besides the one(s) they are using, or of systematic classroom observation techniques that might help them analyze and improve their own teaching.

Organizing for Instructional Improvement.　Many of the meetings teachers attend deal with procedural and bureaucratic matters. As a contrast, consider department meetings in a secondary school or unit meetings in an elementary school where faculty members regularly view excerpts from videotapes made in their classrooms on a revolving basis so that they can analyze and discuss the content, methodology, and techniques of their teaching as a substantial part of the meeting. If this were to become a widespread practice, we should see some striking improvements (assuming that the participants have the interpersonal communication skills mentioned above rather than to "cut each other down").

Being an Advocate for Teachers.　Helping a teacher get a tape recorder for use in the classroom is one example of advocacy; helping to develop appropriate activities is another. Finding materials, equipment, ideas, and printed articles that teachers might use is an explicit means for a leader to show that he or she is an advocate, not a watchdog or inspector. Going to bat for a teacher who is involved in a controversy is another example of advocacy.

Diagnosing Learning Problems.　Teachers who have made observations in others' classrooms as an assignment for a graduate course have often remarked that seeing some of their own current or former students in someone else's class has been an eye opener. If teachers had regular opportunities to engage in such inter-visitations they would add perspective to their understanding of individual students and also have access to the support that a colleague can provide in dealing with individuals.

Selecting Instructional Activities.　We usually think of a teacher as the person who selects activities. The leadership may have a strong hand (often applied subtly) in this process. Some schools have lots of field trips; others don't. The leader's attitude toward these may have been instrumental. Some schools have lots of problem-solving activities, role-playing, group activities; others don't. The philosophy of the leadership is probably reflected in this situation.

Selecting Instructional Materials.　Leadership can be expressed by which maps, supplementary reading materials, things to be manipulated by students, and other devices are purchased. These decisions also influence what may happen in instruction. When censorship becomes an issue, the leadership function sharpens.

Communicating with the Community.　Football teams, marching bands, and other performing groups communicate parts of the schools' program to the public. The instructional program is often not so well shared. A function of leadership is to find ways to let the patrons know about the academic, vocational, and other parts of the curriculum as well as the extracurricular programs.

Communicating with Students.　One principal of a successful (award-winning) high school sometimes sings in the choir, plays in the band, and takes part in various other organizations and activities. The message (stronger than words) is "I approve of what you are doing; it's important." When commended for this behavior, he responded, "I wish I knew how to reach the guys smoking in the parking lot better." It would be interesting to analyze the content of educators' informal conversations with students over a period of time and then speculate as to their impact on the instructional program.

Jo Ann Mazzarella summarized the principal's role as instructional leader in a publication of the ERIC Clearinghouse on Educational Management and the Association of California School Administrators.[5] The point was made that the role is constantly changing; however, a number of the observations made at that time can still be made today. Some of the things that principals or others can do as leaders of the instructional program are as follows:

- orient faculty to new teaching techniques
- make classroom visits, evaluate,* give feedback
- involve parents, teachers, counselors, and administrators in developing the grading system
- supervise the testing program
- schedule time for teachers to discuss their concerns
- visit meetings of teams and departments
- devote faculty meetings to what is happening in instruction
- relate needs of students to school system goals and legal requirements
- supervise in-service education
- provide liaison between the schools and the community
- manage change
- allow discussions directed toward innovations
- provide adequate time and support for innovations
- provide constant evaluation of the entire school*
- coordinate the efforts of unit leaders*

Role as Staff Developer

Staff development is a topic related to the supervision and evaluation of teachers. The instructional leader's responsibility for promoting the professional development of the teaching staff is so important for the school's success as to warrant fuller discussion. Writing about the principal as staff developer, Roland Barth emphasized the need for interacting with teachers in ways that encourage growth rather than merely force compliance.[6] He identified three groups of teachers:

1. Teachers who are unable and unwilling to examine their teaching practice critically and unable to have other adults—teachers, principals, parents— examine what and how they are teaching.

---

*These functions should be performed by line administrators; the others can be carried out by collegial leaders.

2. Teachers who are quite able and willing to scrutinize continually and reflect upon what they do and make use of their insights to effect periodic changes.
3. Teachers, few in number, who are able and willing to scrutinize their practice critically and who are quite able and willing, even desirous, of others having access to what they do.

We agree with Barth that one of the major tasks of the instructional leader (or staff developer) is to move teachers from group 1 to group 3. Of course, teachers examine themselves and respond to feedback from others in more than three ways, but these three are certainly benchmarks along the continuum.

A supervisor of teachers has to deal with the full range of personality types. These vary from aggressive to passive, from authoritarian to laissez-faire, from any extreme to its opposite. We need instructional leaders who understand these variations in personality types. For example, inflexible teachers will not respond well to hints; hypersensitive teachers will not react in a healthy way to harsh criticism. Linear teachers may not be tolerant of digressions; heuristic teachers may scorn dogma.

Leading a Group of Teachers

Until now, we have been considering a supervisor (or other leader) working with individual teachers. In addition, group techniques are needed. Some of the qualities needed to lead a group of teachers are the same ones teachers need to lead a group of students. Let us take a closer look at several of these.

Clarity. It has been shown that the clarity of the teacher's communication is related to student achievement. No doubt the instructional leader's clarity is related to teacher achievement. If what the leader expects is not clear, it is unlikely to happen. When a group is attempting to solve a problem, the ability to clarify what the problem is can be most useful. Being able to clarify what others are saying can also be of great help to the group.

Enthusiasm. Enthusiasm is essential to the leader of a group. We advocate an even stronger word, surgence. To be "up" for the occasion and to be excited about the people involved and the content of the discussion are examples of "surgent" behavior. Its opposite is apathy, one of the symptoms of which is "burnout."

Variety. A variety of strategies, activities, and goals can be as refreshing to a group of teachers as to a class of students. The leader who avoids monotony by varying the approach from meeting to meeting will have less trouble keeping the group engaged in the topic at hand, which is the next quality.

Keeping the Group on Task. Sticking to business has been the strongest variable associated with student achievement in recent research that has tried to link teacher behaviors to student outcomes. Task involvement would seem equally important to the instructional leader working with a group of teachers in a problem-solving, staff development or curriculum development process.

Indirect Behaviors.   Though there are many other useful characteristics of group leadership, dealing with feelings as well as ideas, acknowledging and praising others' ideas, and using others' ideas are all behaviors that can be put to good use. Lecturing, giving directions, and criticizing will also be used when appropriate. The leader of a group of teachers will usually get further with the former than the latter.

The balance between structure or task orientation and human relations is a delicate one. As was suggested earlier, a leader with a high-task and low-relations emphasis will be perceived as authoritarian and will tend to tell the group what to do. One who is high on task and also high on relations will tend to sell them on his or her ideas (especially if he or she is surgent). One who places low emphasis on structure but is high on relations will tend to participate with the group. Finally, one with low emphasis on both task and relations will tend to delegate. Paul Hersey, Kenneth Blanchard and others have written at some length about these relationships.[7] An effective leader should be able to play the role of teller, seller, participator, or delegator depending on the situation. The predominant situation for collegial instructional leaders would seem to call for a participator (low structure and high relations).

In general, what we have found in our surveys is that teachers want an instructional leader who will meet with them individually, discuss their concerns, help select appropriate ways to collect data from observation and other means, cooperatively analyze the data, and consider alternatives. They want a colleague who is skilled at observation, knowledgeable about teaching, and supportive.

Harry Broudy has described three fundamental kinds of teaching in "Didactics, Heuristics, and Philetics."[8] The third approach comes close to what teachers seem to be seeking. It is a mentor model characterized by positive regard, individualized guidance, and strong dependence on the nature of the relationship: Horace Mann at one end of the log and me at the other.

Few school leaders would deny that these teacher preferences are reasonable. The kind of instructional leadership teachers say they prefer is also what a broad range of research findings say they should be receiving. Studies of "coaching" with teachers, for example, have underlined the need for consistent follow-up by trainers or supervisors on the practice of new skills.

Despite general agreement on what should be the ideal state of supervisory practice, it has not yet become reality except in isolated instances. What stands in the way? The chief obstacle may well be the traditional model whereby supervision and evaluation are exercised by only one person in the school: the principal. Several limitations on the principal's role serve to stifle the capacity to realize the full supervisory potential: lack of time, lack of specific training and expertise in the techniques of supervision, and the tension caused by the fact that the principal is usually the evaluator as well as the supervisor of teachers.

NEW ROLE DEFINITIONS

Instructional leadership can be separated into four major categories—curriculum development, supervision, teacher evaluation, and management. Teacher evaluation and supervision are often treated together as two parts of the same process. However, the requirements of evaluation often detract from the potential effectiveness of supervision. The apprehension and defensiveness that are frequently associated with supervision are intensified by formal evaluation. Moreover, the demands of management leave little time for supervision and promote a perspective that may not be sensitive to the central concerns of instruction.

Perhaps we need some new role definitions that permit someone to work with teachers in a way that will encourage them to reach their potential without the threat and apprehension that usually accompany supervision and evaluation. We shall try several scenarios that break up the current combination of manager-evaluator-supervisor-adviser. That combination may be inappropriate to the purposes of instructional leadership.

For our first scenario, let's call our teacher "Cinderella," for she has an adviser who is a fairy godmother, whom we shall call "Wanda." Wanda tends to appear "before the fact" rather than after; that is, she gives encouragement and confidence so that Cinderella can do what she wants to do, despite the obstacles. If Cindy wants to try role-playing, simulation, or games to reach an instructional goal, Wanda is up for it! Furthermore, she'll help get Cindy out of trouble—at midnight! Many of us would have welcomed a Wanda at some point in our teaching career when we might have ventured out, but didn't.

We'll call another teacher "Arthur." His supervisor is "Merlin," who is a wizard. Merlin's ideas about what activities will work and which materials are appropriate are incredible. Whereas Wanda's contributions were affective (they gave us the courage to go ahead with what we thought would work), Merlin's are cognitive (they suggest approaches we would not have thought of).

Let's call another teacher "Prince." His adviser is a supervisor known as "Machiavelli." Mac is a process person. He's had training and experience in interpersonal relations and organizational development. He has a feel for how folks will respond to situations. His analysis of what's going on in a discussion is perceptive and useful. His notions about how one can facilitate learning are helpful to a teacher who wants to give "inside help" to students.

G. Polya[9] distinguishes "inside help" (that which aids students to solve problems using their own powers) from "outside help" (that which makes use of the teacher's prowess). Mac has some ambiguity about this. Taking satisfaction in prowess to give "inside help" rather than "outside help" requires an unusual ego. One must be comfortable with oneself to do so.

Another teacher we shall call "Em Peror." Em's advisers overlook the obvious fact that his clothes are not merely fine but nonexistent. Going before our clients naked on the advice of our counselors is still embarrassing. The difference between Em's advisers and Wanda is that they are sycophants, whereas she only encourages that which is feasible.

Supervisors of teachers may not readily identify with Em's advisers, but flattery can be overdone in dealing with teachers as well as with emperors. Uncritical praise can produce undesirable results; positive reinforcement is best applied to specific, desirable behavior that we wish to encourage. We tend to think of factory foremen as overemphasizing the negative, but educators who are lavish with undeserved praise may be as much at fault.

Another teacher might be called "Othello." His supervisor is "Iago." One finds evidence in teacher dismissal hearings of supervisors who are almost as devious as the treacherous Iago in the "bum steers" they give to teachers who are in need of sincere help, not betrayal.

We could go on with literary and historical allusions; Boswell makes an interesting model as an observer and giver of feedback. We know of chapters in books that were developed using a "Boswellian" approach with one author playing the role of observer while another interacts with practitioners in a workshop or seminar setting. However, it may be more useful to construct some general categories that can contain these various types.

Counselor.   As we noted in chapter 1, many supervisors choose the role of counselor. Provided that personal counsel is not given at the expense of feedback on teaching, it can be a helpful adjunct. The line between teaching concern and personal problems is often a fine one. Iago was a counselor to Othello, albeit not a benign one.

Coach.   Machiavelli might be called a coach today—one who observes closely the performance of others over time and gives advice for improvement. The term "coach" connotes a range of activities that may be appropriate to instructional leadership. The emphasis on explicit, focused feedback based on expert observation of performance is certainly appropriate. Persistent and repeated supervised practice is a feature of coaching that is often missing in the development of teaching skills. Our colleagues who are studying the coaching process in relation to teachers see transfer of training—that is, the continued application of newly learned skills—as the weakest link in most preservice and in-service teacher training efforts.

Consultant.   Many teachers who have learned and practiced observation and feedback techniques with colleagues prefer the label "peer consultant" over "peer coach" because it connotes a collaborative relationship rather than a directive one.

Inspector.   A role that has been associated with supervision in the past and is still used as an official title in some parts of the world is that of inspector. Quality control is a function of supervision or instructional leadership, but it can be achieved without the pejorative overtones we tend to associate with "inspection."

Mentor.   We use the label "mentor" in association with a form of teaching Broudy called "Philetic" (based on love and emphasizing a one-to-one relationship as opposed to Didactic or Heuristic teaching). This notion of a mentor fits our concept of an ideal supervisor. Cinderella's fairy godmother, Wanda, was playing the part of a mentor, a kindly and often indulgent role taken by one, usually older, in shaping the career of a protege. Merlin (at King Arthur's court) played the role of a maestro, or wizard, a master of an art, who shares his or her knowledge and cunning with other, appreciative, persons.

Master.   Like "boss" and "overseer," "master," as a title, seems to belong to the by-gone era when theory X was in common use.[10]

The instructional leader may play any or all of these roles, but will tend to emphasize one over the others. Therefore, let us look at some of the dangers inherent in each. The mentor can work with only a limited number of proteges, whereas the school principal has a whole building full. To be a maestro in the symphony of learning that we conduct in schools requires being a master of many arts. Moreover, the principal is expected to be an impresario as well.

The coaching metaphor has been strongly advocated recently, and we tend to agree that this model fits the schools. One who wants to see teachers develop and improve continuously must observe carefully over time, understand and use a range of strategies, and employ techniques that communicate the knowledge of strategies and the information from observation to the teachers. The counselor role is helpful up to a point; becoming involved in the teacher's nonprofessional, personal affairs may be beyond the scope of an instructional leader.

Because we have expressed a preference for the coaching role, let us pursue it a bit further. Can you imagine an Olympic coach merely saying to an athlete, "That was pretty good, but I know you can do better"? No, we expect to hear, "You're taking your eye off the target at the last instant. Let's look at the videotapes I made and compare them with those of your best performance." We would also be surprised to hear such a coach say that he or she would be around to watch two or three times during the year and then write a final report in the spring. We expect the coaching to be continuous and frequent, even after the athlete achieves world status.

How, then, shall we translate the coaching analogy into the real work of the principal? It seems that in a school of appreciable size (30 or more teachers) the head coach needs some assistants. These need not be additional administrators, but may be other teachers who, during free periods or released time, can observe and meet with teachers who are working to achieve growth needs or to overcome deficiency needs.

The new roles have several advantages in addition to the likelihood that teachers will respond more positively to a new kind of leadership. They can provide a career ladder for teachers who do not wish to become administrators yet do wish to advance in the profession. They can provide a means for teacher organizations to play a positive role in the improvement of competence within the profession.

If successfully implemented, such a program could be cost-beneficial. Two examples may illustrate the point. In one case, litigation brought by a teacher cost nearly a quarter of a million dollars in attorney fees alone; in another, a reinstated teacher became a nonproductive liability that, over the years, may have cost a half million dollars in salary, administrative time, legal fees, and the like. If these cases had been worked out cooperatively by the school districts and teacher organizations rather than as labor-management confrontations, those same funds could have bought a lot of in-service training or released time for collegial supervision. Effective collegial leadership would serve as a preventive in such cases.

Because principals have so many roles to fill and severe limitations on their capacity to carry out those roles, is it unreasonable to expect that they might share some of their responsibilities with other personnel? In instructional matters, particularly, others can share the leadership role. Department heads in high schools have traditionally been responsible for concerns that were specific to the subject matter. Elementary schools that are organized into units often have team leaders for each of the units.

In large schools the supervision and evaluation responsibilities often are shared with other administrators. Many of the management functions can also be delegated. The resource that is least often drawn upon is teachers, who can provide observations, feedback, psychological support, and expert analysis for their colleagues.

Department Heads

Department heads in secondary schools have the advantage of being subject-matter specialists in their field. Thus they avoid the skepticism principals often receive, "How can a former math teacher supervise and evaluate a foreign language teacher?" Department heads are also concerned about, and in immediate contact with, the curriculum in their department. However, they have often shied away from assuming responsibilities for supervising teachers or making major decisions about the curriculum. A redefinition of the role and provision for relevant training are needed to make department heads true instructional leaders.

What might a department head hope to accomplish by taking on a new role as instructional leader? To answer the question, let's imagine a possible case. Pat is head of a high school mathematics department and receives a stipend plus a free period each day for carrying out the tasks of the assignment. Pat has had training and experience in using the skills of observing and analyzing teaching and giving feedback to the seven department members. Some of them have similar skills, so sometimes Pat takes their classes while they observe a colleague. At least ten observations are made each month so each teacher (including Pat) has six to eight per year. These are regarded as formative by the teachers, and they choose goals to work on that are consistent with their growth needs and concerns.

In addition to the personal growth that these teachers achieve, there are some spinoffs. Because they observe one another's classes, there is a coherence to the program. They know what others are doing and can articulate sequences of courses and activities. They have a mutual sense of psychological and professional support. They share teaching ideas, and when curriculum is being modified, they analyze the effects at a concrete level. They have overcome their apprehension about videotaping their own teaching for self-analysis. The students are also accustomed to having observers and recorders in the room. One can see the effects of Pat's leadership (and the cooperation of colleagues) in morale, school climate, student achievement, and job satisfaction.

If department heads are to assume greater responsibility as instructional leaders, several other changes may need to occur. There should be prerequisite training in supervision skills and curriculum matters. Most incumbents will need more time for classroom visits than they now have. There also should be a proportionate increase in authority to accompany any increase in responsibility. For example, the department head might have the authority to change teaching assignments, allocate materials, modify curriculum, establish teaching programs. Writing formal evaluations of their fellow teachers would place the same strain on the trust relationship that has been mentioned earlier; hence we would not recommend it.

Teaching Colleagues

Experiments with team teaching may not have proved that it increased achievement by students, but they did show that teachers can benefit from working closely with colleagues. In a team, teachers vicariously pick up teaching techniques from one another and are exposed to an expanded repertoire of strategies. If teachers were trained in systematic observation procedures, they would be the ideal persons to provide feedback to one another. They and their professional organizations are opposed to becoming evaluators of other teachers, but they are usually enthusiastic when given responsibilities for staff development.

To make use of the talents and skills of teachers, some adjustments need to be made to allow and encourage them to observe in one another's classrooms and to have time to meet and discuss what they have observed. Collegial supervision also has implications for inservice training: teachers must develop the skills of systematic observations and helpful feedback.

Creating instructional leadership roles for teachers requires some imagination. For one thing, teachers in this role will need a label or title. We also need to define the functions. For example, we might call them master teachers and place them in charge of student teachers and teacher aides in addition to setting a minimum number of classroom observations and conferences with each of several other teachers. Another area of special concern could be new teachers. There are other possible functions in connection with curriculum, counseling, testing, and the like. Some states have begun to use "mentor teachers" to perform these functions.

Other Sources of Instructional Leadership

Other Administrators.   Vice principals can perform any of the functions we have discussed. Administrators in the central offices of larger school districts often have skills for working with teachers and could benefit from spending time in the schools, but they tend to become isolated and desk-bound. Subject-matter supervisors for large school districts may visit classrooms, give demonstration lessons, choose or recommend curriculum materials, provide inservice training, and in other ways interact directly with teachers about the instructional program.

Students.   Students can supply useful data for the feedback process. Questionnaires can be used to tap their perceptions, and interviews with them can provide a rich source of information. Students can also operate videotape cameras for the teachers who are undertaking self-analysis.

Self-analysis.   This technique has not had the amount of use that it deserves. Theodore Parsons, in the 1960s, developed guides that can be used to analyze one's own videotapes.[11] Minicourses, which were self-instructional units for teachers who wanted to develop new skills, used self-analysis of videotapes guided by a teacher's handbook as the feedback phase of a demonstration-practice strategy. They were very successful in helping teachers to change their classroom behavior. Recent emphasis on "reflective teaching" revives the need for thoughtful self-analysis.

Creating new roles for teachers requires support at the policy level, administrative cooperation, special training, and some hard work on the part of the teachers. Whatever these roles are called and however they are implemented, the techniques of clinical supervision will be essential.

Role of the Principal

The courts, arbitrators, and hearing panels regard the principal as the person most responsible for making judgments in respect to the evaluation of teachers. In some jurisdictions, the superintendent is responsible by law or regulation but may delegate the responsibility to others, usually principals. Given this responsibility, the principal has the difficult task of also being a clinical supervisor in the collegial, constructively critical mode we have advocated. We know some principals who are able to do so and maintain a high level of trust and mutual respect with their teachers. Their competence in the techniques of clinical supervision is a major source of this respect and trust. Despite the encouragement that such principals provide, the majority of teachers do not feel that they are getting the kind of supervision they want and need.

Our response to the existing situation is twofold. First, we need more principals who are trained and experienced in systematic observation and feedback techniques. When they have become skilled, their evaluation activities can provide useful information for the improvement of instruction. These evaluation activities can be a part of instructional leadership rather than empty ritual. Second, the principal needs to share the instructional leadership of the school with teachers and others who are taking on new roles in the instructional program.

There will be a new role for the principal to play in managing the logistics to make collegial observation and analysis possible. Another role may be to provide inservice training or staff development activities that enable teachers to develop the skills necessary to become effective colleagues in a program that uses peer observation and analysis. Another role for the principal will be to work with probationary teachers (those who have not attained tenure) or with teachers who would prefer not to work with peers.

In addition to the new roles, the principal will still have the old role of summative evaluator. In most districts, this responsibility will require (or imply) at least two observations in a year in which a teacher is being formally evaluated. For many schools, that many observations will represent a quantum leap. Our information from several parts of the world (about how often teachers are observed by their evaluators) substantiates our rash claim that most teachers are rarely observed, and when they are, the feedback from the observer is not regarded as helpful. Hence, being in the classroom as a skilled observer for either formative or summative purposes represents a new role for many principals.[12]

One role we do not advocate for a principal is as a member of the committee administering a program of assistance for a teacher who is on notice if that teacher was put on notice by the principal in question. There is often a question of bias or personal conflict in such cases, and it is best to have a "neutral" administrator on the committee as we suggested in chapter 11.

A role that is necessary is to monitor and encourage the peer observation process. Even though teachers who have participated in such programs are enthusiastic about their beneficial effects, the number of competing events in a school calendar can intrude and diminish the effectiveness of the process (which needs to be consistently pursued).

CONCLUSION

For a number of years we have pondered the plight of the typical principal who must play the double role of supervisor and evaluator. We have tried to say and write things that would help make the situation more tolerable. Probably the best solution to this dilemma is to train teachers to observe one another and to provide feedback for formative purposes as part of the staff development program. Formal evaluation for summative purpose—retention decisions, promotion, tenure—would still be the responsibility of administrators.

Another possibility is to use one set of administrators as supervisors and another as evaluators. Department heads in secondary schools would also be natural choices for the supervisory role. The data from supervisor observations would not be used for evaluation unless the teacher requested it.

Another alternative is peer evaluations. Teachers, beyond just helping each other to improve, can actually write formal, summative evaluations on one another. This has been done successfully at the junior college level, but is unlikely to gain acceptance at the elementary and secondary levels. Teacher organizations appear to be opposed to having their members engage in evaluating one another. The prevalence of collective bargaining and also legal distinctions between supervisors and teachers affect who can evaluate.

As we expand our notions of instructional leadership to include others besides the building principal, various divisions of responsibility will take place. For the time being, evaluation will continue to be the responsibility of the principal in most cases, but there will be increasing pressure to provide supervision for instructional improvement, perhaps using other kinds of leadership roles.

We have emphasized the role of the instructional leader as a special kind of clinical supervisor. The role may be shared by a principal with others. Such matters as curriculum guidance and assistance with student discipline are also important.

Whoever is the instructional leader, he or she cannot neglect direct involvement through classroom observation and interaction with teachers. Our analogies all contain this element of direct involvement: the mentor, the maestro, the coach, and the counselor.

Our experience with principals in the field suggests that they often neglect this role; lack of time is usually the reason. There are other reasons. Interacting with teachers about their teaching can be a sticky business. The teachers are often defensive and resentful, and principals often lack skill and training in the prerequisites for a good relationship.

These prerequisites are as follows: a repertoire of observational skills and recording techniques, a working knowledge of a range of instructional strategies, a set of interpersonal communication skills, and feedback strategies to use in conferences with teachers. A number of these techniques have been discussed in the preceding chapters. Our research indicates that these techniques are what teachers are looking for but in many cases are not getting. The studies of effective schools have placed great importance on the effectiveness of the principal. The principal's effectiveness depends, in large part, on instructional leadership. This leadership can be shared with others.

Training and Practice

In order to have the skills ("techniques," we have called them) necessary to carry out the functions of these new roles, principals and teachers need training and practice. We have found that 20 to 30 hours of instruction plus an equal amount of practice (six to ten observations using different techniques, including three to five full cycles with planning before and feedback after) should be adequate.

It is desirable to have both teachers and administrators in such a class. If the training is undertaken within a school system, then teachers' apprehensions are allayed when they learn what the purposes are and what the effects can be. Administrators with only moderate motivation to become better supervisors can benefit from the competition and modeling by teachers who are enthusiastic and resourceful in completing their assignments.

As part of the training we suggest 5 to 10 hours of practice. The first three to five observations (which can be 20 to 30 minutes in duration) should be strictly to gain experience with several different observation techniques, such as at-task, selective verbatim, interaction patterns, and classroom movement. Teachers are usually willing to let a colleague practice his or her newly acquired skills in their classrooms. They are usually interested in seeing the data even though a feedback conference is not part of the assignment. When the observers feel confident, then planning and feedback should be added as part of the assignment. Observers who are practicing these new skills are often rewarded by the response they get from teachers who find the systematic observational records to be interesting and relevant. Finding ways to allow and encourage teachers to continue observing and giving useful feedback to colleagues is still a challenge.

NOTES

1. Thomas I. Ellis, "Teacher Competency: What Administrators Can Do," *ERIC Digest*, No. 9 (Eugene, OR: ERIC Clearinghouse on Educational Management, 1984).
2. Portions of this chapter are adapted from Keith A. Acheson, "The Principal's Role in Instructional Leadership," *OSSC Bulletin* 28, No. 8 (April 1985); and Keith A. Acheson with Stuart C. Smith, "It Is Time for Principals to Share the Responsibility for Instructional Leadership with Others," *OSSC Bulletin* 29, No. 6 (February 1986). Both were prepared by the ERIC Clearinghouse on Educational Management for the Oregon School Study Council, University of Oregon, Eugene. ERIC/CEM is funded by the U.S. Department of Education. Additional portions are adapted from Keith A. Acheson, "A Central Role for Principals," *OSSC Report* 23, No. 3 (Spring 1983), developed under contract with the Northwest Regional Educational Laboratory and reproduced by permission of the Laboratory.
3. Arthur E. Wise, Linda Darling-Hammond, Milbrey W. McLaughlin, Harriet T. Bernstein, *Teacher Evaluation: A Study of Effective Practices.* Prepared for the National Institute of Education, June 1984, The Rand Corporation, Santa Monica, CA; Milbrey Wallin McLaughlin, "Teacher Evaluation and School Improvement," *Teachers College Record* 86, No. 1 (Fall 1984).
4. Edwin Bridges, *Managing the Incompetent Teacher* (Eugene, OR: The ERIC Clearinghouse on Educational Management, 2d ed., 1990).
5. Jo Ann Mazzarella, "The Principal's Role as an Instructional Leader," *ACSA School Management Digest*, Ser. 1, No. 3 (1977).
6. Roland Barth, "The Principal as Staff Developer," *Journal of Education* (Spring 1981): 144–62.
7. Paul Hersey and Kenneth Blanchard, *Management of Organizational Behavior: Utilizing Human Resources* (Englewood Cliffs, NJ: Prentice-Hall, 1982).
8. H. S. Broudy, "Didactics, Heuristics, and Philetics," *Educational Theory* 22 (Summer 1972): 251–61. Can also be found in Ronald Hyman, *Teaching: Vantage Points for Study* (New York: Lippincott, 1974).
9. G. Polya, *How to Solve It* (Princeton, NJ: Princeton University Press, 1971).
10. Douglas McGregor, *The Human Side of Enterprise* (New York: McGraw-Hill, 1960).
11. Theodore Parsons, *Guided Self-Analysis System for Professional Development Education Series* (Berkeley: University of California Press, 1968).
12. For principals who feel maligned by our skepticism, let us admit that we do not have data on all principals, or even most, but if the few thousand we have met or the several thousand whose teachers have responded to our surveys are representative, then we feel justified in stating that many principals do not treat instructional leadership as their prime concern, except in response to questionnaires.

Unit V Exercises

MULTIPLE-CHOICE ITEMS

Answers are on page 255.

1. Which of the following elements might be an issue in a dismissal hearing?
   a. the district standards
   b. the feedback conference
   c. the plan of assistance
   d. all of the above
   e. none of the above
2. When a supervisor is also the evaluator, what is likely to be lost?
   a. systematic observation
   b. feedback
   c. trust
   d. formal evaluation
3. If the supervisor is also the evaluator of the teacher,
   a. it will be more difficult to establish trust.
   b. the teacher's goals may be negotiated.
   c. the teacher is less likely to list classroom control as a goal.
   d. the teacher is likely to be observed more frequently.
   e. the teacher will be less defensive.
4. Clarity is related to
   a. questions.
   b. vocabulary.
   c. applications.
   d. explanations.

    e. all of the above.
5. Abstract concepts such as warmth, enthusiasm, empathy, and altruism
    a. should not be used as goals.
    b. can be translated into observable behavior.
    c. cannot be observed.
    d. require a psychologist to analyze.
    e. do not apply to teaching or supervision.
6. A plan of assistance for a teacher with severe deficiencies
    a. is a legal requirement in some states.
    b. would not be supported by teacher organizations.
    c. would forego techniques of clinical supervision.
    d. might result in dismissal if the teacher did not approve.
    e. should be conducted by the administrator who put the teacher on notice.

PROBLEMS

The following problems do not have single correct answers. Answers are on pages 259–260. Your answers may differ from these yet be as good or better.

1. In the first edition of this book, there was no chapter about evaluation, although the "sting" of evaluation was mentioned. In the second and third editions there was such a chapter in unit I as part of the overview of clinical supervision. Now it is in unit V as one of the "other applications of the techniques of clinical supervision." What arguments can you adduce for or against these changes over time? Is evaluation (of teaching) a part of clinical supervision or is it an application of the techniques or is it something else?
2. The authors look at the supervision of teachers from several perspectives. One perspective comes from the research and the literature on this and related topics. Another comes from frequent contact with practitioners in the field through workshops, in-service activities, graduate courses. If you were preparing supervisors and instructional leaders to help teachers develop and improve their skills and strategies using the techniques described in this book, where would you place your emphasis? Would it be on learning the techniques through demonstration, practice, and feedback? Would it be on what has been learned from research and other scholarly pursuits? Would it be on the politics required to implement different forms of supervision and instructional leadership in the schools?

The following problems have been posed in previous units. We raise them again in the light of additional thought or understanding on your part. Possible answers are on page 260. Your answers may differ from your earlier ones or they may still be the same. As before, they may differ from ours yet be as good or better.

3. As a clinical supervisor, you are working with a teacher to help develop new skills while making the transition from high school teaching to junior high school teaching. One day the teacher becomes distressed and says she is considering leaving the profession. What do you do in your role as clinical supervisor?

4. You are assigned to be the clinical supervisor of an undergraduate who is just starting a student teaching placement. The undergraduate initiates a conversation with you by asking, "Are you here to evaluate me?" How should you respond?

5. Some educators claim that good teachers are born, not made. Others claim that teaching can never be analyzed because it is an art, not a science. Do you agree or disagree with these claims? Why? Why not?

Answers to Multiple-Choice Questions and Problems

ANSWERS TO MULTIPLE-CHOICE QUESTIONS

Unit I

1c, 2d, 3a, 4b, 5a, 6c, 7d, 8d

Unit II

1e; 2e; 3c, e; 4e

Unit III

1d, 2c, 3b, 4c, 5a, 6c, 7a, 8d, 9b, 10d

Unit IV

1c; 2d; 3b; 4e; 5c, d; 6a, e; 7d; 8c, e

Unit V

1d; 2c; 3a, b, c; 4e; 5b; 6a, d

ANSWERS TO PROBLEMS

Unit I

1. The supervisor might begin by acknowledging the teacher's distress (technique 30), then ask the teacher to clarify why she is distressed (technique 31). If the teacher states that she feels her teaching is inadequate, the supervisor might initiate a clinical supervision cycle in which observation data are collected to help the teacher objectively analyze her teaching. If the teacher's distress is caused by personal problems, the supervisor might assume a counselor role (see pages 14–15) or refer the teacher to an expert source of help.

2. The supervisor might enlarge on the question by discussing all supervisory roles with the student teacher. If the supervisor's roles are both to evaluate the student teacher's performance and to help the student improve in skill, the supervisor might discuss both roles and how they relate to each other (see pages 16–17). A supervisor who has an evaluative role might allay some of the student teacher's concerns by sharing the criteria that will be used to evaluate the student teacher's effectiveness (see pages 182–189).

3. It may well be true that, *to an extent*, good teachers are born, not made. Nevertheless, there is strong evidence that a teacher's classroom performance can be improved, *to an extent*, through training (see pages 19–20). Also, it may be true that certain aspects of effective teaching will always elude technical analysis. But most educators (including critics of analytic methods) can identify *some* teaching techniques that differentiate effective and ineffective teachers. In other words, a possible problem with both claims is that they are too extreme.

Unit II

1, 2. Answers will, of course, vary. Share your answer with a friend.
3. Answers will vary but should attend to:
   a. the kind of lesson you will teach.
   b. what you, as teacher, will do.
   c. what the student will do.
   d. the concern, goal, or focus you have chosen.
   e. the kinds of data you will collect.

Unit III

1. Techniques that focus on specific behaviors, such as selective verbatim and at-task, are probably inappropriate in this situation. You might con-

sider instead a wide-lens technique—for example, an anecdotal record or a video or audio recording. Although more restricted, Flanders Interaction Analysis also may be helpful. These techniques enable a teacher to examine his or her teaching behavior and how students react to it. In examining these records, the teacher may develop a better operational definition of what is meant by "coming across."

2. An at-task analysis would be helpful in determining the percentage of time that each of these students is engaged in learning and the percentage of time that they are off task. Off-task time can be analyzed further into several categories of behavior (e.g., daydreaming, chatting with a classmate). The supervisor might also make an anecdotal record limited to the target students and the teacher's interaction with them. Another observational technique that may be appropriate is a selective verbatim in which the supervisor records all teacher comments directed to the problem student.

3. *Inferences*
   a. Students near the front of the room do more talking than students in the back of the room.
   b. Most of the teacher's questions are addressed to the class as a whole rather than to specific students.
   c. A higher proportion of girls than boys responded to the teacher.
   d. Several students engaged in conversations with each other while the lesson was in progress.
   e. Almost half the students (10 of 21) did not participate in the lesson.
   Recommendations
   a. Have students in the back of the room move into empty seats nearer the front of the room.
   b. The teacher should consider standing so that she has a good view of all students.
   c. If side conversations between students persist, the teacher should explain why this behavior is not desirable or perhaps should move some students to different sections of the room.
   d. Direct more questions to specific students rather than to the class as a whole.

4. *Selective verbatim of feedback statements*
   All right.
   A couple of billion.
   Six million.
   Only a billion.
   About three billion.
   All right, Mary is closest because it is over three billion people in the world today.
   All right, there are a lot of people that are just barely making it.

Timeline coding

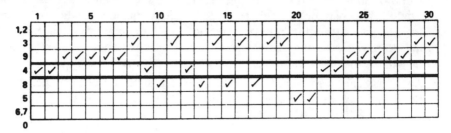

Unit IV

1. **a.** Alternatives will vary. Individual conferences with students are usually better than public rebukes. Attention to planning productive activities to replace negative behavior is advisable. Reinforcing positive behavior is a powerful tool. There are many other reasonable suggestions.
   b. "If I were you, here's what I would try" is not a good opener. "Here are several possibilities; can you suggest others?" is better.

2. Responses will vary depending on the nature of the strategy chosen. Have you considered photographs, checklists, student feedback (questionnaires, reports, evaluations), getting assistance from student teachers, aides, or others?

3. The following examples for student behavior are from Spaulding. The examples for teacher conference behavior are from our own experience; the list can easily be expanded.

   Aggressive Behavior—direct verbal or physical attack, grabbing, destroying:
   "Give me that!"
   "Get out of my room!"
   Negative (Inappropriate) Attention-Getting Behavior—annoying, bothering, belittling, criticizing:
   "You don't know how to jump rope."
   "You've never had to teach a class like this one."
   Manipulating and Directing Others:
   "Tell Cynthia to get out of the wagon."
   "You ought to spend your time on kids, not teachers."
   Resisting Authority (or Delaying):
   "No, I won't do it!"
   "Would you mind repeating the question?"
   Self-Directed Activity:
   "I think I'll make a pie."
   "I'd like to make some tape recordings on my own."

Paying Rapt Attention:

    Listening attentively as teacher gives directions

    Watching supervisor give demonstration lesson

Sharing and Helping:

    Child eagerly takes part in activity or conversation

    Teacher suggests alternative teaching activities

Transacting:

    Mutual give-and-take is present in (child's) activities

Seeking Help:

    "Would you help me fix this?"

    "What would *you* do?"

Following Directions (Passively and Submissively):

    Doing assigned work without enthusiasm or great interest

    Trying the supervisor's suggestion for a class activity, but with a lack of zest

Seeking or Responding to External Stimuli:

    Observing passively, easily diverted

    Listening impassively and attending to any interruption

Responding to Internal Stimuli:

    Daydreaming

    Gazing into the distance

Physical Withdrawal or Avoidance:

    Moving away from teacher and other children

    Missing the conference appointment

Unit V

1. Clinical Supervision, as we have viewed it over the past 16 years, is a strategy for helping teachers study their own teaching with the help of colleagues, either supervisors or fellow teachers. The goal of this strategy is developmental. The goal of evaluation is summative, that is, to decide whether a teacher should be praised, promoted, and retained as opposed to punished, demoted, or dismissed. The tension between these two purposes has made supervision a suspect activity.

    One solution to this dilemma is what we call peer consultation. Implementing such a program requires some new roles for teachers and administrators. We have addressed these in several chapters and continue to explore them in various settings from northern Saskatchewan to tropical Guam. We have watched it work in British Columbia, but not yet across the Pacific.

2. The solutions that appeal to teachers are those that emerged from our experiences with the Teachers' Federation in British Columbia over the past 14 years (chapter 13). A few school principals have made persuasive cases for how they can provide additional clout for teachers who need to im-

prove, or else. Other principals see themselves as colleagues, and so do their teachers. Others see themselves as colleagues, but their teachers do not. Additional experimentation and research needs to be conducted before we announce the millennium for supervision.

3. According to Acheson and Gall you should "avoid direct advice." Don't try to make personal decisions for her. However, you can "translate abstract concerns into observable behavior." You can encourage exploring alternatives. You can "listen more and talk less." There are a number of other techniques that can be applied, such as responding to the teacher's feeling as well as to the verbal content.

4. You might say, "Eventually I must, as part of my responsibility and as part of your recommendations for employment, but for now I see my role as being here to help you become the best teacher you can possibly be. Then evaluation will be no problem for either of us."

5. We believe that teaching can be analyzed in a number of ways, some of which are suggested in chapters 11 and 12. We also believe that some qualities of teaching can either be inherited or learned; enthusiasm is an example. Other qualities, such as genuine empathy, would be difficult (or impossible) to acquire through formal training once one's personality has been set. Teaching as an art form (with connoisseurs) has been explored by Elliot Eisner.

Index